Red-winged
Blackbirds

LES (D.) BELETSKY AND
GORDON H. ORIANS

Red-winged

Blackbirds,

DECISION-MAKING

AND

REPRODUCTIVE

SUCCESS

THE UNIVERSITY OF CHICAGO PRESS
CHICAGO AND LONDON

LES D. BELETSKY is a research scientist in the department
of zoology at the University of Washington. GORDON H.
ORIANS is professor emeritus in the department of zoology
at the University of Washington.

The University of Chicago Press, Chicago 60637
The University of Chicago Press, Ltd., London
© 1996 by The University of Chicago
All rights reserved. Published 1996
Printed in the United States of America

05 04 03 02 01 00 99 98 97 96   1 2 3 4 5

ISBN: 0-226-04186-7 (cloth)
ISBN: 0-226-04187-5 (paper)

Library of Congress Cataloging-in-Publication Data

Beletsky, Leslie David, 1956–
    Red-winged blackbirds : decision-making and reproductive success /
Les D. Beletsky and Gordon H. Orians.
        p.   cm.
    Includes bibliographical references (p.   ) and index.
    ISBN 0-226-04186-7 (cloth : alk. paper). — ISBN 0-226-04187-5
(paper : alk. paper)
    1. Red-winged blackbird—Behavior.   2. Red-winged blackbird—
Reproduction.   I. Orians, Gordon H.   II. Title.
QL696.P2475B45   1996
598.8'81—dc20   96-18894
                                                      CIP

⊚ The paper used in this publication meets the minimum
requirements of the American National Standard for
Information Sciences—Permanence of Paper for Printed
Library Materials, ANSI Z39.48-1984.
This book is printed on acid-free paper.

CONTENTS

ILLUSTRATIONS

TABLES

PREFACE

During recent decades, behavioral ecology has undergone vigorous development. Increasingly detailed and extensive field studies have been guided by significant theoretical and conceptual advances, aided by the ability to analyze large data sets and the availability of new methods of assessing genetic relationships among living individuals. During the 1960s, models of natural selection, most of which were based on actions of individuals, replaced "for the good of the species" views that had dominated most earlier work (Wynne-Edwards 1962; Williams 1966). Nonetheless, the debate over "group selection" continued for some time, eventually leading to more sophisticated models of interdemic selection and kin selection (Hamilton 1964; Maynard Smith 1974; Parker 1974; Dawkins 1986).

More recent evolutionary models are based on the recognition that social systems are composed of individuals that have conflicting genetic interests. Game-theoretic approaches to the the study of social systems have proven to be powerful ways of posing problems and guiding the design and execution of empirical studies. We have used these approaches extensively in our studies, focusing on the decisions made by males and females during the breeding season that ultimately determine within-season and lifetime reproductive success.

Until recently, behavioral ecologists have, of necessity, assumed that social breeding partners were also genetic partners. Application of DNA fingerprinting and other molecular methods during the past decade has revealed the prevalence of significant deviations from these assumptions. These empirical results have stimulated the first major conceptual change in behavioral ecology theory in many decades to be driven by a technological rather than a theoretical advance.

Our studies of blackbirds in Washington began in the 1960s and concentrated on two marsh-nesting, strongly polygynous species, Red-winged (*Agelaius phoeniceus*) and Yellow-headed (*Xanthocephalus*

xanthocephalus) blackbirds. Initially we focused on testing models of natural selection that predicted four types of behavioral characteristics of individuals: habitat selection, foraging behavior, territoriality, and mate selection (Orians 1980). That early work, for the most part, analyzed patterns that could be measured and interpreted without having color-banded populations in which the lifetime performance of individuals could be followed. We approached habitat selection using a hierarchical model based on the concept of the Ideal Free Distribution (Fretwell and Lucas 1970). Our testing consisted of examining settling patterns and nesting success as functions of harem size and female rank in harem. We also assessed the criteria females used to select mates by analyzing temporal patterns of settling and harem sizes.

During the 1960s and 1970s we also gave considerable attention to issues of where to forage and which prey to select. Models of prey choice (Charnov 1973, 1976 a,b) and central place foraging (Orians and Pearson 1979), which we elaborated concurrently with the field study, were used both to design tests of the theory and as means of gaining insights into what should be measured in nature. Our blackbird field study did not yield tests of the theories as definitive as those provided by controlled laboratory studies on other species, but the interaction between theory and observation greatly improved our insights into the dynamics of the blackbird breeding system.

Our early studies of blackbird territoriality focused on identifying the factors that influence the sizes of territories defended by males and the environmental conditions that favor dominance by Red-winged versus Yellow-headed Blackbirds, species whose males defend mutually exclusive territories in marshes of western North America (Orians and Willson 1964). We did not at that time address questions of the causes of territorial dominance and factors determining which males are successful in obtaining and maintaining territories, questions upon which we focused during the fieldwork reported on in this book.

The results we document here build upon the foundation laid by the earlier studies, as anticipated in the final paragraph of the 1980 monograph:

> Many of the questions unasked and unanswered by this study can be investigated only by following the choices of individually marked birds within and between breeding seasons. Obtaining this type of information on patterns of individual choices has been the top priority in the research carried out during the time the results of this intensive study were being analyzed and put into words. This ordering of objectives of the project is appropriate, because the more detailed examination of individual choices

can now be set in the context of the general ecological conditions most likely to influence payoffs from those choices. (Orians, 1980, p. 254)

For our investigation of breeding-season choices we concentrated on Red-winged Blackbirds because they are more catholic in their choices of breeding habitat, more numerous in our study area, and more stable in their local populations than are Yellow-headed Blackbirds (Beletsky and Orians 1994). Also, much more information exists for redwings elsewhere, which enables us to interpret our results more broadly.

Now, with sixteen years of data from our study of color-banded redwings, we can assess the influence of the decisions of individuals on their seasonal and lifetime reproductive success (LRS). We use a combination of extensive observational data and selected experiments to assess the information individuals use to make their decisions and the consequences of those decisions for LRS. Our analysis of breeding-season decisions is novel because we treat the sexes separately. We do so because the major breeding-season decisions made by male and female redwings differ strikingly and because most of these decisions are made independently of the behavior of individuals of the other sex. For females, we look closely at when and where they decide to nest and renest and how much energy they allocate to reproduction. For males, we concentrate on how they establish and maintain territories, without which they have no reproductive success.

Even with our extensive data set, we are able to provide only provisional answers to many of the questions we have posed. We have tried to be conservative in interpreting our data, but we do not hesitate to speculate where we believe that speculation is needed to stimulate future work. We also raise some issues and controversies for which we lack relevant data. We do so because our goal is to paint a comprehensive picture of reproductive decision-making by redwings. Knowing which parts of the canvas remain blank helps to place the other parts in a broader context.

In the initial chapters of the book we introduce our long-term study of redwings and the environment in which it was carried out. Here we draw attention to our main investigative approach, which was to conduct multiple tests (some strong, others weaker) of hypotheses of decision-making and then use the relative balance of positive and negative outcomes to reject or support hypotheses. We will say more about this approach in the final chapter. Our study has been based on the collection of detailed information on the breeding success of hundreds of unmanipulated, color-banded males and females. During our two-decade-long project, the questions we framed at its onset were supplemented by questions suggested by our expanding results and changes taking place in the general field of behavioral ecology; in other words, the questions we attempted to answer continually evolved.

To maintain the consistency of the long-term data set on our core study area, we performed only minor manipulations of the birds or their habitats in that area. The experiments we did perform did not, in our judgment, compromise the integrity of the baseline data and the conclusions based on them. We performed our major experiments on sites peripheral to the core area, where our information was less complete but where most of the individuals were color-banded.

This study of key breeding-season decisions of males and females, and of the information potentially available to birds that affects those decisions, can be viewed from different perspectives. One is to understand variation in individual breeding behavior that leads to variation in LRS. Another is to view decision-making in an environmental context. Variation and predictability of environmental information influence all animal decision-making and thereby most of the behavior of interest to behavioral ecologists. Knowing how and why animals make their breeding decisions is important for understanding life-history strategies.

Unless otherwise stated, means throughout the book are given ± SD.

ACKNOWLEDGMENTS

During our long-term study, many people provided invaluable assistance. The simple acknowledgment we offer them here is inadequate to express our appreciation, for without their help the study could not have been completed.

The following people helped us collect field data, contributing thousands of hours and their enormous energy to the study: C. D'Antonio, E. Davies, C. Halupka, D. Mammen, S. Worlein, C. Monnet, L. Rotterman, C. Patterson, J. Erckmann, T. Johnsen, S. Sharbaugh, R. Sulaiman, S. Birks, M. Dunham, B. Higgins, M. Titcomb, T. Olson, T. Steedle, K. Hanni, G. Stewart, J. McCarty, T. Danufsky, A. Phan, P. Chadwick, E. Gray, L. Davis, L. Gilson, K. Harms, D. Stolley, R. Fuhrmann, M. Hechler, L. Overton, R. Budrys, and C. Calogero.

Elizabeth Gray conducted her doctoral research from 1990 through 1992 at our study site. The results of her work (Gray 1996a,b,c,d), on extrapair copulations in our redwing population, helped us considerably. Many of our analyses and conclusions could not have been carried out and interpreted without important information on redwing behavior and paternity she gathered and shared with us.

During the intensive data-analysis phase of this study—the last five years—a number of University of Washington doctoral students assisted us with expert advice on data analysis, computer programming, and statistical strategies: John Bishop, George Gilchrist, Mark Wells, Robert Matlock, Kevin O'Brien, and William Morris. John Bishop, in particular, sometimes devoted more time to our project than to his own considerable research interests; also, he generated most of the crisp figures in the book.

We also want to thank Ken Yasukawa, Sievert Rohwer, David Westneat, and an unidentified reviewer for reading and commenting upon this manuscript or sections of it. Many of their suggestions significantly improved the book. Lynn Erckmann, BJ Higgins, Sharon Birks, Carla

Calogero, and David Brass helped in various ways with data analysis. Al Dufty taught us the ways of avian radiotelemetry, and Wesley Weathers provided expert advice on quantifying female redwing reproductive energy output. Finally, the staff of the Columbia National Wildlife Refuge and, in particular, the refuge manager, David Goeke, gave us permission to conduct our fieldwork on that fine refuge and assisted us in ways too numerous to itemize. Our long-term study of blackbird breeding success and decisions was supported financially by the National Science Foundation and the National Institute of Mental Health.

Last, we must acknowledge the birds themselves. They assisted us in many ways (usually involuntarily) and were the source of great pleasure as well as scientific data.

Part One

INTRODUCTORY
CONSIDERATIONS

One

Introduction

INTRODUCTION

If living in the world were simple and straightforward, all species would have similar life-history strategies. To maximize fitness, an organism would begin reproducing as soon as possible after birth and thereafter reproduce at the maximum possible rate throughout its lifetime. Real life-histories, however, are characterized by great variability. A major challenge of biology is to explain the evolution and maintenance of the great diversity of life spans, mortality rates, reproductive rates, social systems, and habitat-selection patterns. A life history can be viewed as a sequence of choices made by individuals, each of which influences lifetime reproductive success (LRS) and, hence, fitness. Individuals choose habitats in which to forage and to breed, types of food to hunt, individuals with whom to share genes and produce offspring, and breeding schedules. Early choices can constrain subsequent ones. Thus, choice of a breeding habitat determines the array of nesting sites available, the places within reasonable traveling distance from which food may be sought, and the quality of protection from predators and the physical environment. An individual's options are also influenced by other members of its species and the choices they make, as well as by the activities of individuals of many other species living in the same area. To understand the life history of any organism and why it evolved, we must determine the constraints under which decisions are made and the consequences of those decisions, and then integrate their effects on LRS. The purpose of this book is to attempt such an integration of breeding-season decisions for an intensively studied population of the Red-winged Blackbird (*Agelaius phoeniceus*). Decisions that are important for future reproduction are made during nonbreeding periods as well, but because our investigations have been confined to the breeding season, we are unable to evaluate the decisions made by individuals during the remainder of the year.

Birds have been favored subjects for life-history research because

3

they are diurnal, conspicuous, and easily studied. Individuals of many species are readily trapped and marked with leg bands or tags. In addition, the great differences in life span, foods and foraging, habitat utilization, and social systems among birds offer excellent opportunities for comparative studies. The Red-winged Blackbird, one of the most abundant North American birds, has been the focus of many field studies. Redwings breed from east-central Alaska and the Yukon south to northern Costa Rica and from the Atlantic to the Pacific. Over most of its range, the redwing breeds primarily in marshes, in which habitat it is often the most abundant passerine.

We have studied redwings primarily in the Columbia National Wildlife Refuge (hereafter CNWR) and adjacent areas in the Columbia Basin desert of eastern Washington State. Redwings have bred in this region for thousands of years but today, as a result of extensive irrigation in the region, the number and extent of marshes, and along with them redwings, has increased dramatically.

We have already summarized much information about patterns of LRS in this species (Orians and Beletsky 1989), some of which will be updated here. An earlier book on blackbirds (Orians 1980), which described work conducted at CNWR and other sites during the 1960s, focused primarily on habitat productivity, resource use, and foraging behavior. The present study builds upon that previous work and expands it in several dimensions. Our primary goal in this book is to assess how different decisions made by individual redwings during the breeding season influence LRS, and thereby to understand why redwing decision-making patterns and "rules" evolved as they did. Our use of terms such as "decision" and "choice" does not imply any conscious evaluation of the options by the birds, although we do not assert that such evaluations are absent. Nor do we believe that our investigations reveal whether the birds "think" about their breeding decisions. Our secondary goal is to present some results of our sixteen-year study of territoriality, dispersal, and reproductive success.

THE SEXES ARE VERY DIFFERENT

Among sexually reproducing species, half of the genes in each generation are contributed by males and half by females, no matter what the breeding system. Therefore, if the sex ratio is unity, the average per capita contributions of males and females are equal. However, sex ratios and individual contributions to subsequent generations often vary. By definition, a male is an individual who produces gametes with small amounts of stored energy; a female is an individual who produces gametes with more stored energy. Sperm, being cheap to manufacture, can be produced in large numbers. The contributions of males to subsequent generations are rarely limited by the number of sperm they can produce. Contributions of females, on the other hand, are often limited by the amount of energy they can devote to egg production. Consequently, even when male and female redwings make the same general decisions (e.g., choosing a place to breed), how they make them and the consequences of those decisions differ.

As is typical of polygynous species, redwings are strongly dimorphic in size and plumage. Males, jet black with bright scarlet or red epaulets, weigh 65–85 g in our study area, whereas the streaked brown females weigh only 40–55 g. The striking differences in breeding behavior and morphology suggest that selection pressures and breeding strategies are sufficiently different to require separate treatment. Indeed, despite their genetic union, we treat the two redwing sexes almost as separate species, because their major breeding-season decisions differ. Males choose how to acquire and defend territories and how much time and energy to devote to mate attraction or assisting already-settled females in protecting and provisioning young. The major female decisions are where and when to nest and, perhaps, with whom to copulate.

During the breeding season, male redwings are territorial, each defending a portion of marsh or, in some regions, upland. Redwings also defend their territories against Yellow-headed Blackbirds (*Xanthocephalus xanthocephalus*), but they are often displaced from better quality areas by the larger yellowheads (Orians and Willson 1964; Orians 1980). Redwings are strongly polygynous throughout their range. Harems, which average three to five females but may range up to fifteen or more, tend to be larger in the more productive marshes of western North America than elsewhere (Orians 1980; Beletsky 1996). Male redwings do not participate in nest building or incubation, and, in our study area, most of them do not feed nestlings (Beletsky and Orians 1990). Feeding of nestlings is more prevalent among older males throughout the range of the species and in eastern than in western North America (Searcy and Yasukawa 1983, 1995; Muldal et al. 1986). Apparently, no strong bonds are formed between males and females. Even during the breeding season, mated individuals move around relatively independently of each another—both in daily activities and between breeding efforts.

In this book, we accept polygyny as a given feature of the redwing breeding system rather than attempting to explain its origin. That problem has been dealt with elsewhere (Verner and Willson 1966; Orians 1969, 1972; Wittenberger 1976; Emlen and Oring 1977; Searcy and Yasukawa 1995), although the issue is far from settled. Redwings exemplify resource-defense polygyny, a system in which males settle first and defend sites to which they attract multiple females. Females arrive on and depart from male territories throughout the season, but they overlap extensively in their breeding cycles. Females apparently elect to settle with a male already having a mate because, according to the most widely held theory of avian polygyny, differences in quality among male territories compensate for any penalties associated with secondary or tertiary status. Indeed, all studies of redwings have found either no correlation or a positive correlation between breeding success of individual females and harem size (Holm 1973; Weatherhead and Robertson 1977; Orians and Beletsky 1989, this study). Results of many studies suggest that females choose breeding territories more by attributes of the habitat than by attributes of the males that defend them (Searcy and Yasukawa 1983, 1995).

Female redwings are often aggressive toward other females before nesting begins and subsequently near their nests (Yasukawa and Searcy 1982; Hurly and Robertson 1984; Searcy 1986). Early in the breeding season females settled on male territories are aggressive toward prospecting females and subsequent settlers, but this behavior diminishes as the season progresses. Although the issue of whether females defend a space for the particular resources it contains is controversial, there is little doubt that females engage in space-related aggressive behavior (Searcy and Yasukawa 1995). Analyses of the timing and spacing of nests, however, have provided little evidence that defense of space by females influences the settling patterns of other females (Yasukawa and Searcy 1981; Searcy and Yasukawa 1995; see chapter 4). The bulk of available information suggests that females are able to settle relatively unconstrained by the presence of already-settled birds, and that they can readily shift locations for renestings after nest failure or successful completion of their first nests.

Among both males and females on our study area, cumulative reproductive success, as measured by number of young fledged, on average rises linearly with the number of years breeding. Because of high rates of predation on nests, probable (but unmeasured) high postfledging mortality, and moderately high mortality rates (30 to 40%) between breeding seasons, redwings have a short life expectancy. Most die without having produced any offspring that survive to adulthood. Nonetheless, the decisions they make during the breeding season strongly influence their LRS.

BREEDING-SEASON CHOICES: THE BASICS

We organize our book around the sequences of breeding-season decisions individual redwings make during their adult lifetimes. For females, the major decisions on which we will concentrate our attention are when to nest, when to stop nesting, where to nest, with whom to breed, and how much effort to invest annually in breeding. For males, the major breeding decisions revolve around territory ownership: when, where, and how to acquire first territories, how long to hold territories, and when to change locations.

Each of these decisions is constrained by the intra- and interspecific biological environment and by physical environmental conditions. For males, becoming a breeder requires gaining and maintaining a territory, but territories are usually in short supply. Thus, in any year, many reproductively mature males do not breed even though it would be advantageous for them to do so if they could. Others occupy low-quality territories where their chances of breeding success are low. Changing territories, both within and between years, is socially constrained by the dominance of owners over challengers. Why individuals without territories do not fight harder to gain territories is a feature of the decision-making apparatus of male redwings we explore in some detail.

The criteria by which breeding habitats are evaluated are probably complex. For the most part we have not explored these choices experimentally, but natural perturbations created some "experiments" for us, and our extensive data on settling density and site fidelity provide many clues about habitat preferences. During previous years we sampled and analyzed quantities and temporal patterns of emerging aquatic insects among and within breeding marshes (Orians 1980; Orians and Wittenberger 1991). The abundance of these insects, which are the most important components of the diets of both adults and nestlings during the breeding season, is an important aspect of habitat quality. Other factors include nature of nesting substrates, density of emergent vegetation, and types of upland foraging areas adjacent to the breeding marshes (Beletsky 1996).

Choice of mating partner is exercised primarily by female redwings because males cannot compel females to settle on territories or prevent them from leaving. Males could, of course, reject females that wished to settle, but neither we nor other observers have witnessed such behavior. On theoretical grounds, we would not expect males to reject females because their seasonal RS is positively correlated with harem size. Females can and do make multiple mate choices, both within and between breeding seasons, but a settling choice is both a mate and a habitat choice because the location of the nests determines the nature of the surrounding habitat. Those two choices are in part disaggregated through extrapair copulations (EPCs). However, all females apparently copulate frequently with the owner of the territory on which they nest. About 34% of young on our study area result from extrapair fertilizations (EPFs; Gray 1996a), which is somewhat higher than reported elsewhere (Gibbs et al. 1990; Westneat 1992a, 1993).

Although redwings frequently engage in EPCs, many of which result in fertilized eggs, females very rarely, if ever, deposit eggs in nests other than their own (Harms et al. 1991). Consequently, considerable uncertainty (to investigators and, presumably, to male redwings as well) surrounds paternity, but not maternity, of offspring in redwing nests. Therefore, EPCs influence male and female RS and behavior in different ways. Given that on average about one-third of young are sired by other than the owner of the territory in which the nest is located, the mating decisions of female redwings are more complex than previously recognized. We are at present unable to address these decisions in great detail, but all or nearly all EPF offspring are sired by neighboring territorial males (Gibbs et al. 1990; Westneat 1993; Gray 1996a), and gains in our population from EPFs may approximately balance losses (Gray 1996b). Therefore, EPFs do not substantially affect the variation in male reproduction as estimated under our assumptions of no EPFs (see chapter 2 for details).

Among monogamous species with biparental care, a mate deserted within a breeding season must continue parental care unassisted. Desertion in such cases contributes positively to reproductive success only if the probability of obtaining additional matings is high enough to offset the losses due to poorer parental care, or possible abandonment of the offspring, by the deserted spouse. Mate fidelity between breeding seasons maintains the benefits of past learning and mutual adjustments of pair members, and, if the same breeding site is occupied, knowledge of the area. These benefits are forfeited by desertion, but they may be compensated for by getting a better mate or breeding site.

Among redwings, desertion of a mate is equivalent to a decision to leave the territory. Males do this extremely rarely during a breeding season, and only about 15% of them change territories between breeding seasons (see chapter 8). Females also exhibit considerable site fidelity, but after nest destruction, which happens frequently, many females move to other territories, usually on the same marsh, for renesting (Beletsky and Orians 1991). Female redwings cannot benefit by deserting a nest prior to fledging because males never incubate and, so far as we are aware, in our study area do not initiate nestling feeding when a female dies or leaves.

The level of investment made by male redwings in a breeding effort appears to vary little with the number of active nests on his territory because time devoted to territory defense and harassment of potential predators does not increase with number of nests on a territory. In contrast, the level of reproductive effort by a female is a function of how many nests she builds, the size of her clutch, how much food she brings to her offspring, and how soon and how often she renests after failure or successful completion of a nest. The energetic outputs of female redwings during the breeding season are high and variable, but we do not know how level of investment affects within-season survival. We can, and will, assess the influence of current investment by females on between-year survival and on investment in subsequent breeding seasons.

CASE HISTORIES

The following two typical lifetime breeding case histories illustrate how a male and a female achieved their LRS, the probable decisions they made while doing so, and how we assessed and scored the decisions. Some decisions are known; others are inferred from indirect evidence. Our purpose in presenting these case histories is to provide a quick overview of the types of breeding behavior and decisions we have analyzed, and of how the disparate decisions fit together to produce LRS.

1. Male 54883, more familiarly known as BA-RYA (a blue and an aluminum-colored band on the left leg, and red, yellow, and aluminum-colored bands on the right), was first seen at CNWR in March 1983 as an unbanded adult with a new territory on the east side of McMannamon Lake. Because he had full adult plumage, we knew he was at least two years old, and because he wore no bands, he definitely had not held a territory before on our core study area. He was quickly trapped and banded. He occupied an area that had been defended during the 1982 breeding season by another male who was no longer present. Thus, BA-RYA had "replaced" the previous occupant (as opposed to "inserting" between two previous and still present territory owners), and

he did so sometime between July 1982 and February 1983 (between breeding seasons). He had obtained the real estate either by directly challenging the previous owner or replacing him after he died or deserted. Because very few males gain territories by directly evicting other males, the latter method is the more likely.

BA-RYA held his McMannamon Lake territory for two years. In 1983, 4 females built a total of 7 nests on his territory, from which 15 young successfully fledged. In 1984, he had 3 females and 3 nests, none of which fledged young. Another male owned BA-RYA's McMannamon territory at the start of the 1985 season, but we do not know whether BA-RYA left of his own volition or was evicted. However, BA-RYA appeared on the west side of Juvenile Pocket a few days after 15 May 1985, midway through the breeding season, replacing a male who was never seen again. BA-RYA held that portion of Juvenile Pocket, our most productive redwing marsh, for three years. In 1985, in the remaining breeding period (late May and June), BA-RYA's 4 females built 12 nests, from which they fledged 5 offspring. In 1986, 2 females built 5 nests, from which 5 young fledged; in 1987, 14 females built 19 nests, from which 20 young fledged. BA-RYA was not seen after June 1987; he presumably died during the 1987–1988 winter. His lifetime production of fledged young, assuming that he fathered all of them, was 45. BA-RYA was never observed to feed young.

BA-RYA made, or is suspected to have made, the following breeding decisions during his lifetime:

Instead of risking injury by fighting a current owner for a territory, BA-RYA probably gained breeding status by waiting, searching for a vacant territory; by checking repeatedly, he eventually located one on McMannamon Lake. Rather than bringing insect food to his nestlings and fledglings, BA-RYA spent his time advertising throughout each breeding season for additional mates. Because his efforts in 1984 yielded no fledged young on his territory, BA-RYA may have deserted the territory and searched for another nearby that had a better probability of future success. He monitored Juvenile Pocket and finally obtained a territory there in mid–breeding season by replacing an owner who probably died. The new territory, 600 m from his original one, was better because the previous year it had supported 3 females who had 4 nests and fledged 7 young, whereas his own territory that year had produced no fledged young. Also, there were already nests in progress when he assumed ownership, and although he could not benefit reproductively from active nests, he "inherited" some of the females for future nests. BA-RYA defended his Juvenile Pocket territory through the 1986 and

1987 seasons, retaining his current holdings rather than switching to adjacent territories when those owners died.

2. Female 38053, YA-RBY, was banded as an adult female on 1 May 1988, when she left the eggs she was incubating and flew to a trap near Juvenile Pocket baited with seeds. Her nesting history that follows includes only those nests definitely associated with her by our field observers, i.e., none of these nests were assigned to the female by our HAREMSIZE computer program (see chapter 2). YA-RBY spent her entire reproductive "career" on Juvenile Pocket. Her first nest of 1988, on the territory of male 65451, fledged 2 offspring. She switched locations for her second 1988 nest, to the territory of male 56320, and again fledged 2. In 1989 she returned to nest with her first "mate," 65451, and fledged 3. For her second 1989 nest, which fledged 4, YA-RBY switched to the territory of male 65700. YA-RBY remained to nest on 65700's territory during the next three years. In 1990 she had 1 nest that fledged 3; in 1991 her only nest failed; and in 1992 she had 1 nest that fledged 1. Because we stopped nest monitoring at the end of the 1992 breeding season, we do not know whether YA-RBY bred in subsequent years, but during her five years on Juvenile Pocket, she built nests on the territories of 3 different males and successfully fledged 15 young.

YA-RBY made, or is suspected of having made, the following breeding decisions:

YA-RBY was at least two years old in 1988 (we know she was not a yearling because her epaulets in 1988 already had a reddish hue; see chapter 2), and she probably had bred outside of the core study area in 1987. Searching for a new breeding site in early April 1988, she settled in Juvenile Pocket, perhaps attracted by the high density of male territories there and the high density of already-settled females. She selected the territory of male 65451, a new breeder, settled in among his other 4 females, built the fifth nest on the territory that year, copulated with 65451 and his neighbors, and laid her first egg on 26 April. After successfully fledging 2 from her first nest, and although the end of the breeding season was near, she tried again. YA-RBY moved over the boundary to the adjacent territory of male 56320, laying the first egg of her second clutch on 13 June. The next year, 1989, she returned to the territory of her first mate on Juvenile Pocket, male 65451, and again began laying rather late, starting the fourth nest on the territory on 18 April. For her second nest of 1989, she moved to the territory of another adjacent neighbor, male 65700. For the next three years she remained with 65700, being the primary (first to nest) female on his territory in

1990 and 1991, although she continued to solicit copulations occasionally from his neighbors. During her five years of breeding in the study area, YA-RBY nested on only one marsh but on 3 males' territories, and she copulated with several other adjacent neighbors as well. She made a total of seven separate decisions about when to start nests.

INFORMATION UPON WHICH BREEDING-SEASON CHOICES CAN BE BASED

Redwings do not make their breeding-season decisions randomly, but the extensive variation in decisions among and within individuals indicates that most decisions are not "hard-wired." The decisions of individual birds presumably are influenced by a genetic program of conditional decision-making rules that can be expressed as "if the environmental situation is x, then do y." These conditional rules are expected to evolve in accordance with long-term statistical correlations between situation x and the payoff from behavior y, given x. Because determining the current environmental state requires some investment of time, individuals are expected to invest that time only if their success exceeds that which they would have achieved if they had made their decisions in the absence of the information gained by the investment. Therefore, estimating the value of information, with value measured as the positive influence of possession of that information on reproductive success, has been a major goal of our study.

The environmental factors that most strongly influence redwing reproductive success on our study area are weather, food supply, nest predation, brood parasitism, intraspecific competition, competition with yellowheads, and vegetation changes. These factors change both within and between breeding seasons, at different rates, and with different predictability. Weather changes abruptly and unpredictably, but in our study area the probability of bad weather gradually declines during the breeding season. Emergence of aquatic insects changes annually, seasonally, and on a daily basis in response to weather conditions— aquatic insects, for example, do not emerge on cold, rainy days (Orians 1980). Brood parasitism by Brown-headed Cowbirds (*Molothrus ater*) does not begin at CNWR until early May but it soon reaches a high rate that is maintained throughout the remainder of the redwing breeding season (Orians et al. 1989). The migratory yellowheads arrive on the breeding grounds long after redwing territories have been reoccupied and after many female redwings have begun nesting, but the areas that will be occupied by yellowheads are fairly predictable over periods of several years (Beletsky and Orians 1994). New growth of emergent vegetation begins in March and continues through the breeding season. Between years, the structure of the vegetation may change dramatically as a result of winter blow-down and beaver activity.

Thus, the complex information available from the environment changes in different ways and at different rates, and often has low predictive value. We base our analyses on correlations between environmental states and reproductive success in our sixteen-year data record. Our primary method of estimating the value of different kinds of environmental information has been to determine correlations between particular environmental states and success of reproductive efforts initiated under those conditions. In other words, we ask, If the correlations we observed empirically are assumed to characterize the environment over evolutionarily significant time spans, how should redwings use that information in making their decisions? Of course, conditions during our sixteen-year record probably differed somewhat from the long-term average. Predation patterns and spring weather are both notoriously variable. Brood parasitism rates are certainly much higher than they were just a few decades ago because cowbirds were relatively rare in Washington State until very recently. Nonetheless, correlations between reproductive success and many environmental variables may be sufficiently consistent to enable us to evaluate conditional decision-making rules in response to them. In any event, because the long-term empirical record is the most complete source of data available to us, we use it to the fullest extent reasonable.

We have supplemented our long-term empirical record with selected experimental manipulations of environmental conditions and the states of the birds themselves. We experimentally manipulated old nests to determine whether the clues they provide about the previous year's breeding are used by females when they make their settling decisions (Erckmann et al. 1990; see chapter 4). We artificially increased food supplies to determine female nesting responses (chapter 3). We experimentally removed males from their territories to test theories of territorial dominance (chapters 7 and 8), and we monitored and manipulated hormone levels to determine how physiological conditions influence the outcome of territorial contests (Beletsky and Orians 1989a; Beletsky et al. 1990).

A major limitation in our ability to assess the value of environmental information is the fact that our measures of success are based primarily upon the outcomes of nests initiated by female redwings on our study marshes. Because we could not manipulate where or when females nested, we could not, for example, measure the success of nests if fewer (or more) females had elected to breed on a particular marsh at a particular time. We were also unable to, or did not, manipulate the physiological condition of females, predation rates or patterns, brood parasitism, competition with yellowheads, or the weather (we did *talk* about it a lot). Therefore, our study suffers from the usual problems inherent in any correlational analysis. In an attempt to avoid overinterpreting correlational data, we will assess the strengths and weaknesses of all our judgments that are based exclusively on nonexperimental, long-term data.

PLAN OF THE BOOK

Chapter 2 provides an introduction to our study area and the redwing population that inhabits it, and an overview of our methods for monitoring territoriality, site fidelity, and breeding success. Female breeding decisions—when and where to nest and how much energy to expend each year—are considered in chapters 3, 4, and 5. In chapter 6 we explore theoretical considerations relating to how males acquire their territories and retain dominance there. We then consider male decisions—how, when, and where to acquire territories—in chapter 7, and site fidelity and movements in chapter 8. Finally, in chapter 9 we attempt a synthesis of what we have learned about redwing breeding decisions, their consequences, and the constraints on them, and discuss general implications of the results of our long-term study.

Two

Marshes as Breeding Habitats, Study Site, General Methods, and Lifetime Reproductive Success

INTRODUCTION

In most parts of North America the majority of redwing nests are built in emergent vegetation over water. Relative to many habitat types, marshes are short-lived. At high latitudes, most lakes that support marshes were formed by the action of glaciers during their last advance and retreat. These lakes are filled in slowly over centuries by sediments carried in by rivers, supplemented by atmospheric deposition and organic debris. Some lakes arise as oxbows, former river channels that become isolated when rivers change their courses. Other generators of marshes are beavers, whose dams create many small lakes whose life spans are measured in years to decades, and humans, whose dams often create large lakes. Human-made lakes often fill in rapidly because "good" dam sites are usually in areas where rivers carry heavy sediment loads that quickly accumulate behind the dams. Nonetheless, lakes are long-lived in relation to time frames of blackbird population dynamics. Newly formed marshes are quickly discovered by blackbirds and are occupied as long as they provide suitable breeding conditions.

The variability of their water levels is a feature of many lakes of great significance for breeding blackbirds. In humid regions where most lakes have outlets, water levels are stable enough for beds of emergent vegetation to develop in shallow areas that are protected from strong wave action. In arid and semiarid regions, most lakes lack outlets, and water levels fluctuate markedly in response to seasonal and yearly variations in precipitation. Beds of emergent vegetation fail to develop on most of these lakes, and redwings are unable to nest there. Similar instability of water levels characterizes many impoundments whose waters are used for irrigation or power generation.

In addition to varying in time, features of lakes vary spatially. Beds of emergent vegetation are even more patchy than lakes, and their locations within lakes shift in response to changes in lake levels and local disturbances. On lakes that are moderately steep-sided, emergent vegetation is confined to relatively narrow strips adjacent to shore. Shallower lakes may support broader beds of emergent vegetation of varying degrees of patchiness, and, depending upon water levels, varying portions of those beds may have no standing water below them.

The sizes and shapes of beds of emergent vegetation are significant for blackbirds in a number of ways. They determine the number of territorial neighbors a male redwing has, the vulnerability of nests to terrestrial and aquatic predators, the quantity of food produced on the territories, and the amounts and kinds of undefended foraging areas at different distances from nest sites. Thin strips of emergent vegetation may be only one territory wide, so that each male has no more than two neighbors, and all territories interface with both open water and uplands. In broad marsh beds, only some territories have either an interface with open water or upland, and no territories have both.

MARSHES OF THE COLUMBIA NATIONAL WILDLIFE REFUGE (CNWR)

Our long-term study site, the Columbia National Wildlife Refuge (46.5° N, 119.1° W) and adjacent state-owned and private lands, is located in the heart of the Columbia Basin Desert of eastern Washington. Known locally as the Potholes, the topography consists of basins and buttes scoured in Miocene lava flows by Pleistocene floods when the current channel of the Columbia River was blocked by ice (Bretz 1959). The Potholes lie in the rainshadow of the Cascade Mountains and receive only about 200 mm of precipitation annually. Rainfall is generally light during the blackbird breeding season, but strong winds are very common. Winters are relatively mild, but ice forms on the lakes for at least brief periods during the winter. During unusually cold winters, ice cover lasts up to several months and the lakes may not thaw until early March. Most redwing nesting occurs from the end of March (first eggs laid) through the end of June (last young fledged). March is usually cool, although the weather then is quite variable (chapter 3). April is moderate, but May and June are usually warm; midday temperatures often exceed 30° C. July and August are hot.

Basins in the area were either dry or occupied by vernal ponds prior to the initiation of extensive irrigation about 1951, which caused ground water tables to rise, creating many lakes and ponds. Water is also provided by seepage from the Potholes Reservoir to the north and a major drainage canal that carries water from the reservoir to agricultural lands to the south. Many of the ponds are managed by the U.S. Fish and Wildlife Service, which has installed weirs at their outlets that maintain nearly constant water levels through the spring and summer. Thus, although our study site is located in an arid region, water-level stability is similar to that found in humid areas.

The sides of some of the Potholes lakes are too steep to support emergent vegetation, but where gradients are appropriate, there are stands of cattail (*Typha angustifolia*), bulrushes (*Scirpus*), and sedges (fig. 2.1). When we began the study, scattered stands of peachleaf willow (*Salix amygdaloides*) grew along the streams and edges of lakes, but they have been largely cut down by beavers. Their place has been partly taken by a thorny exotic tree, the Russian olive (*Elaeagnus angustifolia*), whose fruits are readily dispersed by birds. The upland vegetation of the area is a desert dominated by sagebrush (*Artemisia tridentata*) and rabbitbrush (*Chrysothamnus nauseosus* and *C. viscidifolius*), with an understory of perennial grasses (*Agropyron spicatum* and *Poa sandbergii*) and the Eurasian annual cheat-grass (*Bromus tectorum*). Greasewood (*Sarcobatus vermiculatus*), with an understory of saltgrass (*Dactylus glomerata*), dominates alkaline flats.

Two of our major study lakes are adjacent to agricultural lands (fig. 2.2). Morgan Lake is bordered on its north side by a large irrigated pasture. An alfalfa field lies south of McMannamon Lake. Both of these areas are utilized extensively by foraging blackbirds, particularly early in the spring. The entire refuge was heavily grazed by cattle until the early 1970s, but since then Morgan is the only core-area study lake to which cattle have had access.

Our core study area at CNWR consists of marshes on five lakes in a single drainage system (fig. 2.2). Approximately 2,800 m separate the northernmost lake from the southernmost. The core breeding marshes are located along a north-south linear axis, with generally broad areas of dry desert grassland to the east and west. This particular geography has several important implications for the birds' behavior. For example, individuals switching their breeding sites can do so by moving very short distances to the north or south, but to the east or west they must first cross extensive arid areas. Also, breeding activity on all the marshes can easily be monitored by conspecifics because undefended upland areas abut all the marshes. The demographic data analyzed and interpreted in this book were gathered primarily on the core area, but we also monitored populations and performed experiments on some of the peripheral lakes identified in the figure (Frog Lake, Marsh Unit 3, Herman Pond, Coot Lake, Hays Creek).

Fig. 2.1. Typical Red-winged
Blackbird breeding habitat at
the Columbia National Wildlife
Refuge, where the males'
territories occupy stands of
emergent vegetation that grow
in shallow portions of lakes
and waterways. (a) Frog Lake,
where "strip" territories in
cattails line the perimeter of
the lake. (b) Morgan Pocket,
a "pocket" marsh, a large
expanse of vegetation with
many irregularly shaped
redwing territories.

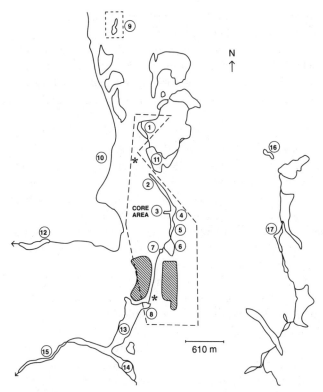

Fig. 2.2. Map of lakes and waterways in the study area showing positions of the core-area marshes and some of the peripheral breeding areas. The locations of the large grain traps where most birds were captured and banded are indicated by asterisks; the Ranch trap was located in the northern part of the study area, the Subheadquarters trap in the southern part. Crosshatched areas are agricultural fields. Frog Lake (9), in the small box at the top of the map, was actually located 5.2 km north of the Subheadquarters trap. Marsh Unit 3 (12) and Hays Creek (15) are long, thin marshes that run farther west than displayed. Core breeding marshes are (1) Hampton Slough, (2) North Juvenile, (3) Juvenile Pocket, (4) SE/SW Juvenile, (5) Para Lake, (6) McMannamon Lake, (7) McMannamon Pocket, and (8) Morgan Pocket. Peripheral breeding marshes are (9) Frog Creek, (10) Crab Creek, (11) Lake Marie, (12) Marsh Unit 3, (13) Morgan Lake, (14) Halfmoon Lake, (15) Hays Creek, (16) Coot Lake, and (17) Herman Pond.

PHYSICAL VARIABILITY OF MARSHES
IN BLACKBIRD TIME

The structure of marsh vegetation exerts a profound influence on breed-ing blackbirds. Marsh vegetation is typically no more than a few meters high at the end of the growing season. Because it is dominated by a few species of herbaceous perennials, the emergent vegetation has a simple, repetitive structure. During the winter in temperate regions, or during dry periods at low latitudes, the emergent plants die back to underwater perennating structures from which new growth develops. Nevertheless, the plants are typically sturdy enough that the dead stalks remain upright through at least one winter and constitute the major structure of the marsh in early spring when blackbird breeding begins.

SEASONAL CHANGES IN MARSH STRUCTURE

In early spring, the structure of a temperate marsh, such as those at CNWR, is formed by dead stalks of emergent vegetation that have survived one or more winters. These stalks provide advertising and sentinel perches for territorial male redwings, and they are the only support available for the nests of early-breeding females. The beds of dead vegetation block sunlight and depress water temperatures. As a result, growth of new emergent stalks is slower within thick beds than in more open areas. Under very dense beds, new growth may be prevented entirely. Growth of new stalks increases stem densities, thereby changing both nest sites and foraging conditions within the beds. Thus, conditions when the first redwing nests are built differ markedly from those only two months later.

Although they are sturdy, dead stalks gradually decay. After a few years, stalks rot at water level and are then severed by ice or wave action. This can result in broad areas of "blow-down" that eventually create conditions highly favorable for growth of new stalks from the underwater rhizomes (fig. 2.3). These changes are often rapid enough to alter dramatically the territories of individual blackbirds between consecutive breeding seasons.

Other rapid changes in marsh vegetation are caused by the action of mammals. Our study area supports a thriving population of beavers. Because lake levels are controlled by weirs, the beavers seldom build dams, although they constantly try to block water flow through weirs (forever frustrating refuge personnel). The beavers forage extensively on cattail corms; a family can virtually destroy the beds of cattails—eliminating all emergent vegetation—on a small lake within two years. Muskrats also harvest many cattails, but they consume only the meristematic regions of individual growing stalks and do not destroy corms. Therefore, they have only minor effects on vegetation structure. Cattle, when present, heavily graze the fresh stalks of cattails and bulrushes during the growing season, and they wander out on the ice to eat dead stalks during the winter. (One bull fell through the ice on Morgan Pocket over the 1987–88 winter, creating an underwater obstacle that

Fig. 2.3. A typical redwing breeding marsh at the Columbia National Wildlife Refuge, showing areas of major overwinter cattail blow-down. Such changes in marsh structure can significantly alter the quality of male territories between years.

we had to detour around each time we checked nests the following
spring.)

Knowledge of the histories of each of the eight core-area breeding
marshes may assist the reader in interpreting the results of our analyses
(see also table 2.1).

MORGAN POCKET. A relatively small marsh on the northeast corner
of a large lake, it was during most of the study a densely populated,
highly productive redwing breeding area. However, strong competition
from yellowheads starting in the mid-1980s, and heavy cattle damage
that began during the winter of 1984–85 and continued each year thereafter, severely reduced the amount of emergent vegetation, redwing
numbers, and breeding success. During the last years of the study,
yellowheads excluded redwings from most of the marsh, confining the
two or three remaining males to territories on the shore edge of the
marsh.

McMANNAMON POCKET. Located along the stream that empties
McMannamon Lake, this marsh varied widely over the years in the
number of male territories it contained. During the last few years of
the study, beavers cut down much of the standing crop of cattail, but
the male redwings that remained still attracted many females that nested
on small cattail islands with only a few stalks, or in sedges along the
stream.

McMANNAMON LAKE. A large, round lake bordered by a strip of
cattail of varying thickness. The southeast part of the lake, with the
widest cattail marsh, was heavily settled by yellowheads starting in the
mid 1980s. Yellowheads peaked there in 1988 and declined in number
each subsequent year until 1993, when there were none (Beletsky and
Orians 1994). The marsh vegetation on the southeast section of the lake
was reduced to about one-half its previous width by beavers during the
1991–92 winter. A major nesting area during the early years of the
study, with over 120 nests per year, only 30 to 40 nests per year were
built on McMannamon during the final years of the study.

PARA LAKE. A long, narrow lake that connects Juvenile Lake to
McMannamon Lake. The northernmost two-thirds of Para has only
very thin strips of cattail marsh a meter or two wide, whereas the
southern third has a section of wider marsh. Beavers began reducing

TABLE 2.1. Major attributes of eight core-area redwing breeding marshes monitored from 1977 through 1992 at CNWR

Marsh	Type[a]	$\bar{X}$ no. of male territories at midseason, 1 May[b]	$\bar{X}$ territory size (m^2)	$\bar{X}$ harem size	$\bar{X}$ start date of first 10 nests each year, 1977–92[c]	Major YHB[d] area?	Years of major perturbations	$\bar{X}$ no. of territorial years/male
Morgan Pocket	P	5.2 ± 2.7	117 ± 64	4.6 ± 2.6	112 ± 12	Y	1985, 1986	2.1 ± 1.9
McMannamon Pocket	P	8.3 ± 1.3	132 ± 79	4.4 ± 2.6	110 ± 9	N	1987	2.1 ± 1.6
Juvenile Pocket	P	14.9 ± 5.0	93 ± 46	5.5 ± 3.4	103 ± 9	N	none	2.7 ± 1.9
North Juvenile	P/S	6.6 ± 2.7	154 ± 72	3.6 ± 1.9	104 ± 9	Y	1990, 1991	2.2 ± 1.7
McMannamon Lake	S	14.2 ± 2.6	157 ± 89	3.3 ± 2.0	108 ± 9	Y	1985, 1987, 1992	2.0 ± 1.6
Para Lake	S	7.7 ± 2.1	173 ± 89	3.2 ± 2.0	111 ± 8	N	1992	2.2 ± 1.7
SE/SW Juvenile	S	6.6 ± 2.6	185 ± 104	3.1 ± 1.6	110 ± 9	N	1991, 1992	1.6 ± 1.0
Hampton Slough	S	12.8 ± 6.4	160 ± 98	3.4 ± 1.9	112 ± 11	N	1985, 1986	2.7 ± 1.9

[a] P = Pocket; S = Strip; North Juvenile had elements of both types.
[b] 1983–92.
[c] Julian dates of first eggs.
[d] Yellow-headed Blackbird.

the emergent vegetation here in 1990, cut down about half of it during the winter of 1991–92, and the remainder in 1993.

SE/SW JUVENILE. We consider together these marshes, which border the southeast and southwest banks of Juvenile Lake, because they are both thin strips, because they are located directly across from each other, and because single male territories frequently spanned the lake to include portions of both strips. Most emergent vegetation was destroyed by beavers during the winters of 1990–91 (SE) and 1991–92 (SE and SW).

JUVENILE POCKET. The emergent vegetation in this small marsh, located in an infolding of south Juvenile Lake that juts to the west, expanded steadily in size each year both because there were no major blow-downs and because there were annual accretions of emergent vegetation to the marsh periphery. Protected to the north and south by cliffs, it was the marsh most sheltered from the wind. By the end of the study, Juvenile Pocket was the only core-area marsh that had not been substantially damaged by beavers or other actors and that was still fledging large numbers of redwings. More than 200 nests annually were built on Juvenile Pocket from 1989 through 1991.

NORTH JUVENILE. A long marsh located along the northeast shore of Juvenile Lake, North Juvenile was heavily colonized by yellowheads early in the study, but their occupancy of the marsh dwindled in the late 1980s. During the winters of 1989–90 and 1990–91, beavers destroyed most of the emergent vegetation. By the 1992 breeding season, fewer than ten redwing nests were built on North Juvenile.

HAMPTON SLOUGH. A long, thin lake bordered for the most part by a thin strip of cattail. At various times during the study, the south end and the midportion of "the Slough" contained broader expanses of cattail and bulrush, but beaver removed them. Beaver caused minor damage to cattail beds during the winter of 1984–85, destroyed half the emergent vegetation during the winter of 1985–86 (virtually eliminating vegetation at the north end of the lake but leaving some at the shallow southern end of the lake), and then removed the rest during the next few years. By 1992 the number of redwing nests on Hampton Slough was only about ten, an order of magnitude less than its peak in the early 1980s.

SEASONAL CHANGES IN PRODUCTION OF BLACKBIRD FOOD

The most striking characteristic of temperate marshes is the seasonal pattern of emergence of insects with aquatic larval but terrestrial adult stages. The number of aquatic insects that emerge on a lake is a function of the chemistry of the lake, its depth and permanence, the kind of predators present, and the nature of submerged and emergent vegetation. CNWR lakes originally lacked fish, but trout (*Salmo spp.*) were introduced for sport fishing, and carp (*Cyprinus carpio*) inadvertently gained access to the Potholes drainage systems from the Columbia River. Studies of insect emergence carried out at CNWR prior to the initiation of the present project revealed that carp may reduce emergences to about 1/100 of their probable previous values (Orians 1980). The effect appears to be caused by habitat destruction rather than direct predation on insects. Carp-infested lakes are characterized by muddy bottoms almost devoid of vegetation, and their water is perpetually murky.

At CNWR, the most important emerging insects from the viewpoint of blackbirds are odonates, particularly damselflies, which greatly outnumber dragonflies. Seasonal emergence of odonates begins in late April, reaches a peak in late June, and continues at a high level through the summer (Orians 1980). During a typical sunny day, larvae begin to crawl out of the water early in the morning and emerge at the highest rate late in the morning. The number emerging declines rapidly during the afternoon. This diurnal pattern is more marked earlier in the blackbird breeding season when the nights are colder than later (Orians 1980). Within lakes, emergence is greatest on shores exposed to open water and on outer edges of beds of emergent vegetation. Emergence is lowest on shores behind emergent vegetation and within expanses of emergent vegetation (Orians 1980). Once teneral odonates have hardened enough to be able to fly, which usually takes about an hour depending upon temperature and humidity, they fly away from the edges of the lakes to the uplands, greatly increasing prey densities there during the afternoon.

For reasons that are not clear, the pattern and quantity of emergences on individual lakes vary greatly among years. Indeed, the ranks of CNWR lakes ordered by densities of emerging aquatic insects may change markedly from year to year. For example, North Juvenile, one of the core marshes, had the greatest damselfly emergence of seven sampled marshes in the study area in 1978, but in 1979 it had the lowest damselfly emergence among the same marshes (Orians and

Wittenberger 1991). We are unable either to explain or predict these changes, and we doubt that blackbirds are able to do so, although we are reluctant to conclude that blackbirds are as ignorant as we are of events that affect them so strongly.

Emerging aquatic insects are an unusual type of animal prey because they are renewed on a daily basis, and the quantity of emergence on day $x + 1$ is not determined by the quantity of emergence on day x. In addition, an individual soft-bodied teneral, the prime prey of breeding blackbirds, is easily captured for only about an hour after it emerges from the water. After that it can fly away when a blackbird approaches and it can usually outmaneuver a blackbird in flight. Thus, the primary food delivered by female redwings to their nestlings is highly variable in space and time on scales ranging from hours to weeks, and quantities and locations of emergences are poorly correlated between years.

GENERAL METHODS

TRAPPING AND BANDING; AGING

We banded all territorial males in the core study area, many males with territories in peripheral areas, many male floaters, and many females with unique combinations of colored aluminum leg bands and U.S. Fish and Wildlife Service numbered bands. Bands were, for the most part, red, blue, yellow, or aluminum-colored. We placed small traps baited with seeds near territories to catch individual birds; we caught most females by this method. We also caught males in one of two larger, multiple-capture traps located some distance from the core marshes (fig. 2.2). One of the larger traps was situated in the northern half of the core study area (through 1990), and one in the southern half. We operated the larger traps, also baited with seeds, several hours at a time, several days per week. Trapped birds, up to ten at a time, were removed usually every twenty minutes. We recorded, weighed, and, if necessary, banded all males when they were captured. We gave females the same treatment but also scored them subjectively for plumage characteristics and determined their reproductive condition by checking for a brood patch.

We captured most territory owners in the area at least once each year; some visited traps repeatedly during a breeding season. From 1987 onwards, many captured individuals also involuntarily donated small quantities of blood (200–300 µl), removed from a wing vein, so that we could determine circulating levels of various steroid hormones. Blood sampling, accomplished in a minute or less, was a very minor procedure. Most birds immediately flew back to their territories after being bled, and many returned to the same trap the same day, suggesting that they were not harmed by the procedure and did not perceive it to be an especially unpleasant experience.

We gave all females full color-band combinations. We were certain of the true ages of only those few females born locally who were captured in future years wearing USFWS numbered bands we had given them as nestlings. However, yearling females almost always have dull, brownish epaulets that get redder with age (Nero 1954; Payne 1969; Miskimen 1980; Langston et al. 1990). In fact, about 80% of the thirty or so locally born, banded females we recovered during their yearling year had no red in their epaulets, i.e., they were dull and brownish. In contrast, 100% of known-age females that were first captured when they were greater than one year old had reddish epaulets. Thus, for the years we scored epaulets when we captured females (1982–92), we assumed that all females with no red in their epaulets were one year old. This assumption permitted us for some analyses to divide our information into that gathered for "yearlings" (females during the year they had no red in their epaulets) and "matures" (which included information for all females initially trapped with red epaulets and information from "yearlings" during their subsequent breeding years).

For two reasons we knew the true ages of many more males than females. First, more locally born and banded males than females returned to the study area and were captured. Second, yearling males, "subadults," have a more female-like plumage than adult males, and are always identifiable as one-year-olds. Thus, we knew the true ages of all males that were first banded as nestlings or subadults. During the early years of the study, yearling males received only an aluminum USFWS numbered band. From 1985 onwards they were given a USFWS band and a single colored band that indicated the month and year the bird was captured. When we captured these males as adults, we gave them full color combinations. However, subadults known to hold territories (very few birds) received full color combinations. We could age males initially trapped and banded in adult plumage, which they first acquire in molt during their second autumn, only as "at least two years old." We aged such males, caught the next year, as "at least three," etc.

MONITORING REPRODUCTIVE SUCCESS

We monitored intensively all core-area marshes to obtain information on when nests were started, when they terminated, causes of termination, clutch size, fledging success, and nest parasitism by Brown-headed Cowbirds. Each year we began searching marshes for nests about 1 April, or earlier if females were observed nest-building. Each nest was marked with a numbered orange and yellow flag placed higher than the nest (so that we could see the flag and its number with a telescope from shore) in nearby vegetation. Most years we checked nests for progress every 3 days; each marsh was searched completely for new nests every 6 days. In 1980 and 1981, nests were checked daily. Nestlings were banded with single USFWS bands at 6 to 8 d of age. Nestlings fledged usually at 11 to 12 d. We considered a nest to have fledged young if (1) fledglings were seen near the empty nest at the appropriate time, or (2) an individually identifiable female was observed feeding fledglings, or (3) nestlings were known to have survived at least 8 days and the nest was found empty with no physical evidence of predation during the next visit. The major source of nest failure was predation by birds, mammals, and snakes (see below). One or two nestlings starved in some nests, but very rarely did entire clutches; losses to starvation were much lower than predation losses. We have no information on survival of fledglings after they left nests. For most of our analyses, we considered a nest to be "successful" if it fledged ≥ 1; "unsuccessful" if it fledged none.

We estimate annual reproductive success (RS) for a male as the sum of all young fledged from nests located within his territory. We assume 100% paternity in these calculations, even though we know that about one-third of offspring are sired by EPCs, because we have no way to adjust for EPCs. The unavoidable error introduced by this procedure is probably very small because males in the population gain, on average, as much as they lose via EPCs and there are no "supermales" that consistently gain reproductively from EPCs (Gray 1996b). Gray was able to identify both participants in 375 copulations during 402 hours of observations, 66 (17%) of which were EPCs. Using DNA fingerprinting methods, she found that 33.7% of 403 nestlings were the result of extrapair fertilizations (EPFs). Seventy-two of 134 broods she examined (53.7%) included one or more EPF nestlings. All but one EPF nestling proved to be fathered by other territory owners on the same marsh, most of them by adjacent neighbors (Gray 1996a).

Although EPFs were common, the overall effect on male RS was minor. During all three years of Gray's study (1990 through 1992), correlations between the apparent and true RS of individual males were highly significant; factoring in EPFs, in fact, did not significantly change among-individual variance in male RS. Within and across breeding seasons, equivalent numbers of males gained and lost paternity from EPFs. For 76 males over three years, 22 increased their paternity via EPFs, 28 had reduced paternity, and 26 experienced no net change, i.e., they gained as much by copulating with neighboring females as they lost from their own females' copulating with neighboring males. Finally, individual males did not consistently gain or lose from EPFs from year to year (Gray 1996b).

We estimated female annual RS as the sum of young fledged from all her nests that year. We assigned most nests to a female because she was observed to build or attend the nest. For some analyses, we assigned additional nests to a female with our HAREMSIZE program, which is described below.

Early in our study we realized that we could never catch and band every female that nested in our marshes—they were too numerous and they moved frequently into and out of the study area between nests and/or between years. In addition, many nests were depredated or abandoned before we could identify their builders. Determining which female builds and tends each nest is a nontrivial task because females usually move low in the vegetation and because two or more females may build nests within a meter of each other. Some of the nests to which no female could be assigned were built by unbanded females but many others were probably built by banded females, some of whom had other nests with which we *were* able to associate them. Thus, we had gaps in our nesting records that prevented us from knowing true RS and reproductive effort for many females, as well as true territorial harem sizes.

To correct for these gaps in our nesting records, we estimated harem sizes using a method outlined by Searcy (1979a). Nests not associated with banded females (those built by unbanded or unknown females) were assigned to the smallest possible number of additional females that could account for those nests, based on known nest dates, and assuming that a female renests (lays a first egg in a new nest) no sooner than four days after destruction of her previous nest (we know definitely that many banded females laid the first egg of a new clutch as soon as 4 days after the failure of a previous nest; other redwing researchers have also reported minimum four-day delays). The harem-estimating program, HAREMSIZE, keyed in on the start dates (date of the first egg) and termination dates (actual or estimated) of each nest. If the known, banded females on the territory, given their known nest timing, could have been responsible for all of the "unknown" nests on the territory, then no additional ("phantom") females were added to the harem. The first phantom female necessary to account for an "unknown-female" nest on a male's territory was considered by the program to be a real female on that territory, available to be assigned to other, subsequent "unknown-female" nests, provided that the timing was appropriate. The process was iterated, the program creating a new phantom female each time another "unknown-female" nest could not be assigned to one of the banded or phantom females already present in that harem. The program also tracked individual banded females so that if they moved to other territories within the core area, they could not be credited with additional nests on their initial territories. Furthermore, the program could assign nests "backwards" in time as well as forwards, e.g., if there was an "unknown" nest that terminated on 15 April and a banded female started her first "known" nest of the year on 22 April, the earlier nest could be assigned to her (provided that no other female on the male's territory provided a better "fit" in time). HAREMSIZE was indispensable for estimating the numbers of females on each male's territory each year, and for estimating female RS and reproductive effort.

HAREMSIZE assigns more females to a harem than the number definitely known to have built nests, but it is a conservative adjustment because some nests that are assigned to females in the harem (either to known or phantom females) were certainly built by additional females that were on the territory only temporarily. Thus, true harem sizes, on average, were larger than those calculated by HAREMSIZE, and some females were credited with nests they did not build, but our estimates using the program are closer to the real values than uncorrected estimates would be.

We cannot provide a systematic assessment of the magnitude of the error introduced to our analyses by HAREMSIZE. The error depends on the distribution of the number of our positive assignments of known banded females to nests for every male territory each year (those with 1 nest, those with 2 nests, those with 3 nests, etc.), as well as on the distribution of nest dates within each territory. If nesting on a territory were fairly simultaneous, HAREMSIZE would introduce only minor error because all simultaneously active nests must be tended by separate females. As the degree of synchronicity of nest dates within territories decreases, the potential for introduced error by HAREMSIZE increases.

True harem sizes and the estimates produced by the program are equal when we know the identity of each nest-tending female on a male's territory. But we have complete information on females and nests for a larger proportion of small harems than of medium or large harems. A few examples may help illustrate the bias. On Juvenile Pocket in 1992, male 62009 had 7 nests. Five of them were positively attributed to 3 banded females. One of the other 2 nests, because of its start date, could not have been built by any of the 3 banded females. Therefore, HAREMSIZE added one phantom female and arrived at a total harem for male 62009 of 4 females. This number is almost certainly the true harem size. At an extreme, however, on Hampton Slough in 1988, male 64009 had 15 nests, but only 3 were assigned in the field to 3 banded females. HAREMSIZE assigned the 12 "unknown-female" nests to the 3 banded females and to 5 phantom females, yielding a total harem size of 8, the minimum number of females that could account for the 15 nests. The true harem could well have been larger. The large harems typical of our study area, and the varying incompleteness of our data set, require us to use this estimating program. This and other similar estimates have been in regular use in avian behavioral ecology for more than fifteen years (e.g., Searcy 1979a), and we have already established its appropriateness for our CNWR blackbird populations (Beletsky and Orians 1987a; Beletsky et al. 1990).

MONITORING TERRITORIES

Each year we made territory maps for the core marshes at the beginning of the breeding season and updated them usually every two weeks thereafter. We also made territory maps for some of the peripheral marshes, such as Frog Lake, Marsh Unit 3, Hays Creek, Herman Pond, and Coot Lake, especially in years when they were sites of experimental manipulations. Territories were mapped by noting positions of males as they engaged in advertising, boundary disputes, and patrolling. At the termination of breeding each year, we used an Alidade surveying instrument to prepare highly detailed maps (2.54 cm = 6.1 m) of the core study marshes that included marsh outlines, territory boundaries, and nest positions. When individual males switched territories, we measured distances that they moved on an aerial photograph of the study area (2.54 cm = 170 m).

Many of our analyses of male territorial behavior are based on the territorial histories of males, on both core and peripheral marshes, as well as their histories as floaters. Information about floaters is provided by the date and location of their first capture, how often and where they were caught subsequently, and how many years they floated. For males that eventually obtained territories, we knew when and where they did so. Because we were interested in male movements—natal dispersal, breeding dispersal, and how far resident floaters roam as they search for territorial vacancies—we surveyed for banded individuals outside our core site. From 1985 through 1992, we censused territorial males in all marshes up to distances of 4 to 5 km in all directions surrounding the core site. We conducted censuses during early mornings and late afternoons, when males were most likely to be present on their territories. Almost all males with territories located 4 to 5 km from the core site were unbanded, suggesting that dispersal beyond this distance was rare (Beletsky and Orians 1993).

We were able to obtain complete censuses of banded male territory owners to a distance of 5 km from the the core study area because habitat that is suitable for redwing breeding covers only very small, disjunct areas on which males are readily observed and their band combinations read. Thus, our knowledge of male dispersal out to that distance is excellent, although we do not know the tail of the dispersal distribution. Fortunately, none of our analyses requires us to know the distances to which the most widely dispersing individuals travel.

VARIATION IN LRS

Long-term population studies of the kind we conducted typically demonstrate substantial temporal and spatial variation in demographic patterns. These variations show how populations respond to slightly different habitats or to similar habitats of differing quality, and, over time, to changing environmental conditions. Because demographic attributes and life-history features of populations evolved in temporally and spatially varying environments, birds should detect and respond to those variations. To set the stage for our analyses of the breeding-season decisions of male and female redwings, we first review briefly and update some of our previously published information on LRS, and describe long-term differences among marshes in factors that influence RS. Consistent differences among our eight marshes could influence male decisions on where to prospect for territories, how hard to fight to retain current territories, and whether, given opportunities, to switch territories. For females, this information could be important for decisions about where to nest, when to start nesting, and whether to remain on the same marsh between nesting attempts or to move.

Lifetime production of fledglings for 461 males, estimated as the number of young fledging from their territories, and 1311 females that began breeding in 1977 and continued from 1977 through 1991, derived

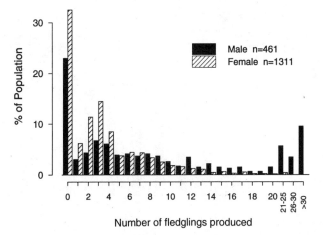

Fig. 2.4. Lifetime fledgling production of male and female redwings that attempted to breed, 1977–92. Information for males assumes 100% paternity of all young produced on their territories.

from information collected through 1992, is shown in fig. 2.4. Because 13% of these females had gaps of one year or more in their breeding records—either because we missed assigning them to nests or because they moved temporarily outside the monitored area—we adjusted their LRS by crediting them with the mean number of fledglings produced by mature females during the year(s) we missed them.

It is evident that a small percentage of males and of females account for most fledged offspring. More than 20% of males who succeeded in acquiring territories, and more than 30% of females who nested, fledged no offspring during their recorded breeding lifetimes. Furthermore, a large but undetermined segment of the adult male population each year fails to establish territories and thus has no chance to breed. Among individuals known to have bred between 1977 and 1992, there was, as expected in a polygamous breeder, a great disparity in variance in LRS between the sexes—for males, mean = 11.3, variance = 245.9, n = 461; for females, mean = 3.2, variance = 15.1, n = 1311. One exceptional male, who bred for eleven years, had 176 young fledge from nests on his territory, 4.2% of all young fledged in the study area during those years (fig. 2.5; Beletsky and Orians 1989c).

The average number of years on territory for 461 males was 2.4 ± 1.8 (range 1 to 11); the average number of breeding years for 1311 females was 2.4 ± 1.9. The lifetime number of fledged young per

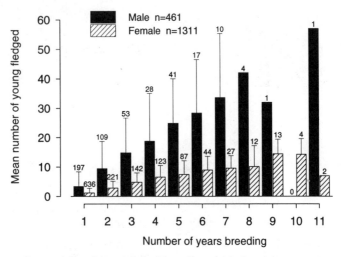

Fig. 2.5. Mean number of young fledged by male and female redwings as a function of the number of years breeding. Information for males assumes 100% paternity of all young produced on their territories. One male bred for eleven years, producing 176 fledged young (more than the number displayed).

individual breeder increased, on average, almost linearly with the number of breeding years, both for males and females (fig. 2.5).

CAUSES OF VARIATION IN LRS

LRS of a male depends primarily on the number of years he holds a territory, on the number of females that nest on his territory, on the average fledging success of those females (Orians and Beletsky 1989), and potentially on his skills at obtaining EPCs and guarding his mates from other males (Gray 1994; Westneat 1994). Female LRS depends primarily on number of years breeding, but environmental features also influence LRS.

On our eight core study marshes, reproductive success and some of its determinants varied in the following ways:

MARSH SHAPE: POCKETS VERSUS STRIPS

The marshes differed in size, as to when and how often they suffered major perturbations, and whether Yellow-headed Blackbirds settled on them (table 2.1). For many of our analyses we found it useful to group the marshes into two broad categories, according to general shape. Four of the core marshes (McMannamon Lake, Para, SE/SW Juvenile, Hampton Slough) were "strips," in which the emergent vegetation existed for the most part as thin strips and patches only one male territory wide. Three others were "pocket" marshes (Morgan, McMannamon, and Juvenile pockets), consisting of broad expanses of vegetation that contained many irregularly shaped territories. North Juvenile was a "hybrid"—a pocket area attached to a long strip; for analysis we usually considered North Juvenile to be a strip.

Marsh shape is important because it determines the spatial arrangement of male territories. Terrestrial nest predators have easy access to all redwing territories on a strip, but only to those territories on pockets that are adjacent to shore. Also, males with territories on pockets had up to five adjacent territorial neighbors, whereas males with territories on strips had, at most, two. Interactions among territorial neighbors affect social behavior and breeding success (e.g., Beletsky and Orians 1989b; Eason and Hannon 1994). Furthermore, females on pocket marshes that elect to change territories between nesting efforts have more adjacent territories from which to choose and, in general, shorter distances to traverse than do females on strip marshes. Highly relevant to our present purposes, significantly more young fledged, on average, from territories located in pockets than from those on strips (table 2.2). Pocket advantage may be due to some combination of the increased remoteness of many nests from shore and because the larger numbers of birds were more effective in antipredator surveillance and mobbing.

MEAN TERRITORY TENURE

The average number of years that males held their territories and bred varied significantly among marshes, from 1.6 ± 1.0 years on SE/SW Juvenile to 2.7 ± 1.9 on Hampton Slough (males that remained on the same marsh during their breeding lifetimes, n = 406; ANOVA, F = 2.24, P = 0.03; table 2.1). However, with one exception, there was no obvious pattern that explained the variation; there was no difference in mean tenure between strips and pockets (ANOVA, F = 0.15, P = 0.70). SE/SW Juvenile was for many years a relatively low-quality marsh which many males, after establishing territories there, deserted to move elsewhere.

HAREM SIZES

Marshes differed in mean harem size (ANOVA, F = 20.11, P < 0.0001). A posteriori tests placed the five strips marshes in one statistically distinct group and the three "pure" pocket marshes in two others (McMannamon Pocket and Morgan Pocket in one, and Juvenile Pocket

TABLE 2.2. Annual differences in some attributes of the redwing population at CNWR, 1977 through 1992

Year	No. of territories on May 1	No. of territorial males with ≥ 1 nest	Estimated no. of breeding females[a]	X̄ harem size[a]	Total no. of nests	X̄ first egg date for first nests of all females[d]	X̄ no. of young fledged/territory	
							Pockets	Strips
1977	65	65	239	3.5 ± 2.2	410	123 ± 15	5.6	3.4
1978	70	74	266	3.8 ± 2.5	453	114 ± 18	7.1	8.5
1979b	36	36	146	4.5 ± 2.7	289	127 ± 15	21.6	7.9
1980c	64	66	326	5.2 ± 2.5	558	119 ± 9	7.8	4.3
1981	76	82	275	3.8 ± 1.8	488	121 ± 10	5.9	3.0
1982	69	68	255	3.8 ± 2.1	418	125 ± 13	7.2	2.8
1983	72	80	285	3.8 ± 2.0	565	107 ± 14	9.3	3.8
1984	82	80	293	4.0 ± 2.3	548	116 ± 16	8.6	3.4
1985	83	84	303	3.7 ± 2.2	565	121 ± 16	7.3	3.4
1986	85	82	237	3.2 ± 2.1	504	119 ± 19	5.5	0.9
1987	79	79	329	4.3 ± 2.7	493	126 ± 16	9.0	4.6
1988	90	92	322	3.8 ± 2.8	539	126 ± 14	5.3	1.5
1989	83	75	304	4.5 ± 2.9	493	129 ± 15	6.5	1.8
1990	65	59	208	3.9 ± 3.2	321	123 ± 16	5.6	1.8
1991	59	57	181	3.4 ± 2.4	322	129 ± 11	2.3	1.8
1992	53	51	178	3.8 ± 3.2	278	122 ± 14	4.8	2.4
1993	37e	—	—	—	—	—	—	—
1994	40	—	—	—	—	—	—	—

aEstimated by HAREMSIZE program.
bFewer marshes were monitored in 1979.
c1980 was the first year in which Juvenile Pocket was monitored.
dJulian date, 100 = 10 April.
eExperimental removal of some territorial males occurred in 1993; see chapter 8.

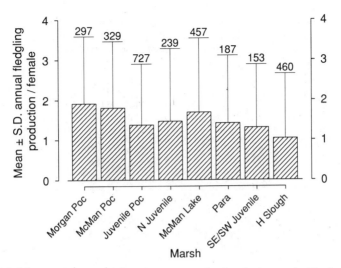

Fig. 2.6. Mean annual reproductive success per nesting female, by marsh. Numbers of females used to calculate each mean are given above error bars.

in another). Therefore, males with territories on pockets had significantly larger harems than males with territories on strips. Although territories were smallest on Juvenile Pocket, harems were largest there.

FLEDGING SUCCESS

Average annual fledging success per female varied among marshes (fig. 2.6; ANOVA, $F = 6.59$, $P < 0.0001$). Three strips (Para, SE/SW Juvenile, Hampton Slough), the pocket/strip hybrid (North Juvenile), and Juvenile Pocket fell into one statistically distinct group in which females had relatively low success per female. Females had intermediate success on McMannamon Lake, a strip, and highest success on two pockets (McMannamon Pocket and Morgan Pocket).

PREDATION RATES

The most frequent cause of nest failure was depredation by an array of predators, particularly Black-billed Magpies (*Pica pica*), Western Harvest Mice (*Reithrodontomys megalotis*), Raccoons (*Procyon lotor*), and snakes (*Pituophis melanoleucus, Crotalus viridis*). Nest predation rates varied among marshes; they were lowest on pockets (fig. 2.7). There was also broad interannual variation in nest predation rates within the study area (summed across all marshes; fig. 2.8), mostly due to changes in the intensity of predation by magpies. Sometimes a single predator

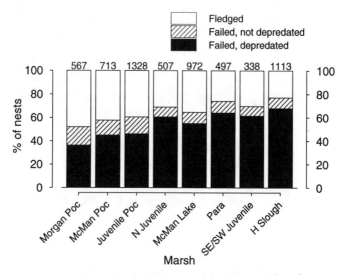

Fig. 2.7. Percentage of nests that failed because of depredation or for other reasons, all years combined, by marsh. Only nests that received ≥ 1 egg are included. Total samples sizes are given above bars.

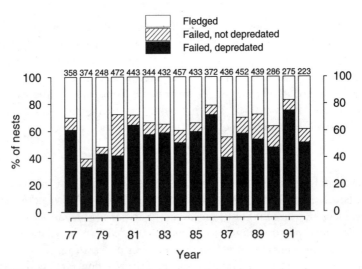

Fig. 2.8. Percentage of nests that failed because of depredation or for other reasons, all marshes combined, by year. Only nests that received ≥ 1 egg are included. Total samples sizes are given above bars.

had a large effect, e.g., the low percentage of successful nests at Juvenile Pocket in 1991 was caused to a large degree by a marauding raccoon that visited the marsh a number of times.

EPCS AND MATE GUARDING

Because the marshes were at different distances from good foraging areas, how long males left their territories to make foraging trips probably differed among marshes. Because Morgan Pocket and the McMannamon area were adjacent to agricultural fields commonly used for foraging, males on those marshes could minimize off-territory time. This is important because males that remain on territories can to some degree guard their mates during their fertilizable periods from neighboring males. When males leave territories frequently on foraging trips, however, they may increase the loss of their paternity to neighboring males through EPCs (Westneat 1994).

DECISION-MAKING AND ENVIRONMENTAL PREDICTABILITY: THE FUTURE FROM A BLACKBIRD PERSPECTIVE

Our focus in this book is on how breeding redwings make decisions about habitats, mates, territories, and nests. We assume that the decision-making rules are conditional, that is, specific choices are based upon a genetically based algorithm that is modified by currently available information or information that can be acquired over blackbird-appropriate time spans. The overview we have just presented of marshes as blackbird habitats emphasizes that making predictions about future conditions, even those in the relatively near future, is probably very difficult. Weather and predation patterns are highly variable, and the changes are unpredictable. The food supply can change dramatically on daily and weekly time frames. Emergent vegetation grows rapidly during a single breeding season, and events during the winter may transform the vegetative structure present when the next breeding season begins.

Given these enviromental fluctuations, it is not surprising to find great variation in breeding success among marshes, and from year to year. Some information redwings could have gathered in one year may have had predictive value—for example, pocket marshes consistently supported better breeding success per individual than did strips. Nevertheless, breeding success varied greatly among years on individual marshes, with the result that success in year x was a poor predictor of success in year y (chapter 4). In such a variable environment, substantial reproductive decisions should be based primarily not on environmental predictability but on other information. Therefore, we focus in this book on these other types of information. Decision-making to maximize reproductive success would be easy in a highly predictable environment, but the male and female redwings we studied did not have that luxury.

Part Two

FEMALE
DECISIONS

In this section we focus on decisions female redwings make during the breeding season. We concentrate our attention on when to begin nesting each year, where to settle and build first nests, where to build subsequent nests, how much effort to invest in the nestlings and fledglings in each breeding cycle, and when to stop breeding. Other important decisions, such as where to forage and what prey to select, have been treated in detail elsewhere (Orians 1980). They will be mentioned only in passing here even though they are important determinants of breeding success.

Females could base their settling decisions on the quality of breeding sites, the features of the males that own them, the identities of neighboring territory holders, and the number and identities of already-settled females. All of these factors change significantly during a breeding season, with the result that no two females confront exactly the same overall breeding situation when they make their decisions. For the same reason, no two decisions by a given female are made under the same circumstances.

Throughout their range, male redwings establish territories before females choose their breeding situations. Therefore, any choice by a female of a male is also a choice of breeding habitat and vice versa. Except for the first one to settle on a marsh, every arriving female is confronted with some pattern of already-settled females. The later she arrives, the larger the number of females that are already settled and/or breeding. If a female wishes to be the primary (first to nest) female on a territory, both the number and quality of territories on which she can achieve that status decline during the breeding season. The great majority of females cannot simultaneously optimize their timing, male, location, and harem rank, each of which may affect RS. Also, environmental factors interact with such intrinsic qualities of females as their age, size, aggressiveness, and genotype. The best compromise depends upon the available opportunities and the relative importance of the different factors over the course of a breeding season.

Although time, male, location, harem rank, condition, and genotype may all interact to influence fitness, it is useful to identify what constraints are imposed if a female chooses on the basis of just one criterion. If a female simply selects when she will start breeding, her settling location may be little constrained. Early-settling female redwings are aggressive toward other females, especially close to their nests. However, most of the available evidence suggests that this aggression exerts little influence on subsequent settling decisions. A female's rank in harem is set by the number and distribution of already-settled or already-breeding females and the location she selects. If a female chooses her breeding location on the basis of the male holding the territory, she must follow in rank all previously settled females on that territory, but she can have him as a mate at any time during the breeding season. If a female picks the best location in which to settle independently of the male holding the territory, she also must follow in rank all previously settled females on that territory, but she is not time-constrained in her choice. If a female wishes to achieve a particular rank, she is at all times location-constrained and usually time-constrained. Early in the season, many options exist to become first-ranked, but options to become second- or third-ranked are few. The relative proportions of various rank options continuously change during the season, with first-rank options declining and subsequent-rank options increasing.

If seasonal reproductive success is positively correlated with earliness of starting date, females should begin breeding as soon as they have accumulated enough energy reserves to be able to start. Highly synchronized initiation of breeding is a likely consequence if timing is important, but other patterns are possible if optimal timing is location-dependent. If either location or male is important, times of initiation of breeding are likely to be more variable, but strong aggregations in space are expected. If rank is a major factor, timing of breeding can assume many patterns depending upon which rank or ranks are preferred.

In this section, we will explore these complications by analyzing our data for evidence of the importance of several factors for breeding success. We begin, in chapter 3, by considering several environmental factors and factors intrinsic to females that could influence initiation of breeding. In chapter 4 we analyze the importance of where to nest by looking at settling patterns of females and the influences of harem size and rank in harem on reproductive success. We also examine the influence of behavior of already-settled females toward new arrivals. Finally, in chapter 5 we consider how much effort females expend for reproduction during a breeding season and how they decide to terminate breeding for the year.

Three

When to Nest:
Influences and Constraints
on Starting Dates

INTRODUCTION AND THEORY

Breeding seasons of tropical species are, on average, longer than those of higher-latitude breeders, but no species of bird is known to breed uninterruptedly throughout the year (Ricklefs 1966, 1983). Among Temperate Zone breeders, nesting begins when food supplies and other conditions improve sufficiently that parents can accumulate energy reserves for sperm and egg production, and can gather enough food to raise offspring while maintaining themselves (Lack 1966, 1968; Perrins 1970). These conditions develop during the spring for most species, but some, such as cardueline finches, depend upon food supplies that do not reach peak levels until well into the summer. Because winter and early spring weather is variable at high latitudes, when suitable breeding conditions develop is also variable. Rate of development of suitable conditions for breeding often varies spatially on local scales in relation to topography, exposure, and soils.

Although initiation of breeding is strongly influenced by weather and weather-dependent environmental conditions, other factors, such as the condition of individual birds and their social environment, also play important roles. For example, initiation of breeding in Great Tits (*Parus major*) is closely tied to temperature and to caterpillar emergence (Lack 1966); but breeding begins earlier when over-winter survival is high, suggesting that individuals are able to breed sooner if they survive the winter in good condition (Perrins 1979). Female Pied Flycatchers (*Ficedula hypoleuca*) start laying shortly after the first warm day in spring, but first they must find mates; the breeding season is short and annual RS falls sharply over periods of only a few days (Lack 1966; Harvey et al. 1985; Lundberg and Alatalo 1992). When individual female redwings start and stop nesting each year on our study area is highly variable, both within and between marshes (see tables 2.1 and 2.2). As we pointed out in chapter 2, our study marshes differ in many characteristics that could influence when female redwings initiate breeding during a given

TABLE 3.1. Factors potentially influencing initiation of breeding by female redwings at CNWR

| Factor | Variability component potentially influenced[a] | | |
	Within-marsh	Between-marsh	Between-season
General environment			
Local food supplies and weather[b]	o	++	++
Emergent vegetation	+	+	+
Wintering conditions	++	++	+
Social environment			
Territorial males	+	+	o
Already-settled females	++	+	o
Individual female attributes			
Age[b]	++	++	o
Previous reproductive effort[b]	++	++	+
Genotype[b]	++	+	o

[a]Number of pluses indicates potential relative strength of effect; o = no effect.
[b]Tested in the present work.

year. Also, within each marsh, females begin nesting over a two-month period, that is, over a substantial portion of the spring breeding season. In this chapter, we attempt to explain this striking amount of variability in timing of breeding. Factors that potentially influence when female redwings initiate breeding, some of which we investigate here, and which component of variability they are likely to influence, are shown in table 3.1.

TEMPORAL PATTERN OF NEST STARTS AND NEST SUCCESS

Females built nests and began laying as early as week 13 (24–31 March), but the mode for first egg of the season was week 17 (22–28 April), and the median was week 18 (fig. 3.1). Many of the nests from week 20 onwards that are categorized as first nests in figure 3.1 were probably second nests of females whose first nests were missed—either as a result of our failure to assign first nests to some females within the study area, or because they first nested outside the study area and then moved into the monitored area after nest failure. However, these errors certainly contribute relatively little to the general pattern shown in figure 3.1.

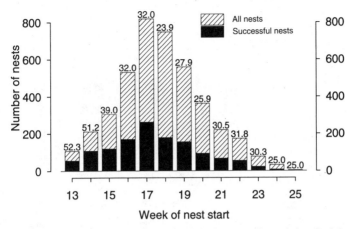

Fig. 3.1. Distribution of nest starts, by week, of the first nests for each female each year, 1977 through 1992. Week 13 is 24–31 March; week 25 is 17–23 June. All fully constructed nests, whether or not they received eggs, are included. The number of successful nests, i.e., those resulting in at least one fledged young, are indicated by the dark portions of bars; the percentage of nests that were successful is given above bars (all nests, n = 4147; successful nests, n = 1298).

The percent of nests begun each week that were eventually successful (fledged ≥ 1) is indicated in figure 3.1 by the darker shaded portion of each bar. The mean number of young fledged from *successful* nests that were begun each week varied over the season (fig. 3.2). There was a significant relationship between nest start week and fledging success for mature females, earlier successful nests tending to fledge more young (rank correlation, $z = -2.68$, $P = 0.007$). For yearlings, however, there was no significant variation over time in the number of fledglings produced per successful nest ($z = -1.25$, $P = 0.21$). Part of the higher fledging rate for early successful nests of matures may be attributable to the trend in redwings for average clutch size to decrease during the breeding season (Orians 1980; Strehl and White 1986). These results suggest that starvation of young early during the breeding season was not a constraint for females during the study. Negative relationships between laying date and nest success characterize redwing populations elsewhere as well (e.g., Dolbeer 1976).

We also found a striking positive association between starting date and accrued annual fledging success. A mature female's total seasonal production of fledglings was significantly correlated with week in which she initiated breeding (fig. 3.3; ANCOVA, number of young fledged per capita by matures vs. yearlings; $F = 33.35$, $P \ll 0.0001$; r value

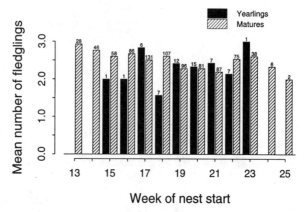

Fig. 3.2. Distributions, for yearling and mature females, of the mean number of young fledged from successful nests that were started each week of the breeding season, 1982 through 1992. Week 13 is the last week of March. Values above bars are sample sizes.

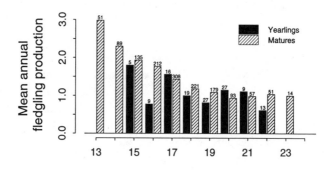

Fig. 3.3. Annual RS (per capita fledgling production) for yearling and mature females, by week of the start of each female's first nest (week of first egg date), 1982 through 1992. Week 13 is 24–31 March; week 23 is 3–9 June. Matures, n = 1413; yearlings, n = 133. Values above bars are sample sizes.

for success of mature females vs. week = -0.013, P ≪ 0.0001; r value for yearlings = -0.003, P = 0.50). The data shown in figure 3.3 are not normally distributed because of the disproportionate number of females whose annual fledgling production was zero; thus the normality assumption of ANCOVA is violated. We provide the ANCOVA result because the pattern in the histogram is obvious, the P value extremely low. Thus, at CNWR, selection for early initiation of breeding by mature females appears to be strong. Nonetheless, because females begin nesting over a two-month period, other factors must be influencing when they start.

Differences in arrival times cannot explain most of the variation in starting dates because many females are present on the study area for periods of up to several weeks before they begin building nests. When we arrived at CNWR each year in late February or early March, small flocks of females were usually present in the area, and a few individuals were already settled on male territories. We do not know whether these females are early migrants or individuals that wintered near the study area (redwing females at CNWR are migratory; adult males are not). More females arrive and/or settle during mid- and late March, but the first females generally do not begin to lay until about 1 April (day 91).

We estimated minimum "waiting periods"—intervals between settling on a territory and starting a nest—by determining intervals between each female's first egg of the season and when she was first captured that year, provided that the latter date was earlier than the former. Some "waiting periods" were as long as 70 days, but some of those greater than 30 days must have been caused by our missing earlier nests of those females. Plotted in figure 3.4 are the average waiting periods of females of 30 days or less, by week of first capture ($n = 829$ periods; only one waiting period for each female is included). The average interval between when a female arrived in spring in the study area and when she started her first nest decreased during the breeding season, from about 24 d to less than 5 d (fig. 3.4).

At Juvenile Pocket, Elizabeth Gray gathered detailed information on settlement dates and first egg dates for color-banded females. "Settling" was defined as having occurred when a female was sighted on the marsh during three consecutive days, subsequently was seen there regularly, and then nested there. Settlement date was the first day of the three consecutive days. The mean ($\pm$ SD) waiting periods for females that settled prior to 1 May in 1990, 1991, and 1992, respectively, were 27.4 $\pm$ 13.5 d, $n = 31$ females; 35.1 $\pm$ 13.6 d, $n = 34$; and 35.7 $\pm$ 21.2 d, $n = 23$.

These estimated and actual CNWR waiting periods accord with those found by Langston et al. (1990) elsewhere in eastern Washington. Although they had no banded females, Langston et al. estimated that the average settlement date for primary females was 14 March, and their average first egg date was 20 April ($n = 14$), a mean interval duration of 37 days; for secondary females, who, by definition in that study,

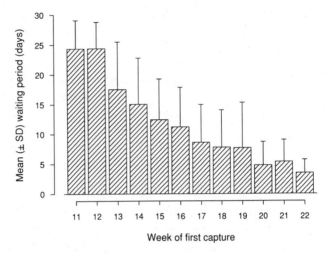

Fig. 3.4. Mean waiting periods (duration between first capture date and first egg date) for females by week of start date of periods. Distribution includes only one waiting period per female and only those ≤ 30 d; n = 829. Week 11 is 10–16 March; week 23 is 3–9 June.

settled later in the season, the mean interval was 17 days. Nero (1956a) noted waiting periods of about 21 days (n = 4 pairs) between female settlement ("pair formation") and first egg dates in Wisconsin, and Teather et al. (1988) found the mean waiting periods of 17 females in Ontario to be 14.1 ± 9.3 days.

After arriving in the study area, females may use the time before they nest to gather information about marshes and territories for use in making their settling decisions. But even after they have chosen a territory, many continue to delay nesting. Two factors might affect the durations of waiting periods. One is a genetic program that exerts gross control of reproduction via endocrine function, with effects such as timing of gonadal maturation. Wingfield et al. (1992) call the cues that grossly regulate the onset of breeding "initial predictive information." Such cues are changing daylengths and endogenous rhythms. The other factor, which Wingfield et al. term "supplementary information," is local environmental conditions. Supplementary information, which "fine-tunes" when individuals begin, can take the form of an accelerator or an inhibitor (Marshall 1970), either slightly advancing or delaying the onset of breeding. Below we explore supplementary information as it may influence nesting times.

TESTS OF HYPOTHESES TO EXPLAIN
TIMING OF NESTING

GENERAL ENVIRONMENTAL FACTORS

Local environmental factors, such as weather, structure of previous years' dead emergent vegetation, growth of new emergent vegetation, and early spring food supplies, may influence timing of breeding. Because our study marshes are within a few kilometers of one another, weather conditions can contribute only to interyear variation in initiation of breeding (although some marshes are more sheltered than others from the frequent high winds that buffet the area in spring). Our study marshes do differ, however, in the state of previous years' emergent vegetation and the timing of new growth. Therefore, availability of good nest sites early in spring varies enough among marshes and between years to account potentially for some of both within- and between-year variability in initiation of breeding among marshes, but it is likely to have less influence on within-marsh variability. We have insufficient data on marsh vegetation to address this factor.

Early in spring, our study marshes provide almost no food for redwings. At this time, the birds feed almost exclusively in the surrounding uplands. These upland feeding areas vary greatly in structure and, probably, in the kinds and abundances of early spring food supplies they offer, but we have not measured food availability there. These areas are undefended and, hence, are available to all birds, but individuals usually forage relatively close to the marshes in which they eventually nest. Our trapping data show that male redwings at CNWR rarely forage more than 2 km from their territories during the breeding season (Beletsky and Orians 1987a), and we have no reason to believe that females travel farther. Thus, females may differ in how soon they are able to store enough energy to begin nesting. Differences in the proximity of good, upland feeding sites could contribute to among- but not within-marsh differences in nest-starting dates.

Influence of Early Spring Weather

We gathered weather information from annual summaries of climatological data published for Washington State by the National Oceanic and Atmospheric Administration. The specific data we used were collected from the weather monitoring station closest to CNWR, located about 20 km southeast. We noted the average temperature for February, March, and April in each year of our study, the number of days each month on which the maximum temperature did not rise above freezing (0° C), the total monthly precipitation, and the number of days of precipitation each month.

Females should respond strongly to weather in making their decisions about when to start their nests each year only if March weather is positively correlated with April weather. That is, females should delay breeding if March weather is bad only if (a) bad weather in March is strongly correlated with bad weather in April, when they will be incubating and feeding young; and if (b) bad weather in April lowers fledging success of nests started during the early portion of the breeding season.

These necessary correlations appear to be lacking at our study site. Although there were significant correlations between February and March temperatures (regression of average monthly temperatures, March on February, $r^2 = 0.41$, $P = 0.008$; regression of number of days below freezing, March on February, $r^2 = 0.32$, $P = 0.02$), there were no significant correlations between any of the weather factors in March, when females arrive, and April, when they normally start nesting. That is, April weather during this sixteen-year period could not be predicted from knowledge of March weather. In addition to being difficult to predict, spring weather did not appear to influence strongly redwing nesting success. There were no significant regression relationships between the weather factors and the average number of fledglings produced per nest, for all first nests started before 1 May. Further, there were no significant relationships between the weather factors and the percentage of nests started before 1 May that were successful (fledged ≥ 1).

Not surprisingly, given that weather is unpredictable and not of major consequence, early spring weather exerted little influence on initiation of breeding. We regressed the average start date for the first 10 nests on the study area each year on each of the four weather components for February and March. The only significant relationship was a positive one between total precipitation and average first egg dates (February, $r^2 = 0.32$, $P = 0.02$; March, $r^2 = 0.30$, $P = 0.03$). Contrary to our expectations, average temperature in March was almost negatively significantly related to average nest-start date ($r^2 = 0.24$, $P = 0.055$), that is, nesting tended to start later when early spring was warmer. Further, the direction of the significant regression found between February and March precipitation and nesting date (regression line for March given in figure 3.5) was opposite to what we would have predicted: more precipitation was significantly associated with earlier

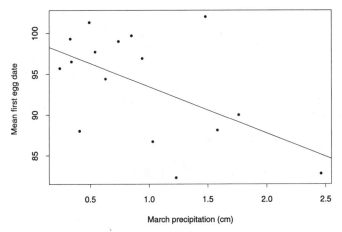

Fig. 3.5. Regression of average start date of the first ten nests on the study area each year on total precipitation in March of each year (n = 16 years).

nesting. We also performed these analyses on the mean dates of the first 20 nests each year, and also on just those nests (first 10, first 20) that received at least one egg; the results were virtually identical to that indicated above for the first 10 nests, although in these cases the regression of average temperature in March vs. average start date was farther from significance.

The inability of females to predict early spring weather is also suggested by the temporal distribution of fully constructed nests that never get eggs (fig. 3.6). Females that nest very early may have to abandon nests if the weather deteriorates. March at CNWR is often cold and windy, and it often turns cold again after an initial warming. Many early nests never receive any eggs, in most cases probably because weather deteriorates after females build them. For example, in 1991 on Juvenile Pocket, 12 of the first 21 nests never received eggs (n = 10) or did not receive eggs until many weeks after being built (n = 2). Nests begun during the first three weeks of the season had the highest probability of never receiving eggs (fig. 3.6). This analysis includes only fully built nests that never received eggs. Thus, they were highly unlikely to have been "practice" nests or to have been built by inexperienced females, because almost all nests during the first few weeks of the season are built by females at least two years old. The percentage of nests each week that were abandoned prior to laying declined incrementally until, after week 16, 85% or more of completed nests received eggs. Thus, at CNWR there is a three- to four-week "window of oppor-

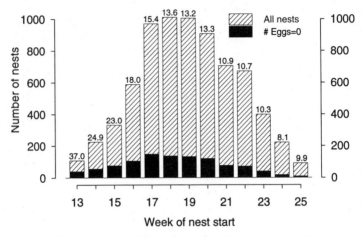

Fig. 3.6. Distribution, by week, of all nests started on the study area, 1977 through 1992. Dark portion of each bar shows the number of nests begun that week that never received eggs; percentage not receiving eggs is given above bars (all nests, n = 7236; nests that never received eggs, n = 1035).

tunity" for early-arriving females to start early nests, which historically do well (figs. 3.1 and 3.2), but females starting early are likely to have their breeding effort interrupted by bad weather, as suggested by the higher percentages of their nests that never receive eggs. However, the risk may not be great because females can quickly renest after the weather ameliorates. (We do not know why the females tend to build new nests in these situations, rather than laying in their already-completed ones.)

Early Spring Food Supplies

Local food abundance may influence initiation of nesting because early food supplies could be good indicators of the food levels that will be necessary to raise young. Also, early abundant food may allow females to accumulate more rapidly sufficient energy reserves for egg formation and nesting (Lack 1966, Perrins 1970). Local differences in food abundance could thus influence both between-marsh and between-year variability in start dates. There is both correlational and experimental evidence that earlier-than-usual seasonal food availability can advance breeding dates in Temperate Zone birds (Newton 1973; Nolan and Thompson 1975; Yom-Tov 1974; Drent and Daan 1980; Smith et al. 1980).

Two experiments that provided extra food before nesting began produced strong effects on nest initiation dates in redwings. Ewald and

Rohwer (1982) placed feeders stocked with sunflower seeds, cracked corn, and commercial puppy chow, all items of high protein content, on experimental territories at a site about 50 km northwest of CNWR. They then monitored nesting on the experimental territories and on control, unmanipulated territories on another marsh. In 1977 supplemental feeding started on 31 March, with single feeders on 8 experimental territories. Feeders were refilled soon (1 to 3 d) after they were emptied. The average first egg date was 17 d earlier on the experimental than on the control territories. In 1978, with many more feeders arranged in a grid on a marsh with 36 male territories (the marsh that contained the 1977 control territories), and with food supplements begun about 40 d earlier, average first egg date was 26 d earlier on the experimental than on control territories. Several aspects of Ewald and Rohwer's experiments make their results difficult to interpret (Searcy and Yasukawa 1995). For example, in 1977, experimental and control territories were on four separate marshes that could have differed naturally in average harem sizes and nest-start dates; in 1978, the investigators removed many experimental males from territories before feeders were placed, attracting many new territory owners, and possibly biasing results. Wimberger (1988) conducted a similar experiment, but he controlled for marsh effects by randomly assigning territories on the same marsh to fed or unfed treatments. First nest-start dates averaged 10 to 12 d earlier on fed than on unfed territories.

These experiments demonstrated the importance of food supplies on initiation of redwing breeding, but they did not show whether the location of food supplies was important because all feeders were placed on male territories. To test whether food abundance close to but not on territories would also advance breeding, we designed an experiment in which some territories had feeders but all birds had access to undefended feeders on adjacent uplands. If finding good food supplies on the territory itself is the important trigger for advancing breeding, then we expected nest initiations to advance only on territories with feeders.

We conducted this experiment in 1990 at Frog Lake, one of our peripheral-area strip marshes where all males but few females were banded. We installed eight seed trays around the lake on 13 March, when the first females were arriving at the marsh. Four trays were placed in the marsh such that every other territory had one, and four were placed 25 to 35 m upland from the marsh in undefended foraging areas directly opposite those territories that did not have a tray. Unhusked sunflower seeds (up to approximately 350 g) were added daily to refill each tray until 20 April, when we removed the trays. Many male redwing floaters were attracted to the four upland feeders, and, indeed, once they found the free food, floaters were present at or near the feeders every day. During our daily trip to the lake, we observed few females at the upland feeders, which were constantly visited by the male flock of, usually, 10 to 15 floaters intermittently joined by individual Frog Lake territory owners. Both females and territory owners used the feeders on their territories. The upland trays were emptied by the birds daily, but the marsh trays always had seeds.

We first searched Frog Lake for nests on 30 March, finding a single completed nest. The marsh was searched for new nests and nests were checked for progress every 4 d thereafter. By 16 April, 20 nests had been built on Frog Lake, 13 on "unfed" territories, 7 on "fed" territories, and at least 1 on each of the original male territories. Only 13 of these first 20 nests received eggs. The mean first egg date of the 4 nests on territories with feeders was day 101.8 ± 5.8; for the 9 nests on territories without feeders it was day 105.3 ± 3.8 (Julian dates, day $100 = 10$ April). The similarity of these mean dates suggests that the effect of supplemental feeding was largely independent of the location of the food source. Females on territories without feeders may have fed regularly at the upland feeders when we were not present at the site, and male territory owners with feeders may have permitted neighboring females to feed at them, as found by Gray (1996c).

Supplemental feeding apparently did advance nesting at Frog Lake. The mean first egg dates for the first 5 and for the first 10 nests on Frog Lake, and for three unmanipulated core-area marshes, in 1990 and other years, are given in table 3.2. Juvenile Pocket, which often had the first nests of the season on the core study area (table 2.1), had the earliest average first egg dates in 1990, but nesting at Frog Lake began only a day or two later. In other years, nesting often began on Frog Lake two to four weeks after it began on Juvenile Pocket. But Frog Lake is best compared to the other strip marshes in table 3.2, McMannamon Lake and Hampton Slough. Frog Lake nest starts in 1990 were somewhat earlier than at McMannamon and much earlier than at Hampton Slough, whereas in other years, Frog Lake nesting generally began later than on those marshes.

Environmental Conditions Elsewhere

When a female begins to breed may depend upon environmental conditions elsewhere. Females that breed in our study area migrate to other, mostly unknown, wintering areas. Some may winter in the Columbia Basin of eastern Washington but others probably migrate as far as the

TABLE 3.2. Mean dates of first eggs of nests on Frog Lake during 1990
supplemental feeding experiment and in other years, and on some
unmanipulated core marshes in those years

Marsh	Mean first egg date[a]	
	First 5 nests	First 10 nests
Frog Lake		
1986	116 ± 0	119 ± 3.7
1987	115 ± 5.2	117 ± 5.2
1989	126 ± 1.8	127 ± 1.7
1990	100 ± 4.5	103 ± 4.1
McMannamon Lake		
1986	093 ± 1.1	098 ± 7.3
1987	110 ± 3.9	114 ± 4.9
1989	118 ± 4.3	122 ± 5.6
1990	102 ± 2.4	107 ± 5.2
Hampton Slough		
1986	111 ± 1.9	113 ± 2.7
1987	112 ± 1.1	113 ± 1.4
1989	116 ± 1.6	119 ± 3.9
1990	123 ± 1.6	135 ± 13.9
Juvenile Pocket		
1986	084 ± 0.9	086 ± 2.8
1987	099 ± 8.4	103 ± 6.9
1989	101 ± 4.3	104 ± 4.8
1990	099 ± 1.5	101 ± 1.6

[a]Julian date, day 091 = 1 April; day 100 = 10 April.

Central Valley of California. Birds that winter farther from our study
area may arrive later on the breeding grounds, and they may have
depleted their energy reserves during their migratory flight. Alternatively, more southerly wintering individuals may experience better winter foraging conditions and be able to accumulate sufficient energy reserves for migration and breeding sooner than those individuals that
winter farther north. Also, harshness of winter conditions may vary
considerably in the geographic area over which our breeding females
winter. Therefore, variable wintering grounds are potentially major
sources of variability in initiation of breeding, especially within
marshes. Unfortunately, none of our banded females (nor any others
banded in Washington during the past thirty years) has been recovered
outside Washington. Thus, we cannot allocate females to migration

routes or wintering sites, and we are unable to assess the influence of wintering area on timing of initiation of breeding.

SOCIAL ENVIRONMENT

Although social constraints on nesting might be expected, given the conspicuous aggressive behavior among females early during the breeding season, the weight of evidence to date suggests that interactions with males or with other females only weakly affect female nesting decisions. Females are not prevented from settling on a territory by resistance from the resident male. Because a male's annual RS increases, on average, almost linearly with his harem size (Orians and Beletsky 1989; Beletsky 1996; see also chapter 2), it is to his advantage to accept all females. When males are overtly aggressive toward females, their aggression is directed to already-settled mates. The objective appears to be to prevent their mates from harassing newly arriving females (Nero 1956a; O'Connor 1976; Searcy 1986; Searcy and Yasukawa 1995; personal observations). Females may respond positively to familiar neighboring males when making their settling decisions (Beletsky and Orians 1991), but we have no evidence to suggest that familiar neighbors influence the timing of nests.

Although female redwings are highly aggressive toward one another early in the breeding season, chasing and fighting, the point of the aggression is still unclear. Early observations suggested that females defend small "sub-territories" on their mates' larger territories, in which they locate their nests (Nero 1956a; Orians 1961; Beletsky 1983), but subsequent tests for subterritories yielded only equivocal evidence. Females are more aggressive toward each other the nearer they are to their nests, i.e., their aggression is space-centered (Searcy and Yasukawa 1995), but results of analyses of nest-start dates within harems, and of female removal experiments, suggest that already-settled females neither prevent other females from settling nor affect one another's timing of nesting (Yasukawa and Searcy 1981; Searcy 1988; Searcy and Yasukawa 1995). Thus, even if females defend areas around their nests and early females exhibit other space-related aggression, such behavior does not prevent other females from settling and nesting. These issues are explored in detail in the next chapter.

Females may actually benefit from the presence of other nesting females through improved cooperative nest defense or predator dilution or by nesting in the center of a large group (Picman et al. 1988). Females may even delay breeding in order to wait for others to start. Westneat (1992b), for example, found a significant positive effect of "synchronous" nesting on fledging success of individual females in his New York redwing population.

Variation in initiation of breeding may be due to intrinsic variability among females. Young, inexperienced females may be unable to breed as soon as older, more experienced individuals. Variability in foraging skills could also influence how soon females can begin to nest, and a female's unusually large energetic investment during one breeding season could negatively influence her physiological condition to a point where she must delay her initiation of breeding the subsequent year. Finally, females may be genetically programmed to start at different times in the spring. Such genetically based variability could be maintained by stochastic variation in environmental conditions that cause the best starting time to vary considerably among years. With our long-term data we can address some of these potential factors.

Age

Most first females to settle on male territories in spring have bright red epaulets and so are at least two years old (Crawford 1977, Miskimen 1980); this was the case at CNWR. To test whether age influences start date, we made histograms of annual start dates for yearlings and for mature females (nest data from 1982 through 1992, plumage-scored females only). Mature females, on average, began nesting one week earlier than did yearlings (cf. figs. 3.7, 3.8; ANOVA on mean first egg dates; $F = 41.87$, $P < 0.0001$). Female age therefore influences mean starting date, but starting dates of both yearling and older females are highly variable. Therefore, age effects cannot explain why initiation of breeding by females of all ages is spread out over a period of nearly two months.

Previous Reproductive Effort

Female redwings at CNWR build nests, incubate, and feed nestlings and fledglings largely without assistance from their mates. Also, since most females attempt to fledge offspring several times during the season, they may be in poor physiological condition at the end of the breeding season. One possible outcome is that females who invest heavily in a given year might be unable to achieve breeding condition as early the following year. We will explore the cost of reproduction in detail in chapter 5. Here we note only that our data show that magnitude of reproductive effort in year x does not affect starting date in year $x + 1$.

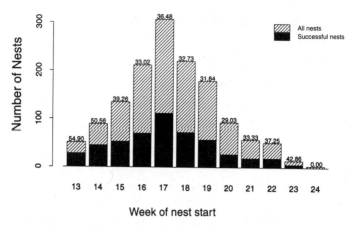

Fig. 3.7. Distribution of first nest starts, by week, for all mature females, 1982 through 1992. Dark portion of each bar shows the number of successful nests; percentage values are given above bars (all nests, n = 1411; successful nests, n = 508.

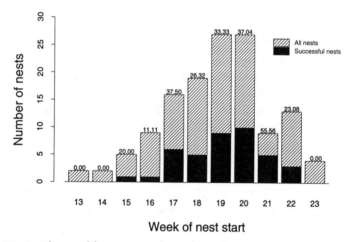

Fig. 3.8. Distribution of first nest starts by week for all yearling females, 1982 through 1992. Dark portion of each bar shows the number of successful nests; percentage values are given above bars (all nests, n = 133; successful nests, n = 40).

Therefore, prior year's investment in reproduction cannot explain any of the variability in annual starting dates.

If females tire themselves significantly with each nesting effort, to the point where subsequent efforts are threatened, then initiation of first nests could be delayed until nesting becomes less stressful. To test whether females wear themselves out from first nesting attempts, we compared success of females starting their first nests and second nests

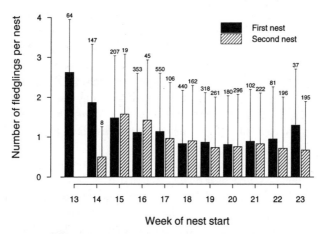

Fig. 3.9. Mean (±SD) nesting success (number of fledglings per nest) of first nests of females versus second nests of females started during the same week, based on first egg dates. Only nests that received at least one egg were included. Samples sizes are given above error bars.

during the same week. Mean fledging success by week for females' first and females' second nests started during the same week are plotted in figure 3.9. We compared fledging success between the two groups only during weeks 15 through 19 because there were zero or few "second nesters" during weeks 13 and 14, and after week 19 (mid-May) many "first nesters" must have been errors of assignment of status (either we missed their earlier nests or they moved into the monitored area after their earlier nests terminated). For no week was there a significant difference in fledging rate from nests of first and second nesters (2-sample t-tests; week 15, t = -0.26, 1-tailed P = 0.40; week 16, t = -1.30, P = 0.10; week 17, t = 1.13, P = 0.13; week 18, t = -0.56, P = 0.29; week 19, t = 1.26, P = 0.10). Therefore, the hypothesis that females tire themselves from first nesting attempts is not supported; females should thus not take this possible cost of nesting into account when making their initial nest-timing decisions.

Genetic Differences

Given the highly variable environment in which redwings breed, considerable genetic variation in responses to environmental cues could readily be maintained in the population. We have very little data on relatedness of females on our study area because so few of them banded as nestlings become local breeders. Therefore, we must resort to indirect evidence to assess whether genetic variability might account for some of the variation in starting dates among females in our population. Our best evidence is provided by the relative starting dates of individual females in subsequent years. Genetic variability would be indicated if individual females consistently started earlier or later than the average starting dates of the population during different years. Such genetic variability could express itself via hormone levels, differential responses to changing daylengths, different wintering grounds, and different foraging abilities. An analysis of starting dates cannot discriminate among these potential causes.

We compared the deviation from the population mean annual nest date of a female's first nest during her first nonyearling year, with the deviation from the mean date of her subsequent-year first nest. We found a significant positive correlation between these dates (r = 0.29, P < 0.001, n = 241), that is, a female that starts late one year also tends to start late the next. This finding does not prove heritability of nest-timing behavior but is consistent with a genetic influence. Thus, genetic differences may explain some of the variability in initiation of breeding among female redwings in our population. Variability in genetic predisposition to initiate breeding could be maintained if the time of initiation that resulted in the largest number of young being fledged varied among years, if the optimal timing depended on where females winter, or if morphology influenced temporal patterns of success.

RENESTING

Because predation rates on redwing nests on our study marshes are high (chapter 2), as they are in other areas (e.g., Orians 1961; Caccamise 1976; Weatherhead and Robertson 1977; Lenington 1980; Picman et al. 1988; Westneat 1992b), most females have opportunities to renest at least once during a breeding season. Except for renesting after failure during laying or incubation of the earliest nests, environmental conditions are good by the time females renest. We know of no reason why a female could increase her fitness by waiting to renest longer than the time she requires to readjust physiologically and recover her energy reserves. Therefore, we predicted that most females would renest quickly.

Factors that could influence physiological readjustment times include age of female, stage in the nesting cycle when the nest was destroyed, and her genotype. The minimum delay between nest destruction and laying the first egg of a new clutch must be at least 3 to 4 d, because the female's physiology must be reset and she must construct a new

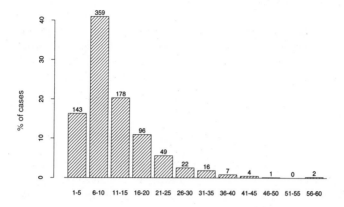

Fig. 3.10. Durations between date of loss of first nest and initiation of second nests (date of first egg), for all females, 1982 through 1992 (mean = 8.6 ± 7.6 days, n = 877).

nest; intervals as brief as this have been observed (e.g., Dolbeer 1976; Beletsky and Orians, unpublished data). The histogram in figure 3.10, which plots intervals between termination dates of failed first nests and first egg dates of the females' second nests, shows that about 55% of these periods fall within 10 d of failure of the first nest, and about 75% within two weeks. Thus, although there is some variation, the great majority of first renests are started quickly after nest destruction. Both yearling and mature females tend to renest quickly, but, on average, yearlings do so significantly faster (mean delay duration for matures = 8.8 ± 7.7 d, n = 820; and for yearlings, 6.0 ± 5.1 d, n = 57; t = 2.70, 2-tailed P = 0.007). The difference may be due to the fact that yearlings, which on average start their annual nesting later than do matures, renest later in the season when environmental conditions are highly favorable.

The stage at which the first nest is destroyed is likely to influence the time required to be ready to renest. Females whose first nests progressed to the nestling stage may have greater depletion of energy reserves as a result of feeding young, and thus may have to delay longer before starting their next nests, than females whose first nests terminated during the egg stage. We tested for such a relationship, but found a significant effect in the direction opposite to the one we expected: females whose first nests terminated during the egg stage tended to have longer delays (mean = 8.4 ± 8.1 d, n = 1421) than those whose nests terminated in the nestling stage (mean = 7.4 ± 7.2 d, n = 263;

t = 1.88, 1-tailed P = 0.03). This trend may indicate that hormonal readjustments are faster if a female has progressed to the nestling feeding stage than if she is still incubating; that the later in the season, the stronger the reason to renest quickly; or that renesting is easier later in the season.

DISCUSSION: WHY INITIATION OF NESTING IS SO VARIABLE

Some aspects of the considerable variation among females in seasonal nest-starting dates remain unexplained, but we have excluded a number of possible causative factors and we have evidence that suggests the importance of others. Explanations of the variation must take into account our findings that the earliest nests had the highest probability of successful fledging and the greatest success when they did fledge, and that mature females that started earlier had significantly greater annual RS than did later starters.

Most early-arriving females wait for a while, up to four weeks, before initiating nesting. Some of the delay may be explained by the need of females to accumulate energy reserves because supplemental feeding does accelerate nesting to a moderate degree. Although our food-manipulation experiment and those of Ewald and Rohwer (1982) and Wimberger (1988) indicate that initiation of breeding may be influenced by the ability of females to accumulate energy reserves, food availability cannot explain important aspects of initiation of breeding on our study area. First, by mid-April food is always abundant, so food supplies could account for only differences in nest starts in early April on our study marshes; they cannot explain why so many females do not begin to nest until late April or May. Second, marshes close to abundant early spring food supplies do not necessarily have early starting dates. For example, McMannamon Lake and McMannamon Pocket are adjacent to a cultivated field rich in seeds early in spring (fig. 2.2). Large numbers of resident and migrant redwings, including those that breed on McMannamon, feed in that field in February and March, yet nesting starts later on McMannamon than on Juvenile Pocket (see tables 2.1, 3.2), which has no rich food supplies nearby. In fact, we know from our trapping records that females who build their nests on Juvenile Pocket early during the breeding season forage daily in the McMannamon area, about 600 m distant. Also, nesting starts slightly later on McMannamon Pocket than on McMannamon Lake (table 2.1), even though the two areas are equidistant from the rich foraging area. The combined evidence strongly suggests that many female redwings have accumulated, or could easily accumulate, sufficient energy reserves to nest earlier than they do.

Early spring weather apparently exerts little effect on timing of nesting. Females start to breed sooner if March is wetter than normal, but March temperatures have no effect. The lack of responsiveness to March temperatures can be explained by the lack of correlation between March weather and April weather. In the absence of such correlations, we would not expect females to respond to March temperatures, and they do not.

Environmental conditions elsewhere could be having an important influence on starting dates of females, but, unfortunately, we cannot evaluate this factor because we have no recoveries of our banded females during the winter. However, we do know that females arrive on the breeding grounds over at least a two-month period, and many late-breeding females do not arrive until shortly before they start their first nests. Some of this variability in arrival times may be correlated with where the birds wintered and environmental conditions during the winter. Some of the variability may be caused by genetic differences in females with respect to where they winter and when they initiate spring migration. We have no direct data on genetic variability, but individual females are consistent in when they initiate breeding relative to the overall population pattern. That is, some females consistently breed early; others consistently breed late. Also, genetic differences have been implicated at least partly in the regulation of other components of breeding behavior of redwing females, such as how often they change nesting locations (Picman 1981).

Age of female also explains some of the variability because yearling females initiate breeding on average one week after older females. Nonetheless, both yearling and older females are about equally variable in their starting dates, so age explains little of the within-marsh or between-marsh variability in starting dates.

The existence of conspicuous aggressive behavior among females, particularly early in the breeding season, suggests that social constraints might be important determinants of when and where females nest. However, our data and those of other investigators have failed to demonstrate a strong effect of already-settled females on the nesting times and locations of subsequently-settling females. We will explore this and other aspects of the social environment, particularly rank in harem, more fully in the next chapter.

Settling females probably attend to a variety of factors in making their nest-start decisions each spring, with the relative importance of each factor waxing and waning as spring progresses. Although nest-timing decisions are made with respect to social and physical environments that change subtly during the breeding season, our data suggest that it is useful to divide female nest initiation decisions into two "decision-making environments." One is the early breeding environ-ment, in March and early April, during which experienced females in particular can benefit strongly by attempting very early nests, but in doing so they assume risks of unpredictable bad weather that can termi-nate their nests. The advantage to females who start very early was pronounced during the years of our study, and is evident in figure 3.3: average per capita annual fledging production was highest for females who started earliest. These early nesters benefit because their first nests experience lower rates of nest predation (chapter 5), because they fledge more young when they do fledge, and because, by starting earlier, they have more time for renests. But our data also reveal a special risk of early breeding, that is, that nests begun during the earliest weeks have the highest probability of being abandoned before they receive eggs (fig. 3.6).

A second "decision-making environment" occurs from mid-April through June, and applies to later-arriving females and to renesters. Food for the young during this period is reliably available, weather is improved, and nest predation is common. Under these circumstances, there are no potential benefits for breeding delays, and females appar-ently breed as soon as they are able, i.e., nest-initiation decisions are wholly dependent on hormonal and other physiological adjustments. Also, whereas early nesters may compete for specific nesting ranks, rank may be irrelevant to later nesters (see chapter 4).

CONCLUSION

The results from our study area may not generalize to all redwing populations. For example, because eastern populations have shorter breeding seasons and, hence, greater nesting synchrony, females have fewer options in choosing nesting times. Indeed, Westneat (1992b) found a positive association between a female's first egg date of first nest and annual RS in only one of three years of his study; and almost all first nests were started within the same two- to three-week period. Moreover, perhaps atypically, the CNWR population suffers from little early-season nestling starvation. In other regions, females may risk losing young to starvation should they nest before insects are widely available.

Our data, though incomplete, suggest that a variety of factors influence when females begin to nest. Given that our females differ in age, in experience, probably in where they winter and when they begin their spring migrations, in their skills in foraging, and in the marshes they inhabit, it is perhaps not surprising that they begin nesting over a long time-period each year. In contrast, when females lose their nests, they quickly renest, usually within ten days, suggesting that whatever factors lead to variation in initial starting dates, there is little variation in the rapidity of renesting and trying again. Variation in when individual females terminate their breeding efforts each year will be explored in chapter 5.

Females achieve a higher annual reproductive success if they begin nesting early in the spring, but seasonal reproductive success is fairly constant after the first few weeks. Therefore, selection on starting date would appear to be weak if a female cannot initiate breeding very early.

Four

Where to Nest:
Influences and Constraints
on Settling Decisions

INTRODUCTION

In addition to deciding *when* to initiate breeding, which we analyzed in chapter 3, a female redwing must also decide *where* to settle and nest. When a female selects the territory in which she will place her nest, she simultaneously chooses (1) a physical location, which influences the probability of nest success by providing cover from predators, protection from weather, and proximity to food resources; (2) a territorial male, who influences nest success and fitness by protecting her nests and contributing genes to some of her young; (3) a set of male neighbors, who may also help protect her nests and contribute genes to her brood; (4) harem mates, if other females are already settled on the territory; and (5) a rank in the harem, which depends upon how many other females have already settled on the territory.

To evaluate her choices, a female must assess environmental features at several different spatial scales (Orians and Wittenberger 1991). The choice of a general habitat determines which patches are available for use. Choice of a patch, in turn, determines the types of objects that will be encountered. A suitable habitat needs to contain a mixture of patches that provide opportunities for all of the activities required for successful reproduction. Some activities, such as foraging, are usually extensive in nature, whereas others, such as selection and use of a nest site, are local but intensive in nature. Some choices are made only once, whereas others are made repeatedly over the entire period during which the habitat is used. Because a nest site is a critical resource to which a female redwing is committed for a period of more than a month if her nest is successful, selection of nest sites may dominate other components of habitat selection. Because of high nest predation rates, female redwings, on average, make more than one nest-site decision each breeding season, but they make many more decisions as to foraging location. Females at CNWR and in many other populations regularly travel long distances from their nests to gather nest material, food for themselves, and food for their nestlings.

Information is also relevant at different temporal scales. When a migratory female arrives on a breeding ground at the beginning of the nesting season, little information may be available to her on which to judge the quality of the breeding environment. The food supply that is present when she must make her decision may not be strongly correlated with what will be available when she is feeding nestlings. The foliage that conceals nests from predators or supports the nests may not be fully developed, and potential predators and parasites may be absent or present at different densities than they will be weeks later. The later a female arrives, the more information is available to her. For example, a late arriver will be able to assess the progress of settled females on local territories. Vegetation will be developed, and food supplies and predator abundances may closely approximate what they will be when she will be provisioning her own nest.

Settling time also influences the options available to a female. Because female redwings are not territorial, newly arriving individuals can potentially settle wherever they wish, although agonistic behavior from already-settled females may prevent settling in particular areas for limited periods of time. The number and distribution of already-settled females constrains the choices of rank open to a female. The number of territories on which a female can be the primary female in a harem declines as more females settle and becomes zero when all territories have at least one female. Other rank choices become similarly constrained as more females settle.

Some information about habitat features that influence breeding success may be available from former breeding seasons. The previous year's vegetation provides both a substrate for new nests and information about the likely structure of the current year's vegetation. The nests of most passerine birds are used only once and are not designed for great longevity. Nonetheless, many nests survive from one breeding season to the next. They provide information on how many birds nested there the previous year and, less accurately, the success of those nests (Erckmann et al. 1990).

Most of the factors that influence breeding success of females cannot be manipulated by them. A female cannot alter the structure of vegetation, the identities of territory owners or locations of territory boundaries, or the numbers, identities, and locations of already-settled females. She can choose only from among the available options. She can, however, influence the assistance offered to her by neighboring males by copulating with them (Gray 1994, 1996c), and perhaps she can, by being aggressive, influence when and where later-arriving females settle.

Some of the information available to a settling female is relevant for the duration of her breeding season, but some of it is not. A female redwing breeding in eastern Washington generally makes more than one settling decision each year. She does so after her nest is destroyed by a predator or fails for other reasons, or if her first nest is successful and she decides to renest. At the time of each decision, different kinds and amounts of information are available and a different social matrix exists. The male on whose territory a female first decides to settle and his neighbors are likely to be present most of the breeding season, but the females that are already present may move elsewhere for renesting. The identity and precise number of females that will arrive subsequently on any territory is unknowable.

In this chapter, we present what is known about how female redwings choose their breeding situation and analyze and discuss our data on where females settle to nest. We consider what information they appear to use in making settling decisions, the nature and reliability of environmental information potentially available to them, and the consequences of having made decisions as they did. We take a detailed look at the potential effect of female ranks on settling decisions.

ENVIRONMENTAL INFORMATION

The territory on which a female redwing elects to nest provides a matrix of vegetation within which the female constructs her nest and forages for some of her own food and food for her nestlings. The territory is also bordered by one or more contiguous territories and, in nearly all cases in our study area, by sagebrush-dominated uplands. Evidence from several previous studies indirectly suggests that habitat characteristics, particularly vegetation structure, influence the females' settlement decisions. For example, Lenington (1980) showed that nest success in a New Jersey population of redwings was consistently positively correlated with such habitat attributes as cattail density, water depth below nests, and number of plant stems supporting nests, suggesting that females may have based settlement decisons on those attributes. Yasukawa et al. (1992) found that nest success in Wisconsin was positively correlated with the presence near nests of tall plants, on which males perched and acted as sentinels, and females preferentially installed nests near experimentally placed, prominent perches. Also, females in both Washington and Indiana have been shown to prefer particular marsh areas rather than the territories of particular males (Searcy 1979a; Yasukawa 1981).

We discuss four sources of environmental information that may influence where females decide to nest: vegetation structure, food supply, previous nests, and year-to-year predictability of nesting success on particular marshes.

VEGETATION STRUCTURE

In our study area, most redwing nests are built in emergent vegetation over water. During the 1960s, a few nests were built in sagebrush bushes near water and one was in a willow tree in a remodeled Bullock's Oriole's (*Icterus bullockii*) nest (Orians 1980), but upland nesting sites were not used during the years of our current study. Because of water-level fluctuations, parts of some cattail beds at times lack standing water, and redwings sometimes nest in those areas. All early nests are supported by the previous year's vegetation, but later nests may be supported partly or entirely by current season's vegetation growth. Previous year's growth may survive the winter relatively intact, but ice damage or collapse of cattail beds as part of a natural cycle of bed decay and renewal regularly results in conditions of poor cover and support for nests until new growth has reached a height of a meter or more.

Our study was not designed to measure changes in vegetation, but natural forces produced some dramatic alterations in vegetation structures. To evaluate whether gross deterioration in a marsh's vegetation structure would negatively influence female settlement decisions, we compared female settlement and reproductive success on one of our core marshes, Hampton Slough, before and after beavers substantially damaged the beds of emergent vegetation. Beavers began destroying Hampton Slough's cattail beds during the winter of 1984–85, but damage was minor until the following winter, when approximately half the vegetation was destroyed. Damage by beavers continued intermittently until, by the 1990 redwing breeding season, only a thin fringe of cattail—a few stalks—remained on about one-third of the south part of the lake and one small, thick patch of bulrush survived on the north end. The number of male territories was reduced from a high of 22 in 1981 to 5 in 1990, and average harem sizes declined concurrently (table 4.1). Average annual fledging success per female was quite variable both before and during periods of vegetation damage. Annual return rates of females to Hampton Slough were in the 45 to 60% range prior to 1985,

TABLE 4.1. Return rates and success of female redwings breeding on
Hampton Slough before (1981 through 1984) and during (1985 through 1992)
major destruction of marsh vegetation by beavers

Year	No. of male territories	No. of nests	Harem size ($\overline{X} \pm SD$)	Fledgling success/ female ($\overline{X} \pm SD$)	Return rate of females to marsh %	No.	No. of new females settling on marsh
1981	22	179	4.1 ± 1.5	0.9 ± 1.4	n.a.	n.a.	n.a.
1982	21	133	3.2 ± 1.7	0.4 ± 1.0	59.6	28	31
1983	20	147	3.6 ± 1.7	0.6 ± 1.3	50.0	22	39
1984	16	102	3.6 ± 1.3	1.0 ± 1.4	46.3	19	33
1985	21	111	3.4 ± 1.7	1.4 ± 1.9	41.7	15	48
1986	18	86	2.8 ± 1.4	0.3 ± 0.7	42.3	11	36
1987	15	80	3.4 ± 2.2	0.8 ± 1.4	28.6	6	43
1988	11	70	2.9 ± 1.8	0.4 ± 1.0	45.5	5	27
1989	9	34	2.2 ± 1.3	0.5 ± 1.3	62.5	5	14
1990	5	11	1.6 ± 0.9	0.3 ± 0.8	0	0	7
1991	5	19	2.6 ± 1.3	1.1 ± 1.6	0	0	13
1992	4	17	2.5 ± 1.3	0.2 ± 0.6	25.0	1	9

then continued in that range through 1989. Also, new females in good
numbers continued to select the lake as their nesting site through that
year (table 4.1). Thus, although the marsh underwent extensive physical degradation that appeared seriously to compromise its suitability for
breeding, returning and new females continued to nest there. Only the
near-total destruction of emergent vegetation, from 1990 to 1992, kept
females from settling there.

FOOD SUPPLY

Redwings breeding in our study area obtain some of their food from
their territories, but most food is gathered along undefended margins
of lakes and in uplands. Where the sides of lakes at CNWR are steep,
beds of emergent vegetation often are too narrow to support redwing
territories. These lake edges are excellent undefended, communal foraging areas that are regularly used by redwings during the breeding season. Most territories are not adjacent to undefended lake edges, but the
amount of such areas and their proximity to a nesting marsh may
influence its desirability. Most redwings forage in the uplands during
the afternoon, when few aquatic insects are emerging. However, many
of the insects captured in the uplands are members of taxa having
aquatic larval stages (Orians 1980). Emergence of the aquatic insects

that are the main food delivered to nestling redwings at CNWR normally begins in early May, after most females have built their first nests.

Because the food supply that will support the breeding effort is not immediately apparent at the time most females select their first nesting sites, only indirect information about future food supplies can be available. Two potential indirect sources of information are clues about food supplies the previous year and aquatic insects visible to a bird foraging at the water's surface. Later-arriving females and renesting females can use more directly observable information to assess current food supplies. Unfortunately, we do not know what early-arriving females can learn by peering into the water.

A returning female could remember a significant amount of information about food supplies in the area in which she nested the previous year. How useful would such information be to her? We did not measure insect emergence quantitatively during the current study, but detailed information on interseasonal variability of insect emergences is available from earlier studies at CNWR (Orians 1980; Orians and Wittenberger 1991). These empirical data indicate that the amount of interseasonal variability in emergences from study lakes is so great that information from the previous year is a poor predictor of emergence rates during the current year.

PREVIOUS NESTS

Another indirect source of information is the number and fate of nests built the previous year. Overwinter survival of nests on our study area is high. Of 142 nests built on several CNWR marshes in 1983, 131 (92%) were still present in February 1984. Therefore, a returning female can estimate the density of breeding birds the previous year by counting old nests. She can also estimate the success rate of those nests. In February 1984 "naive" human observers classified as successful 12 (63%) of 19 nests that actually fledged young and as unsuccessful 66 (81%) of 81 nests that failed to receive eggs or that lost eggs or small nestlings to predators in 1983. Their success rate in assessing the fate of old nests was significantly above that predicted by chance (Erckmann et al. 1990). If female redwings are at least as good as biologists at judging the fate of old nests by their appearances, they should be able to derive information about nesting success the previous year by examining old nests.

Experiments in which old nests were removed from some portions of nesting habitat and added to other areas were performed in 1983 and

1984 on McMannamon Lake and Hampton Slough. Females significantly preferred to nest on plots with old nests in 1983 but not in 1984. An analysis of the combined data from both years revealed no significant preference for plots with old nests (Erckmann et al. 1990). Old nests apparently have little influence on settling decisions by female redwings at CNWR, but females might use old nests as an indicator of the overall quality of a breeding area, while choosing specific nesting sites within a marsh using factors other than local density of nests. The nest-manipulation experiments could not have revealed an effect at the whole marsh scale.

MARSH FIDELITY AND ENVIRONMENTAL PREDICTABILITY

The relatively high fidelity of females to Hampton Slough during years when the marsh was destroyed by beavers shows that even major alterations of nesting substrates do not strongly influence female choices of general settling sites, especially by returning females. Therefore, it is not surprising that under conditions of less drastic changes in the structure of emergent beds, returning females are strongly faithful to their previous breeding areas, regardless of their nesting success the previous year. Within a year, more than 90% of females remained on the same marsh for their first and second nests, even when their first nests failed. Between years, more females whose final year x nests failed changed marshes in year $x + 1$ than did females successful in year x, but the great majority nested on the same marshes regardless of their success or lack of it (Beletsky and Orians 1991; Beletsky 1996). These data indicate that after an initial settling decision is made, the benefits of site familiarity most often outweigh potential benefits of moving to new locations.

Fidelity to particular marshes may also be favored because females cannot reliably use year x nesting success information to assess whether a move to a new location in year $x + 1$ would improve their reproductive success. Although nest success rates varied significantly among marshes, within marshes success rates were not consistent between years. Figure 4.1 plots the mean percentages of successful nests, i.e., those fledging ≥ 1, on the eight core marshes. Each bar in the box plot shows the median and surrounding quartile values of the percent success rates on each marsh over the sixteen-year study. The mean values were significantly different among marshes (ANOVA, F = 3.68, P = 0.001). But autocorrelations from year x to year $x + 1$ of the percentage of successful nests on each of the marshes were not significant; thus, on our study area, nest success rates in one year were not, in general, good indicators

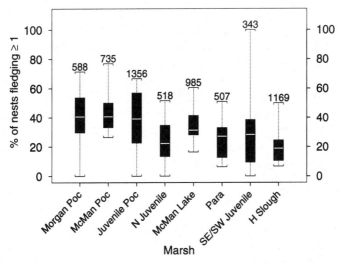

Fig. 4.1. Box plot of the percentages of successful nests each year, by marsh. Each bar shows the median ± one quartile of the percent success rates on each marsh for n = 16 years. Values above error bars show the total numbers of nests per marsh.

of success rates the next. Therefore, even if current information on nest success over a wide area were ascertainable by females, it would not have good year-to-year predictive value.

SOCIAL INFORMATION

A MATE

The presence of a male is apparently necessary to induce a female redwing to settle because females have never been observed to attempt to breed other than on the territory of a male. But do the traits of the male, as opposed to or in addition to the features of his territory, influence female settling decisions? Traits of a male that might influence his desirability as a mate include the genes he will provide to his offspring, his health (current vigor and likelihood that he will transmit parasites to his mate or offspring), and the quality of parental care he will provide (nest defense, provisioning offspring). A male's genes are a fixed trait, but his health and his future behavior can vary. A male's current health can presumably be assessed by a female when she settles, but his future health cannot. Although some studies have identified significant correlations between some aspects of male redwing morphology or behavior and whether a particular male will be a "good" parent, i.e., his probability of provisioning nestlings or being a vigorous nest defender, females apparently do not use that information in their settlement decisions. No correlations existed between the physical or behavioral male attributes that could indicate good parenting and the males' "attractiveness" to females, as measured by female settling order on their territories and the number of females eventually attracted to their territories (e.g., Searcy 1979a; Eckert and Weatherhead 1987a; Shutler and Weatherhead 1991a; Weatherhead et al. 1993). In our study area, male redwings rarely feed nestlings, so females could gain little from attempting to assess this component of parenting even if it were possible to do so.

We did not attempt to measure directly the influence of male size, plumage, health, or parental behavior on mate choices of females. Nonetheless, our information on extrapair copulations (EPCs) and our long-term data set on female site fidelity provide some indirect evidence of the extent to which females respond to traits of males when selecting a territory. If females are responding to genetic traits of males in making settling decisions, they should be less likely to seek EPCs if they are mated to a high-quality male than if they are mated to a low-quality male, and they should selectively seek particular males for EPCs. Neither pattern characterizes our study population. Males that participate in a large number of EPCs in a given year are no more likely than other males to participate in a large number in subsequent years, nor are females mated to particular males more likely to engage in EPCs than females mated to other males (Gray 1996b; see also chapter 2). Thus, the data on patterns of EPCs do not support the hypothesis that female settling decisions are strongly influenced by genetic traits of males.

Another indicator of the influence of male quality on settling decisions is the mate fidelity of females. If females are responding positively to the traits of males when they settle, they should be less likely to nest on the same territory the following year if the former occupant has not returned than if he has. Similarly, if a male moves to another territory nearby, his mates should have a tendency to move with him. Our long-term data set supports neither of these predictions. Females often switch their nesting among territorial males, both within and between years. Between years, females abandon males with whom they had bred successfully the previous year about 50% of the time (Beletsky and Orians 1991; Beletsky 1996). A female is no more likely to breed on the same territory the following year if the former owner returns than if he does not. In addition, females do not follow males who shift their territories between years to new locations, even if they are nearby

(Orians and Beletsky 1989; Beletsky 1996). Female fidelity to particular territories or marsh areas rather than to particular males is strong in other populations as well (Picman 1981; Westneat 1992b). All extensive studies of redwings have shown that females apparently are little influenced by the qualities of males when they select their breeding territories.

MALE NEIGHBORS

Although the traits of a territory owner appear not to influence females, the presence and identities of male neighbors may influence female settling decisions. Although a female probably cannot influence the parental care provided by the male on whose territory she nests, or who the neighboring males are, she can influence the behavior of those neighbors by copulating with them. Neighboring males are potential sources of genes for her offspring, they own territories on which she may be allowed to forage, and they may assist in defending her nest. A male redwing known to have copulated with a particular female, either because he was observed to do so or because DNA fingerprinting revealed that he had fathered at least one of her offspring, is more likely to permit her to forage on his territory and is more likely to engage in active defense of her nest against a predator than are males not known to have copulated with her (Gray 1996c).

The ability of females to influence the behavior of neighboring males may help to explain the surprising fact that the number of familiar males resident on a breeding marsh appears to influence female settling choices and breeding success more than the identity of the male on whose territory she nests. Females nesting with males whose neighbors have been present for more than one breeding season have higher fledging success than females on territories with unfamiliar male neighbors (Beletsky and Orians 1989b). For females whose final year x nests were unsuccessful, the presence of familiar neighboring males in year $x+1$ was positively correlated with the probability that they would return to the same marsh. If a female's final year x male was not present the next year, then her probability of remaining on the same marsh to breed was positively correlated with the number of resident, familiar males, whether or not her final year x nest was successful or not (Beletsky and Orians 1991). We have no data with which to test the possibility, suggested by these results, that males who have copulated with a female for more than one breeding season are more vigorous in the defense of her nests or more tolerant of her use of their territories for foraging than are males copulating with her for the first breeding season. But the *breeding group* of males on a marsh apparently affects female settlement.

Most female redwings share the territory on which they nest with one or more additional females. Both the number and identity of these females could influence a female's settling decision and nesting success. Harem mates with whom a female shared a territory during a previous breeding season may be more likely to assist her in defense than are unfamiliar females, and she may need to expend less time and energy to establish stable relationships with them (Picman 1981). Because between-year marsh fidelity is strong and harems on our study area are large, some females may be harem mates for several years. They may also associate during nonbreeding months, but we gathered no data during those months.

A female arriving early in the breeding season who has the option of becoming a primary female on some of the territories or a secondary female on others might be more likely to accept secondary status on a territory with a familiar harem mate than on a territory with an unfamiliar first female. Likewise, already-settled females might be strongly aggressive toward unfamiliar females and less aggressive toward familiar females trying to settle on their territories. We explore these ideas briefly in the chapter's discussion section.

Theoretical Considerations

HAREM SIZE. When deciding to settle, a female can determine the number and identity of females already settled on nearby territories. She cannot know when or how many other females will settle on the territory she chooses or who they will be. However, because high-quality territories attract females first and eventually accumulate larger harems, and because returning females may remember the density of females the previous year, an experienced female might be able to judge roughly the number of females likely to arrive after she settles.

Estimating the future size of her harem might be beneficial to a female because, in Washington populations at least, there is a positive correlation between average annual RS of females and harem size (Holm 1973; Beletsky 1996); other investigators, working in Ontario, found no significant association (Weatherhead and Robertson 1977; Muldal et al. 1986). Several factors could explain increased female success on territories with larger harems. First, territories with better food supplies and nest sites usually attract more females. Second, females settle earlier on better territories, and the earliest females to breed generally have the highest annual RS (chapter 3). Third, the increased density of females could itself reduce nest predation rate because more individuals are present to detect predators. The higher density of nests may facilitate group mobbing of predators (Picman 1980; Picman et al. 1988), "swamping" of predators, and mutual nest defense (Westneat 1992b). Larger harems also potentially can have negative effects on a female's breeding success. Large numbers of females sharing a territory could depress the local food supply, decrease the amount of parental care a female receives from the male, and/or increase the attractiveness of the area to predators.

FEMALE-FEMALE AGGRESSION. Once a female has settled, she may, by means of aggressive behavior, influence to some degree the temporal pattern of settling by subsequent females. Many observers have noted high levels of aggression by already-settled female redwings toward newly arriving females. Primary females are often very aggressive toward secondary females, chasing and displaying at them, and sometimes fighting with them. Already-settled and even actively nesting females give hundreds of aggressive vocalizations each day, both to harem mates and to prospecting females flying over their marshes (Beletsky and Orians 1985). Such aggression in other species is known to function in maintaining exclusive access to resources, reducing local densities, monopolizing male parental care, or reducing intraspecific brood parasitism (Gowaty and Wagner 1988; Petrie and Møller 1991). The most comprehensive review of redwing studies to date failed, however, to detect any influence of aggression by settled female redwings on settling times of other females, locations of their nests on territories, or eventual harem sizes (Searcy and Yasukawa 1995). Yet the conspicuousness of intrasexual aggressive behavior in this species strongly suggests that it in some way benefits its practitioners.

Aggression among female redwings may affect access to resources and reduce overlap in nesting activities. Thus, a female not yet ready to breed could maintain both her rank and the interval between her nest and the next one by delaying nesting by other females. Aggressive interactions among female redwings are conspicuous only early during the breeding season (Nero 1956a; Case and Hewitt 1963; Orians 1969; Holm 1973; personal observations), when food is more likely to be in short supply and when, because fewer females are present, internest intervals are easier to maintain.

Once a female redwing initiates incubation, she cannot prevent another female from settling unless she is willing to lose her clutch by neglecting her eggs so that they are killed by chilling. Therefore, aggression toward other female redwings could function to delay settling of other females until a female starts incubating, thereby preserving the rank a female had when she settled and/or achieving a minimum interval between initiation of her clutch and clutches of successive harem mates.

RANK IN HAREM. When a female settles, she acquires a potential nesting-order rank in a male's harem. Settling order probably correlates strongly with eventual nesting order, as has been shown in some but not all other redwing populations, and as is true for our CNWR population. If nesting rank influences annual RS, females may defend their rank and settle to achieve a particular rank. A female, unless she is the first one to settle on a marsh, has a choice of ranks, and unless she delays her own nesting so that a later-arriving female begins nesting before she does, or she is delayed by other females, she knows her nesting rank when she settles.

A female's rank could influence her fitness in at least two ways. First, the aggression of primary females toward secondaries suggests that behavioral dominance is correlated with nest rank. Thus, rank could be of importance to females because of the dominance it may confer. Dominance may affect access to resources that influence breeding success. Also, it could function to reduce overlap in nesting activities. A female of high rank not yet ready to breed could maintain her rank by delaying the nesting of other females. That dominance interactions are conspicuous only early during the breeding season suggests that they are important primarily to high-ranked, early nesters. Subtle dominance interactions may exist among lower-ranked females, but no redwing researchers have yet observed them.

Second, rank order may influence the quality and quantity of paternal care the female's offspring receive. In Pied Flycatchers, only the primary female receives male assistance in raising young (Lundberg and Alatalo 1992). Among some other blackbirds, including the Yellow-headed Blackbird, males preferentially feed nestlings at the first nests to hatch on their territories (Willson 1966; Patterson et al. 1980; Gori 1984). However, male redwings do not assist with nest building or incubation, and at CNWR, if they feed young at all, usually do not do so until relatively late in the season, when opportunities to attract additional females are poor. The primary female is no more likely to have nestlings at that time than are lower-ranking females in the harem. When males fed nestlings at our study site they always did so at the most advanced active nest on their territories; but the ranks of those nests ranged from primary to sixth (Beletsky and Orians 1990). However, greater percentages of males help feed young in other regions, generally at the primary or secondary nest (Searcy and Yasukawa 1995), so rank could be a more important factor for deciding female settling in those areas.

Tests

We assess the significance of nesting-order rank by analyzing nesting success and some other factors as functions of rank in harem. Also, to elucidate how females view the number of females associated with them on a territory, we test whether the conspicuous aggression of high-ranked females could function to prevent others from settling and, hence, preserve a primary female's status (i.e., aggression to defend rank), or to delay subsequent females from beginning their nests (aggression to defend low nesting density and/or long internest intervals). We also investigate rank as a settling choice by looking at the settling patterns of females on territories within marshes.

We rank females within a harem by *the date of the first egg in the first nest each female builds in a given year*. A female must have made her settling and nest-initiation decisions at least five to seven days prior to the laying of her first egg, but for the most part we do not know exactly when females arrived on the study area or made those decisions. First egg date is, in any case, a good basis for analyses of within-harem female interactions because it defines how much females actually overlap in their nesting activities. Other investigators of redwings have also used order of first egg dates to reflect female settlement dates and to assign ranks (Garson et al. 1981; Teather et al. 1988). We refer to the first female to lay on a territory as the primary female and the one with the highest rank (lowest number, 1). Subsequent nesters are termed secondary, tertiary, etc. The last female to nest has the lowest rank (highest number) in the harem.

Rank and Settling Patterns: Do Females Prefer High Rank or Large Harems?

If females prefer the highest possible rank, then all territories in a local area should attract one female before any territory attracts a second female, and so on through increasing harem sizes. Also, females should settle as early as possible during the breeding season, and the first female to settle on a territory should defend her rank against other females until she has begun nesting. Alternatively, if females prefer to be members of large harems, that is, if they seek out lower ranks even though higher ranks are available, then a clumped settling pattern should result. In this analysis we use first egg dates as a surrogate of female settlement order.

We determined, for each of our eight marshes each year, the number of territories on which two or more nests were started before every territory had a first nest start. In 77.4% of the cases (total n = 124 marsh-years), one or more territories within a marsh had two or more nests before all territories had one. Sometimes half or more of the territories on a marsh had two or more nests before some had first nests (table 4.2). In contrast, studies in other regions have found that a primary female settled on each male territory in a given area prior to the settlement of any secondaries (Langston et al. 1990, in Washington; Teather et al. 1988, in Ontario). The fact that harems were smaller in those areas may partly explain the difference.

We also have precise early settling patterns for females that nested on Juvenile Pocket from 1990 through 1992 (provided by Elizabeth Gray). Observers watched the marsh four or more hours each day from mid-March to mid-April and recorded the identities of females and their locations. We consider a female to have settled if she was sighted on the marsh during three consecutive days, subsequently was seen there regularly, and then nested there. Her settlement date is taken as the first of the three consecutive days. There is uncertainty in some of our assignments of females to male territories because during the long waiting periods between settling and laying (see chapter 3), some territory boundaries changed. Thus, a female could have settled on one male's territory, but by the time she nested she was on another's. However, because the proportion of such changes was low, only a minor error is probably introduced. Data on all females that settled *prior to the laying of the first egg on the marsh* show clearly that two or more females settled on many territories before all territories within the marsh attracted first females. Indeed, two or more females settle on many individual territories before first eggs were produced on those territories (table 4.3).

Therefore, both our estimates of female settling patterns, based on first egg dates, and our more limited information on real settling dates show that CNWR females do not settle in ways to achieve the highest rank available to them. Even early in the season they elect to settle in larger harems. Moreover, from the point of view of already-settled

TABLE 4.2. Number of territories on each marsh that had two or more nest-starts (first egg dates) before each territory on the marsh had one

Year	Hampton Slough A[a]	B[b]	North Juvenile A	B	Juvenile Pocket A	B	SE/SW Juvenile A	B
1977	15	6	6	1	—	—	4	1
1978	20	13	9	5	4	0	2	0
1979	—	—	—	—	—	—	2	0
1980	20	17	7	2	4	1	7	5
1981	20	8	10	6	5	2	5	4
1982	16	3	6	0	3	0	4	2
1983	19	9	9	6	7	5	7	2
1984	15	5	6	3	8	5	6	4
1985	19	10	7	1	12	8	6	2
1986	15	3	9	5	14	7	6	3
1987	9	2	5	2	15	8	9	5
1988	11	6	7	1	20	15	6	3
1989	6	1	6	1	21	15	5	4
1990	1	0	2	0	15	6	4	0
1991	2	0	1	0	14	5	2	0
1992	3	0	3	1	18	13	2	0

Year	Para Lake A[a]	B[b]	McMannamon Lake A	B	McMannamon Pocket A	B	Morgan Pocket A	B
1977	8	5	19	6	8	6	2	1
1978	7	3	17	6	7	3	3	0
1979	4	2	15	7	3	1	3	2
1980	3	1	12	10	4	2	5	0
1981	6	1	13	7	3	0	7	6
1982	2	0	9	3	3	0	7	5
1983	8	6	16	11	6	2	9	6
1984	4	1	13	7	7	5	8	0
1985	6	0	6	3	6	0	11	5
1986	7	3	13	7	7	4	3	2
1987	7	4	8	4	8	2	6	5
1988	8	3	12	7	12	5	6	4
1989	8	4	4	0	10	5	2	1
1990	5	3	8	2	8	1	3	0
1991	4	0	9	2	2	0	3	1
1992	4	1	10	5	2	0	2	0

Note: Includes only territories that had ≥ 1 egg by 30 April.

[a]Number of territories.

[b]Number of territories with two or more nest-starts (dates of first eggs) before each had one.

TABLE 4.3. Settling patterns of female redwings on Juvenile Pocket before
laying began in 1990, 1991, and 1992

	1990	1991	1992
Total no. of male territories	17	18	18
No. of females on marsh prior to any laying	31	34	14
Mean no. of females/territory prior to any			
laying on the marsh	1.8	1.9	0.8
No. of territories with two females before each			
got one	2	6	1
With three females	7	4	0
With four females	0	2	1
No. (%) of territories[a] on which primary settler			
was also primary nester	12/15 (80)	9/15 (60)	11/13 (85)
No. (%) of territories[a] on which more than one			
female settled prior to first egg date on the			
territory	9/15 (60)	11/15 (73)	2/13 (15)

[a]These analyses include only territories that had one or more settled females prior to the marsh's
first egg date.

primary females, these results show that at CNWR they do not or
cannot prevent secondaries from settling on their territories prior to
laying. However, they may be able to delay the nesting of secondary
females, because primary settlers were usually the first to nest even if
they delayed initiation of their nests until long after they settled (table
4.3). These data support the assumption we use in many of our analyses
that nesting order of females within a harem closely tracks settlement
order, at least for the first few nests per male territory. In New Jersey,
Lenington (1980) found that female redwing settlement date was *not*
correlated with first egg date. However, because only about a third of
the females in her study were banded, errors in determining settling
dates may have obscured the relationships between true settling times
and nest-initiation times. In a New York redwing population, settling
date and first egg date were significantly correlated (Westneat 1992b).

Is Reproductive Success Correlated with Rank in Harem?
We assess the significance of rank by analyzing nesting success as a
function of rank in harem. If high rank is advantageous, then high-
ranked females should, on average, have higher annual RS than lower-
ranked females. Several investigators have found correlations between
rank and reproductive success, but they used only females' first nests

(Crawford 1977; Muldal et al. 1986; Langston et al. 1990) because they did not have enough color-banded females to estimate seasonal reproductive success. This method of analysis may result in serious biases because until late in the breeding season, female redwings in all populations renest quickly when their nests fail. At CNWR, where the nesting period spans 90 to 100 days, some females build as many as five nests, and the mean number of nests built per female per season is 1.9 ± 1.0. On average, 3.8% of females annually fledge two broods. Therefore, only annual fledging success is a meaningful measure of the reproductive significance of rank.

To test the hypothesis that rank and RS are positively correlated, we performed a multiple linear regression, with annual fledging success per female as the dependent variable, to control for the effects of female age and territory (marsh) quality. Variability in territory quality could substantially influence the analysis if, for example, primary females on very poor territories consistently experienced poorer average success than lower-ranked females on good territories. Because mean RS per male and per female is consistently higher on pockets than on strips (Beletsky and Orians 1989b; chapter 2), we included marsh type in the analysis.

We tested the effects of breeding experience (yearling or mature) and marsh type (pocket or strip). Female rank (assigned by the rank order of her first nest of the season) and harem size (the eventual harem size on the male territory on which she placed her first nest of the season) were tested within each marsh type. We used for this analysis only ranks 1 to 4, only females that had at least one nest with $\geq$ 1 egg, and, because we separated females into age groups, only information from 1982 through 1992. Testing only ranks 1 to 4 is appropriate because for the most part these females built their nests during the early portions of breeding seasons, when female-female aggression is most pronounced.

The only two significant effects in the regression model (table 4.4a) were a positive effect on annual RS of breeding experience (mature females performing better than yearlings; mean annual RS for matures = 1.55 ± 1.74 fledged young, n = 900; and for yearlings, 0.95 ± 1.49 young, n = 80) and, on pockets only, a positive effect of harem size (females in larger harems having better annual RS; see below). We repeated the analysis using female ranks up to 9. In this multiple regression model, breeding experience and harem size on pocket marshes had the same significant positive effects on annual RS. Marsh type, pocket vs. strip, also contributed significantly to annual RS (table 4.4b). But

TABLE 4.4. Multiple linear regressions (MLR) of breeding experience, marsh type, rank, and harem size on the annual fledging success of females, and mean annual RS for females of various ranks

a. MLR using only ranks 1 to 4

Value	SE	t	P	
0.846	0.178	4.74	0.0000	Intercept
0.095	0.157	0.61	0.54	Marsh type
-0.259	0.101	-2.58	0.01	Breeding experience
0.055	0.086	0.64	0.52	Rank/strip marshes
0.026	0.071	0.36	0.72	Rank/pocket marshes
0.050	0.049	1.02	0.31	Harem size/strip marshes
0.077	0.026	2.98	0.003	Harem size/pocket marshes

F = 5.71, df = 6 and 973, P < 0.00001

b. MLR using all ranks

Value	SE	t	P	
1.013	0.133	7.60	0.0000	Intercept
0.241	0.117	2.06	0.040	Marsh type
-0.206	0.081	-2.54	0.011	Breeding experience
0.068	0.055	1.22	0.22	Rank/strip marshes
-0.054	0.033	-1.61	0.11	Rank/pocket marshes
0.048	0.046	1.03	0.30	Harem size/strip marshes
0.060	0.022	2.79	0.005	Harem size/pocket marshes

F = 5.62, df = 6 and 1271, P < 0.00001

c. Mean annual RS for females of various ranks

Rank	Strips		Pockets	
	Mean ± SD annual RS	n	Mean ± SD annual RS	n
1	1.13 ± 1.65	144	1.53 ± 1.56	156
2	1.37 ± 1.83	141	1.68 ± 1.76	138
3	1.26 ± 1.59	98	1.86 ± 1.91	140
4	1.42 ± 1.72	52	1.67 ± 1.62	111
5	1.43 ± 1.57	28	1.58 ± 1.57	86
6	1.72 ± 1.51	25	1.60 ± 1.30	63
7	1.14 ± 1.57	7	1.29 ± 1.42	41
8	2.67 ± 1.51	6	1.58 ± 1.33	26
9	3.00	1	1.73 ± 1.71	15

again, there was no effect of a female's rank on her RS. Moreover, for ranks 1 to 4, the trend is clearly in the opposite direction: lower-ranked females had greater annual RS (table 4.4c).

For comparison with previous studies, we also tested whether rank and RS, estimated from first nests only, were positively correlated. Female ranks were again assigned by first egg dates, using only those nests that received ≥ 1 egg. We performed a 2-way ANOVA, with fledging success of females' first nests as the dependent variable and ranks (1 to 4) and territory type (pocket or strip) as main effects. The mean fledging success for nests in the four rank categories and on the two marsh types are given in table 4.5, together with the ANOVA table. There was a strong significant effect of rank on first-nest RS, but in the direction opposite to our expectation: secondary females fared better than primaries, and tertiaries fared better than secondaries. There was also a significant effect of marsh type on RS. The interaction term between rank and marsh type was not significant, indicating that the negative effect of high rank on first-nest fledging success was present on all marsh types (territory quality).

Previous tests of the relationship between female rank in redwings and fledging success have often identified a benefit of being primary. Crawford (1977) examined the nesting success of approximately 70 banded females (about half of them yearlings) over a two-year period in marsh areas in Iowa where harems were small. He found that primary females had significantly higher fledging success from their first nests than did secondaries; he did not monitor any subsequent nests. Muldal et al. (1986) worked for two years on marshes in southern Ontario, where harems ranged from 1 to 6 females (mean = 1.7 in one year and 2.7 the next). Because they had banded few females, they assigned later-season nests to females from the same territories whose previous nests had failed. On territories with more than one female, they found that *secondary* females had the highest mean fledging success if males assisted them in provisioning their nestlings. Males apparently were more likely to help secondaries because when primary nests had nestlings the males were still actively engaged in attracting mates. On those territories where males did not feed nestlings, primary females had the highest mean fledging success. In Washington, Langston et al. (1990) found a strong, positive effect of female rank on RS because earlier nests had lower probabilities of being depredated than later nests. However, because they did not band females, they could monitor and report only first nest success. In a Wisconsin study, nearly 70% (n = 54) of primary females' first nests, but only 39.2% (n = 51) of the first nests of lower-ranked females, fledged offspring (Yasukawa 1989).

TABLE 4.5. Two-way ANOVA, fledging success of first nest versus female rank and marsh type

| | Rank | | | | Marsh type | |
	1	2	3	4	Pockets	Strips
Mean ± SD fledging success/nest	0.73 ± 1.33	1.04 ± 1.41	1.18 ± 1.49	1.30 ± 1.43	1.21 ± 1.43	0.89 ± 1.40
n	590	560	446	314	817	1093

ANOVA table

	df	Sum of squares	Mean square	F	P
Rank	1	76.71	76.71	38.89	<<0.0001
Marsh type	1	38.03	38.03	19.28	<0.0001
Rank x marsh type	1	0.49	0.49	0.25	0.62
Residuals	1906	3759.66	1.97		

Thus, several studies based on analyses of first nests only of females offer evidence that having primary status is beneficial. Whether we analyze our data using first nests only or seasonal RS, primary female redwings in the CNWR population *do not* have higher RS than second-ary females. Therefore, the difference between our results and those of other investigators is not simply the result of differences in methods of analysis.

SIGNIFICANCE OF FEMALE AGGRESSION: DOES IT DELAY NESTING OF OTHER FEMALES? At CNWR most primary settlers are also pri-mary nesters, even though additional females settle on their territories before the primaries begin laying. Thus, the aggression characteristic of early settlers might function to delay nesting of later-settling females. We tested three predictions that should be supported if aggression by primary females delays nesting of secondaries; all are based on observed internest intervals (INIs). First, the observed means of primary-secondary INIs should be significantly longer than expected primary-secondary INI means generated by random female settlement and nest initiation. Second, if the temporal spacing of nests is more valuable to early-settling females than to those settling later (as indicated by the seasonal decline in female-female aggression), then primary-secondary INIs should be significantly longer than those between nests of lower-ranked females. Third, if the primary female's first nest fails quickly and she renests before the secondary female on the same territory begins nesting, the interval between the primary female's second nest and the secondary female's first nest should be, on average, no shorter than primary-secondary INIs in the usual situation in which the primary female has only a single nest before the secondary female begins nest-ing. In other words, even if the primary female's first nest quickly fails, delaying the secondary female should give her the same potential advantage to being "primary" on the territory for her second nesting attempt as it had during her first attempt.

1. We tested the hypothesis that observed mean INIs were signifi-cantly larger than those expected if females initiated nests on the same actual, observed dates but chose territories at random, by conducting permutation tests on subsets of our data. We used for our observed INIs temporal nesting patterns on Juvenile Pocket from 1983 to 1992. First we computed for each year the mean primary-secondary INI for all territories on the marsh in which both primary and secondary nests started prior to 1 May. Territories in which primary or secondary nests began after 1 May were unrepresentative, relatively very poor-quality

TABLE 4.6. Comparison of observed mean internest intervals (INIs) between primary and secondary females on Juvenile Pocket from 1983 to 1992 with mean intervals expected if the same number of females on the marsh settled randomly

Year	Observed INI[a] Mean (days)	n[b]	No. of females[c]	Expected INI Mean (days)	Frequency that actual mean is ≥ the expected, randomly generated mean No./6000	p[e]
1983	5.0	6	31	7.3	930[d]	0.16
1984	4.4	7	31	5.2	2122	0.35
1985	3.3	8	30	4.0	1311	0.22
1986	9.9	10	32	11.9	1485	0.25
1987	9.5	11	34	8.2	4603	0.77
1988	6.6	16	63	6.5	3266	0.54
1989	10.7	14	47	10.6	2425	0.40
1990	6.0	14	53	5.3	4684	0.78
1991	2.2	5	22	9.9	30	0.01
1992	7.1	14	44	7.2	1266	0.21
Grand mean	6.8	105	387	7.6	565	0.09

[a]Observed mean primary-secondary INI for all territories that had secondary nests by 1 May.
[b]The number of territories on which the observed and expected means are based.
[c]The total number of different females responsible for all nests on the marsh by 1 May.
[d]In 930 of 6000 permutation runs the actual mean was ≥ the mean of the randomly generated intervals.
[e]A probability of ≥ 0.95 would indicate that 95% or more of randomly generated means were as small as or smaller than the observed means, i.e., that they are significantly different.

ones, with relatively few females; using them would bias the result by including exceptionally long primary-secondary INIs. Mean observed INIs are given in table 4.6. We calculated expected INI distributions in the following manner: First we determined the first egg dates for all females on each territory each year. Females with first egg dates after 30 April were discarded. The remaining first egg dates for females were then used as the sample from which randomly drawn "females" were picked to reconstitute "harems" that were the same sizes as the original, observed harems. (All females, and not solely primary and secondary females, were used because we wanted our randomly generated nesting orders to reflect the true patterns of female settlement on the marsh, where, for example, some females might settle and nest as tertiary females before other territories acquired primary or secondary nesters.) For instance, in 1983 the procedure resulted in 31 first egg dates of females, ranging from day 86 (27 March) to day 120 (30 April); the 31 dates were randomized and placed into "harems" according to the observed number of females on each territory. The two earliest first egg dates on each "territory" were then defined to be from the primary and secondary nests, and the primary-secondary INI was the interval between them. The mean interval for the n number of territories was calculated. The random sampling (in 1983, of the 31 first egg dates) was repeated 6,000 times for each year, producing 6,000 mean primary-secondary INIs for each year. Thus, our permutation test compared actual mean INIs with a distribution of randomly generated mean INIs that were based each year on real first egg dates.

We then asked, With what frequency were the randomly generated means less than or equal to the observed means? This frequency, or percentage, would be the P-value. If in 95% or more of the randomized trials the generated mean was less than the observed mean that year, we would reject the hypothesis that the observed and randomized means were the same and, instead, accept the alternative, that the observed mean INI was longer than the one predicted by chance alone. In other words, we would accept that some factor, such as female-female aggression, had produced INIs that were longer than those expected if females settled and initiated nesting by random chance. However, we found nonsignificant results in each of the ten years tested (table 4.6).

2. To test the second prediction, that primary-secondary INIs should be significantly longer than those between nests of lower-ranked females, we computed the intervals between nests for all territories with eventual harems of at least four females; we used each female only once per year (i.e., females were not included twice if they had, for example, the first and third nests on a male's territory; nor were cases included in which, for example, a primary female had two nests before a secondary female had a first nest, or a secondary female had two nests before a tertiary had a first, etc.). Mean intervals among the first five nests on male territories were quite uniform—about six days (fig. 4.2). There was no significant difference between the mean intervals between primary and secondary nests and secondary and tertiary nests, although the trend was for intervals to decrease with rank (Wilcoxon matched-pairs test, $t = 1.45$, 1-tailed $P = 0.07$, $n = 397$). The nonsignificance of the result does not preclude the possibility that maintaining larger internest intervals is more important for primary females than for females of lower rank because we restricted our analysis to first nests of females, and thus most of the intervals we computed came from early in the breeding season, when aggression is strongest. These data—mean

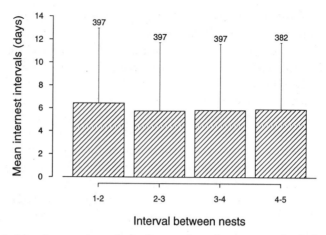

Fig. 4.2. Mean internest intervals, by first egg dates, for territories that had eventual harems of four or more females. Error bars are SD; sample sizes are given above error bars.

six-day INIs among the first four nests per territory—are also consistent with a tactic in which each female delayed the nesting of the next-lowest-ranked female on the territory.

3. Among territories with four or more females, we had 51 cases in which the primary female started two nests (the first having failed early in the cycle) before the secondary started her first. The mean interval between the primary females' second nest starts and the secondary females' first nest starts was 5.8 ± 6.0 d; for 519 cases in which the secondary female had the second nest on the territory, the mean primary-secondary INI was 6.5 ± 6.6 d. A two-sample t-test on these means (t = 0.78) yields a two-tailed P value of 0.44. Thus we accept the hypothesis that the means come from the same population, a result consistent with the hypothesis that the primary female delayed nest initiation by the secondary female.

When considered together, results of these analyses are only partly consistent with a nest-delaying function for female-female aggression. Our randomized permutation tests yielded no indication that the mean primary-secondary INIs on Juvenile Pocket were influenced by social interactions, but they do not rule it out. Our analysis also allows us to reject the hypothesis that primary-secondary INIs are longer than subsequent ones, which would be the case if primary females used aggression to delay secondary females, but later-nesting females did not, or did so to a lesser degree. Our final test, however, of INIs where primary females had two nests before secondaries have one, provides some support for delaying effect of female-female aggression. However, this result is also consistent with the hypothesis that subsequent females voluntarily delay settling or starting their nest because they also benefit from temporal spacing of nests on a territory. An argument against this interpretation, however, is that if secondary females prefer longer intervals between nests, then no aggression on the part of primary females would be needed if the aggression's function is to delay nesting of secondary females.

From an analysis of the results of all investigations of female-female aggression in redwings, Searcy and Yasukawa (1995) concluded that such aggression had no effect on further female settlement or on the timing and spacing of nests. This conclusion was based on a variety of evidence including female removal experiments and their effect on subsequent female settlement (Searcy 1988), correlations between the aggressiveness of individual females and further settlement on their territories (Searcy 1988), analysis of the temporal spacing of nests in Washington (Yasukawa and Searcy 1981), computer simulations of female settlement (Yasukawa and Searcy 1986), and androgen implants to primary females to enhance their aggressiveness (Searcy 1988). A few studies, however, did suggest a negative affect of female-female aggression on subsequent female settlement: an analysis of the temporal spacing of nests in Indiana (Yasukawa and Searcy 1981), female removals by Hurly and Robertson (1985), and correlations of female aggression and nesting sequences and success by Langston et al. (1990). Nevertheless, Searcy (1988) and Searcy and Yasukawa (1995) conclude that female aggression probably has no current functional significance. They suggest that aggressive behavior between same-sexed individuals in redwings is highly advantageous only to males, and that females are genetically "dragged along" by selection on males. Our results provide only weak evidence to the contrary.

CORRELATIONS BETWEEN RANK AND AGE. Female rank should change with age because older, more brightly colored females usually arrive and begin nesting before the duller yearlings, which lack red on their shoulders. Therefore, females should, on average, advance in rank between their first and subsequent breeding seasons. On average, yearlings began their first nests each year about a week and a half after mature females did (figs. 3.7 and 3.8); therefore, yearlings must have had lower ranks than matures. To determine how individuals change in rank between years, we followed the rank histories of 133 banded yearlings. Only 15% of these yearlings, evenly distributed among the sixteen years of the study, were primary females (fig. 4.3a); thus, very few yearlings in any one year are primary. On average, yearlings advanced in rank during their second and third breeding years (fig. 4.3b,c).

HAREM SIZE VERSUS SEASONAL RS. Harem size was positively correlated with annual fledging success of females at CNWR, but only on pocket marshes (table 4.4a,b). The difference between marsh types is not surprising because fledging success per male and per female, and average harem size, are generally higher on pockets (Beletsky and Orians 1989b; table 2.1). The cause of improved RS on pockets is probably better predator detection and antipredator nest defense on the high-breeding-density pockets. This could explain why there is no reproduction-enhancing effect of harem size on the lower-density strip marshes, where territories have, at most, two contiguous neighbors. Mean annual RS for females that nested on territories with differing harem sizes are given in table 4.7.

RANK AND MATE FIDELITY. Rank would be expected to influence mate fidelity if males preferentially assisted females of particular ranks and if that assistance improved females' reproductive success and influenced their future settling decisions. For example, if a male assisted only his primary female by feeding her young (as found by Patterson [1991] in Indiana [85% of the time] and Yasukawa and Searcy [1982] in New York [93% of the time]), she might be more faithful to the male than would a lower-ranked female. In other words, mate fidelity could vary with rank if the bond between a primary female and her mate differed qualitatively from the bonds males form with other females. We are not aware of such bond differences in the CNWR population, although Yasukawa (1989) found that primary females in Wisconsin vocalized from their nests more often when males were near the nest than did lower-ranked females, and that primary nests were also more strongly defended by males. This suggests either that males were more attentive to primary nests, spending more time near them, or that the females' vocalizations stimulated the males to be more attentive. Knight and Temple (1988) found that male redwings presented with a choice defended primary more than secondary nests. The amount of time invested in the seasonal bond might also influence between-year fidelity. The higher a female's rank, the more time she spends on a male's territory, and so the more familiar with him she is. At CNWR, a primary female who remains with a male throughout the season could

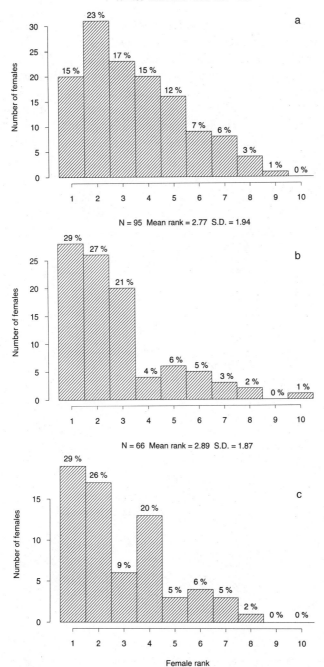

Fig. 4.3. Distribution of ranks of females known to be yearlings during the first year that they were detected breeding at CNWR, 1982 through 1992, (a) during their first breeding year; (b) during their second breeding year; (c) during their third breeding year.

be associated with him for up to 120 d; a female with a low rank would, on average, be on his territory for much less time.

We examined the effect of a female's rank on her fidelity to her mate by determining the percentage of females of different ranks who remained with their mates between nesting attempts. The percentage of females that remained on the same male's territory for their first and second nests of a year was not correlated with rank of the females (fig. 4.4). The results are the same when the behavior of females with

TABLE 4.7. Mean annual fledging success for females that nested on territories with various harem sizes

Harem size[a]	Mean ± SD annual fledging success/female			
	Pockets	n	Strips	n
1	0.81 ± 1.32	15	1.14 ± 1.46	21
2	1.04 ± 1.26	27	1.25 ± 1.72	67
3	1.37 ± 1.45	78	0.99 ± 1.47	96
4	1.72 ± 1.73	86	1.11 ± 1.59	104
5	1.71 ± 1.68	87	1.78 ± 2.06	92
6	1.70 ± 1.75	89	1.60 ± 1.53	50
7	1.39 ± 1.48	103	0.95 ± 1.08	19
8	1.87 ± 1.75	93	1.39 ± 1.64	38
9	1.90 ± 1.72	67	1.24 ± 1.89	15
10	1.84 ± 1.93	58	—	—

[a]Seasonal total harem size on the territory on which female placed her first nest.

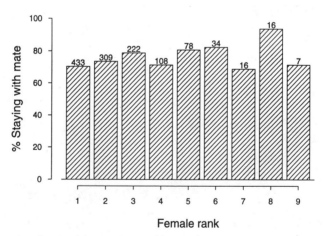

Fig. 4.4. Distribution of the percentages of females, by their first nest rank, that remained on their first mate's territory for their second nest of the season. Females that had both successful and unsuccessful first nests are included. Sample sizes are given above bars.

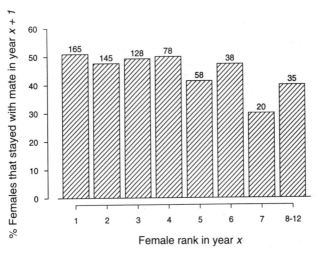

Fig. 4.5. Distribution of the percentages of females, by their first nest rank in year x, that returned to the same male's territory for their first nests of year $x + 1$, provided that the female's mate from her final nest in year x survived and owned the same territory in $x + 1$. Includes only those females that had all of their year x nests on one male's territory. Sample sizes are given above bars.

successful and unsuccessful first nests is analyzed separately. Rank order also did not influence mate fidelity from a female's last nest in year x to her first nest in $x + 1$, provided that the female's mate from her final nest in year x owned the same territory in $x + 1$ (fig. 4.5). Thus, faithfulness is not correlated with rank, an expected result where rank is not correlated with female fledging success.

DISCUSSION

The results of our long-term study of settling decisions indicate that female redwings use a variety of data when making their initial settling decisions and when selecting sites for renesting within breeding seasons. The kinds and amounts of information available to a female vary with time during the breeding season and with age. Because between-year fidelity to particular marshes is very high, initial seasonal settling decisions of yearling and mature females must be made somewhat differently.

The gross physical structure of marshes, including type and condition of vegetation, propensity for food production, and the presence of nests from previous years, may exert influences on the initial decisions of yearlings—although yearlings also have to guide them the settling choices of more experienced females, who usually precede them. Experienced females making settling decisons apparently are less influenced by current physical traits of marshes because between-year marsh fidelity is always very high, even though the condition of marsh vegetation often changes for the worse and there is poor year-to-year consistency in insect emergence and nest success rates.

Females making settling decisions may pay more attention to social cues. As described above, familiar male neighbors may influence female breeding success and thus their presence appears to affect settling decisions. And, as surprising as it would have seemed thirty-five years ago, we must conclude—from the accumulated evidence of many different investigations from various regions—that the particular male owner of a territory does not in any discernible way influence a female's settling decision.

RANK IN HAREM

The result of our long-term monitoring is that at CNWR the order in which females nested on male territories early in the breeding season (ranks 1 to 4), when female-female aggression was most pronounced, was not correlated with annual RS. When we examined the potential effect of rank on first nest success, as have most previous studies, we found a significant effect in the direction opposite that expected: secondary nesters, on average, had greater success than primary females, and those that began third or fourth did even better. We cannot say whether females chose specific ranks, but during the years of our study, a female behaving in ways to maximize her annual RS should have avoided primary status. On average, a female would have accrued the maximum number of fledglings had she started her first nest very early (chapter 3), but not as the primary female on a male's territory.

The apparent paradox in our data, that starting earlier in the season is better (chapter 3) but that primary females, who by definition begin earliest on each territory, have, on average, slightly lower annual RS than secondaries and tertiaries, can be explained by two factors: (1) not all primaries started their nests during the earliest possible nesting weeks of the season (i.e., primary females on poor-quality territories often began their nests several weeks after secondary or tertiary nesters on high-quality territories began theirs, and in some years virtually no females began their nests during the very earliest possible nesting weeks—last week of March and first week of April); and (2) mean primary-secondary and secondary-tertiary INIs are only five to six days long (fig. 4.2) and therefore, on average, many secondaries and tertiaries nested very quickly after primary nesters and so also experienced any reproduction-enhancing effect of very early nesting.

Redwing breeding ecology at CNWR helps explain the patterns we found. Most arguments about potential advantages of high rank hinge on male assistance in feeding young (i.e., on "nonshareable" parental care). But at CNWR, few males feed nestlings, and when they do, they are more likely to feed later nests than primary ones (Beletsky and Orians 1990). This assistance pattern probably reflects the long period over which males devote most of their energy to territory and mate defense and mate advertisement. CNWR marshes are highly productive; females are routinely able to provision three or four nestlings without male assistance, even early during the nesting season. Also, the major CNWR nest predators, Black-billed Magpies, snakes, and large mammals, are not strongly deterred by the attacks of male redwings. Therefore, even if males preferentially defended primary nests, that defense may not be effective in the CNWR area. Thus, high female rank, if important in some populations in gleaning a greater share of male assistance, may be unimportant at CNWR. Further, although many early nests do well, if nest "clumping" or synchrony has strong positive effects on nest success (as indicated by Picman 1980; Picman et al. 1988; Westneat 1992b), then many primary nests at CNWR, begun early and in isolation on male territories, may partly miss out on reproduction-enhancing effects of high nest density.

Although the earliest nests, which include most primary nests, had the highest success rate during the years of our study (fig. 3.1), they are also exposed to the most variable and severe weather conditions. Over the long term, benefits that accrue to nesting success due to early starts that escaped predation may regularly be canceled by poor weather conditions, with the result that females of different ranks on average have similar annual RS. In other words, starting very early entails both great risks and great potential rewards (fig. 3.3). Redwing populations in the CNWR area have larger harems and longer breeding seasons than most redwing populations in the region. For example, harem sizes among redwings breeding at the Turnbull National Wildlife Refuge in extreme eastern Washington, at a higher elevation, are on average only half as large as those at CNWR (Orians 1980). Therefore, the evolution of redwings in the Columbia Basin may have been molded by conditions that, on average, differ from those we studied. Until recently, the warm, dry areas of the lower parts of the Columbia Basin had few marshes because rainfall was insufficient.

The decline of female aggression during the breeding season is consistent with the idea of a continuum of changing "choice environments." At first, when food is relatively scarce and bad weather more likely, females may benefit from keeping others from nesting because competition for food close to their nests would be reduced. Also, in some regions, primary nesters may garner a larger share of male parental care. Later during the breeding season, aggression is low, rank is unimportant, and the most vital nesting factor might be the amount of time remaining before the end of the breeding season. The strategy then might be to ignore other females and simply nest or renest as quickly as possible. At CNWR, although early weather is uncertain, it did not have a strong effect on nest success (chapter 3). Also, we have no indication that our females would benefit from defending food around their nests (fig. 3.2).

We have not traced the rank histories of all females during their entire lifetimes, but the yearling cohort we followed for three years (fig. 4.3) suggests that some females at CNWR never advance to primary status. The combination of no advantage to being primary and a genetic influence on when females begin to nest each year could easily yield the result that many females always begin to nest well after other females have started.

HAREM MATES AND FEMALE-FEMALE AGGRESSION

Our data on settling and nesting patterns provide weak evidence that already-settled females may delay initiation of breeding by later females. However, two or more females often settled per male territory before nesting began, indicating that aggression of primary settlers toward prospecting females did not prevent their settlement. At Winchester Wasteway, 50 km from CNWR, however, Langston et al. (1990) obtained a markedly different result: secondaries did not settle until primaries began incubating. The difference may be related to differences in territory quality and associated female densities. Average harem sizes at CNWR are among the highest recorded anywhere. On marshes such as Juvenile Pocket, where harems commonly ranged up to ten or more, several mature females with equivalent breeding experience may return each year to the same small marsh area or territory. In contrast, when harems are small (two or three females), often only a single female per harem may survive the winter to return the next year. These females may assume primary rank on their same territories, and because few subsequent females arrive, it may be much easier for them to dissuade others—particularly yearlings—from settling.

Thus, the difference between the CNWR population and some others that have been studied may be not in the behavior of primary settlers (they all may be aggressive toward females that subsequently try to settle) but in the typical identities of females who try to settle as second- and lower-ranked females. At CNWR, with large harems and high between-year marsh fidelity, primary, secondary and even tertiary nesters on a single territory often may be females that returned at nearly the same time to the same small area of marsh, if not the same territory. In other regions, with smaller harems, secondaries and tertiaries are less likely to be former harem mates. A returning female who is primary and a prospecting female who was in the same harem with the primary the previous year may have a previous social bond or knowledge of each other that either reduces aggression between them (Picman 1981), facilitating settling of the secondary, or gives the secondary an advantage in "handling" the aggression of the primary that a female new to the area would lack. In fact, aggression between primaries and secondaries when they are returning harem mates may have less to do with preventing settlement than with reestablishing dominance relationships between them. In Indiana, where males preferentially feed at primary nests and male assistance is important to females, and where harems are small such that harem mates are usually new to each other each year, a primary female's early aggression may be used to defend her rank. At CNWR, where male assistance is much less important, harems are large, and long-term familiarity of females within harems is more likely, aggression among females may have more to do with establishing and maintaining within-harem dominance relationships, the functions of which are currently obscure.

Primary settlers are usually primary nesters, a pattern consistent with a use of aggression by primaries to delay the nesting of secondaries. This interpretation is supported by the fact that many secondaries on Juvenile Pocket settled before primaries nested (table 4.3). Also consistent with a role of aggression in delaying nesting by other females is our finding that average intervals between primary and secondary nests and subsequent INIs are similar, and that secondary nesters, on average, start their nests the same number of days after the primary does, regardless of whether it is the primary female's first or second nest. The lack of an RS advantage to primary status is consistent with the idea that primary females use aggressive behavior to delay the nesting of secondaries, rather than to defend rank per se.

Five

How Much Effort
to Invest in Breeding
and When to Stop

INTRODUCTION

One important decision made by breeding female redwings is the amount of time and energy to invest in reproductive activities within a given breeding season. Components of this decision include how much to invest in provisioning the offspring of a given nest and how long to continue breeding. If investment in reproduction during one bout reduces the ability of the parent to invest in future offspring, the trade-off may lead to the evolution of constraints on short-term reproductive efforts (Trivers 1972). The overall goal of this chapter is to determine whether reproductive effort of female redwings within breeding seasons has a parental investment (PI) component.

The optimal level of investment in feeding nestlings and fledglings is determined by the marginal improvement in offspring survival resulting from additional provisioning, offset by delays in initiating a new nest and possible negative effect on survival and vigor of the female. Among many bird species, investment efforts by females may influence and be influenced by compensatory investments by their mates. However, fewer than 10% of males in our study population of redwings feed offspring prior to fledging. At least 12% of our territorial males feed fledglings (Beletsky and Orians 1990), but there is no evidence to indicate that whether or not a male feeds offspring depends upon what his mate does. Therefore, we ignore possible compensatory behavioral adjustments by males as factors affecting female breeding investment decisions.

A key element in theoretical considerations of optimal levels of parental investment is an expectation of inverse relationships between the energetic investment in a current breeding effort and survival and/or investment in future breeding efforts (Trivers 1972; Pianka 1976; Stearns 1976). There are two major reasons for expecting such fitness costs of reproduction. First, because reproduction is energetically expensive, individuals may lower their physiological condition in ways that reduce future performances. Second, reproducing individuals are likely to incur higher predation rates because they behave in ways that make them more conspicuous, while at the same time they are less alert to the presence of predators (Robinson 1986; Stearns 1992).

Studies of birds have yielded both positive (Bryant 1979; Slagsvold 1984; Nur 1984, 1988a; Røskaft 1985; Ekman and Askenmo 1986) and negative (Lack 1966; DeSteven 1980; Smith 1981; Högstedt 1981; Gustafsson and Pärt 1990) evidence for trade-offs between current and future reproduction. The best evidence is provided by experiments in which broods were artificially enlarged. For example, when Blue Tit (*Parus caeruleus*) breeding pairs were provided with 3, 6, 9, 12, or 15 nestlings to raise, interannual survival of adult females was inversely related to experimental brood size, and individuals with enlarged broods tended to have fewer surviving offspring the next year (Nur 1988a). Similarly, one-year-old Collared Flycatchers (*Ficedula albicollis*) that had experimentally enlarged clutches had smaller clutches in the future than did controls (Gustafsson and Pärt 1990). Nur (1988b) concluded that the balance of evidence supports the existence of a cost of reproduction for birds, as do the data gathered on other taxa as well (reviewed by Lessells 1991).

Redwing females at CNWR have sole responsibility for nest building, incubation, brooding young, and, almost entirely, provisioning nestlings. Thus, their direct energetic investment in nesting is considerable. Furthermore, as a consequence of a long breeding season and a high rate of nest destruction, many females nest several times in one season. On average, females in our study population build 1.9 ± 0.9 nests per year, with a range from one to five. Most females who build only one nest have successful first nests. Females whose nests fail typically renest quickly (chapter 3). Roughly 4% of females each year fledge two broods. Thus, female redwings naturally invest highly variable amounts of energy in reproduction.

Because most females breeding on our study area were color-banded, we can estimate their annual reproductive energy investment (RE) scores. We devised a scoring scheme that estimates the total energetic output of each female that is attributable to her reproductive activities. That is, we attempted to determine how much more energy she expended because she engaged in reproductive activities than she would have if she had merely lived in the area without breeding. We assigned energy values to building nests, producing eggs, incubating, and feeding young, according to the best estimates available to us from the literature. Each RE value was scaled as some multiple of basal metabolic rate

(BMR), which was taken as a surrogate expenditure of a nonbreeding female.

If our energy scoring system approximates the actual relative energy costs of various breeding activities, we should be able to detect any reproductive trade-offs between present and future breeding efforts. However, we emphasize that our data are nonexperimental. We simply recorded the natural reproductive investments of females without manipulating them. Therefore, females with high REs may have been in better physiological condition and, hence, able to invest more without incurring future costs. Also, much variation in RE is beyond the control of the females themselves. Rates and timing of nest predation, food supply variations, and weather conditions, which are imposed upon the birds, are therefore a source of considerable noise in the data set.

Future reproductive success could be reduced in any of several ways. First, the probability of survival to year $x + 1$ could be negatively correlated with RE during year x. Increased mortality rates might occur during molt or during the subsequent winter if females were unable to recover fully from their high investments before having to deal with inclement weather and reduced food supplies. This is the strongest effect we tested.

Second, even if females' survival between breeding seasons is unrelated to their level of reproductive investment, females that invested heavily during year x may not be able to achieve the necessary physiological condition as early the next spring as females that had invested less during year x. If so, then there should be a negative correlation between RE in year x and date of initiation of breeding in year $x + 1$.

Third, high RE in year x could dull the "brightness," or red coloration, of a female's shoulder epaulets, perhaps negatively influencing her ability to compete in year $x + 1$ aggressive interactions. One hypothesis of the function of red epaulets in redwing females is that they serve in status signaling during female-female aggression (Muma and Weatherhead 1989, 1991). If a female's ability to achieve high physiological condition early during a breeding season is reduced by heavy RE the previous year, this hypothesis would predict a negative relationship between year x RE score and brightness of epaulets in year $x + 1$. Thus, females with high RE scores are expected not only to initiate breeding later the next year but also to assume a plumage that signals subordinance.

Fourth, a female that invested heavily in reproduction in year x may not be able to maintain a comparable level of investment in year $x + 1$.

If so, there should be a negative correlation between RE in year x and RE in year $x + 1$.

METHODS

From our nest records, we determined for each banded female each year the number of nests she built, the number of eggs she laid, the number of young hatched, the number of days she incubated (defined to be 12 if ≥ 1 egg hatched), the number of days she fed nestlings (defined to be 12 if ≥ 1 fledged), and the number of nests from which young fledged. Because nests were typically visited only once every three days, we did not know exact dates when nests failed. Therefore, we used the "halfway" rule to estimate the number of incubation or nestling-feeding days for nests that failed during those stages. For example, a nest that had three nestlings five days old on 15 May and that was found depredated on 18 May, was assumed to have terminated on 17 May (the convention was to round up); the number of nestling-feeding days for the female would be 7.

All energy cost assignments were made relative to rest phase BMR in units of kJ/d. BMR was determined by the equation

$$kJ/d = 3.18M^{0.726}$$

where M is body mass in grams (after Aschoff and Pohl 1970). Using the breeding-season population mean of 47 g as the mass of a female redwing, BMR is calculated to be 52 kJ/d.

NEST BUILDING. There is little information on the energetic cost of nest building. Gauthier and Thomas (1993), using the doubly labeled water (DLW) technique to measure daily energy expenditure (DEE) of nest-building Cliff Swallows (*Hirundo pyrrhonota*), found the net per day cost to be 0.13–0.23 BMR. Redwing nests probably cost less to build than do those of Cliff Swallows because redwings can gather nest materials much closer to their nests. Therefore, we used 0.2 BMR/d as a reasonable estimate. Thus, for each nest she built, a female was assigned a $(0.2 \times 52 \text{ kJ}) \times 4$ building days = 41.6 kJ cost.

EGG FORMATION. Walsberg (1983) gives the cost of egg formation in a redwing as 0.39 BMR. We assigned a female $0.39 \times 52 \text{ kJ} = 20.3$ kJ/egg. This is an underestimate because it does not account for the extra foraging a female must do to obtain the energy necessary to produce an egg.

INCUBATION. Existing data on DEE during incubation are contradictory. On the one hand, Walsberg (1983) suggests that the DEE of an incubating bird is lower than a nonincubating one because of reduced activity and insulation provided by the nest. On the other hand, an incubating bird transfers a great deal of heat to the clutch of eggs. Moreno and Sanz (1994), using DLW to measure DEE of incubating Pied Flycatchers, estimated the per egg daily cost for incubation to be between 0.13 and 0.38 BMR. We used the larger value as a constant per day incubation cost, regardless of clutch size (0.38 × 52 KJ = 19.8 kJ/incubation day). Ours was a conservative estimate, both because some studies suggest that energy costs increase with clutch size, and because other studies measured field metabolic rates during incubation as high as 1.75 to 2.00 × BMR (e.g., Williams and Dwinnel 1990).

NESTLING FEEDING. The net cost of feeding is the difference between the DEE of a female feeding nestlings and that of a comparable female feeding only herself. Weathers and Sullivan (1989) give DEE values during incubation and nestling feeding for seven species (four passerines, three seabirds), all, unlike redwings, with biparental care. The data indicate that DEE increases on average by 1.54 BMR from incubation to feeding, with seabirds exhibiting a larger increase than passerines (2.57 vs. 1.05 BMR). We used 1.5 BMR for female redwings (1.5 × 52 kJ = 78 kJ/d) because they provide all the food for nestlings, whereas females of the other species share those responsibilities with their mates.

Whether DEE increases with brood size is uncertain. Several studies have found, counter to expectations, that parental DEE is unrelated to brood size (Bryant and Westerterp 1983; Ricklefs and Williams 1984; Williams 1987; Bryant and Tatner 1988; Moreno 1989; Mock 1991), but Williams (1987) found at least some evidence for a positive relationship. Whereas we believe that daily RE of female redwings probably increases with brood size—because the quantity of food the female must deliver to the nest scales with brood size—we follow the majority of studies cited above and use a single value for a day of feeding nestlings regardless of their number. Thus, our estimates of the energetic cost of feeding nestlings are conservative.

FLEDGLING FEEDING. There is little published information from which to estimate the energy cost of feeding fledglings. Relative to feeding nestlings, DEE of Yellow-eyed Juncos (*Junco phaeonotus*) increased slightly (Weathers and Sullivan 1989), but that of European Kestrels

(*Falco tinnunculus*) decreased slightly (Masman et al. 1988). Lacking any clear evidence to favor significant changes, we use the same value of DEE for female redwings feeding either nestlings or fledglings (1.5 × 52kJ = 78 kJ/d).

Females feed fledglings for up to two weeks after they leave the nest. Because we have little information on fledgling survival, we assumed that at least some young from a fledged brood survived 50% of the period to independence. Some fledglings were fed for the full fourteen days; others died shortly after leaving the nest. On average, then, our seven-day assumption is a reasonable estimate of the actual number of fledgling-feeding days for female redwings.

Following is an example of our calculation of the annual reproductive energy expenditure of a female associated with only one nest that had four eggs and fledged four:

nest = (1 nest × 41.6 kJ) = 41.6
eggs = (4 eggs × 20.3 kJ/egg) = 81.2
incubation = (12 d × 19.8 kJ/d) = 237.6
nestling feeding = (12 d × 78 kJ/d) = 936
fledgling feeding = (7 d × 78 kJ/d) = 546
total = 1842.4 kJ

The female expended 1842.4 kJ of energy more than a hypothetical female that did not breed or engage in any other energy-demanding activities. A nonbreeding female doubtlessly expends more energy than her BMR, but given that most of our estimates are conservative, scaling against BMR is a reasonable approximation.

We performed our analysis with data gathered from 1982 through 1992, the years during which we scored female epaulets and so could distinguish yearlings from older females. Yearlings generally arrive on the breeding grounds later than older females. Because they have less available nesting time, yearlings on average invest less than older females during their first breeding season. However, because yearlings are inexperienced, they may expend more energy to perform the same tasks, and the same RE may stress yearlings more. For these reasons, after testing for differences, we deleted yearlings from our RE analyses. We used the HAREMSIZE program to assign "unknown-female" nests to known, banded females when, by known nest-initiation and -termination dates, they could have been responsible for them. Some analyses include females credited with nests by this means; others include only females whose entire breeding activities we knew reliably.

To test for a relationship between female coloration and past RE, we first scored all females caught between 1982 and 1991 for epaulet brightness. Then we determined whether mature females whose year x RE scores were in the top and bottom quartile of values had their year $x+1$ epaulet scores increase, decrease, or remain the same. Epaulet scoring was done subjectively by us and by a host of field helpers. Assigned scores were 0 (= no red), 1 (= faint red), 2 (= medium bright red), or 3 (= very bright red). We used only females at least two years old in this analysis and only the first two consecutive years of epaulet information for each female.

RESULTS

RE SCORES OF YEARLING VERSUS MATURE FEMALES

As expected, yearling females had significantly lower annual RE scores than older females. This difference existed when we included unknown-female nests that were assigned to known-banded females by HAR-EMSIZE (mean ± SE RE score for yearlings = 1398 ± 42, n = 133, and for older females, 1560 ± 14, n = 1411; Wilcoxon 2-sample test, z = −3.71, 1-tailed P = 0.0002) and when we analyzed only nests positively associated with known-banded females (mean = 1313 ± 41, n = 133, for yearlings, and 1473 ± 14, n = 1411, for older females; z = −3.76, P = 0.0002). RE scores for yearling females were only about 10% less than those of older females probably because yearlings begin nesting, on average, only 1.5 weeks later than matures (chapter 3). The small difference indicates that, once they start, yearlings are as active reproductively as older females.

RE SCORES VERSUS SURVIVAL

To evaluate the relationship between RE score in year x and survival to year $x+1$, we compared the mean year x RE scores for females known to breed in year $x+1$ with those of females not observed to breed again, in $x+1$ or later. We assume that nonreturning females died prior to the start of the $x+1$ breeding season. To control for possible effects of age or experience, we tested for differences among females who bred for the first time as adults on the study area (year x) and had bred for the same number of years. Yearling females, who on average had lower RE scores, were not included in the analysis. Contrary to our prediction, mean annual RE scores were significantly higher for females that survived to breed in year $x+1$ in three of four comparisons (females breeding for the first time in the study area: mean ± SE RE score for survivors to year $x+1$ = 1641 ± 26, n = 318, and for nonsurvivors, 1412 ± 27, n = 394; Wilcoxon 2-sample test, z = 6.17, 1-tailed P ≪ 0.001; females breeding for the second time: mean = 1705 ± 32, n = 167, for survivors, and 1465 ± 42, n = 152, for nonsurvivors; z = 4.45, P ≪ 0.001; for the third time: mean = 1715 ± 44, n = 110, for survivors, and 1491 ± 57, n = 91, for nonsurvivors; z = 2.99, P = 0.003; for the fourth time: mean = 1592 ± 72, n = 62, for survivors, and 1509 ± 55, n = 73, for nonsurvivors; z = 0.66, P = 0.51).

RE SCORE IN YEAR X VERSUS FIRST LAYING DATE IN $X+1$

To detect a possible trade-off between a female's reproductive energy expenditure in one year and the date she can begin nesting the next year, we calculated mean first egg dates (for their first nests) for non-yearlings each year and then correlated the individual females' RE scores in year x with their deviations, in days, from the mean nest-start dates in year $x+1$. We found nonsignificant relationships in three of four comparisons (year x = females breeding for the first time at CNWR, r = −0.05, n = 318, P = 0.41; year x = their second breeding year, r = −0.05, n = 167, P = 0.54; year x = their third breeding year, r = −0.20, n = 95, P = 0.048; and year x = their fourth breeding year, r = −0.14, n = 48, P = 0.34). Thus, when a female initiated breeding in a given year was apparently uninfluenced by her energy expenditure the previous breeding season.

RE SCORES VERSUS COLORATION

To test for a relationship between RE and plumage changes during the following molt, we compared the percentage of females whose epaulet scores increased, decreased, or remained the same between years for those females with year x RE scores in the top and bottom quartiles of values (2 × 3 contingency table). We predicted that the epaulets of females with the highest RE scores would tend to become duller between years, whereas the epaulets of females with particularly low RE scores would tend to brighten. However, there was no significant relationship (χ^2 = 0.20, P = 0.9), indicating that between-year coloration changes were independent of previous RE scores. Further, the percentages of females whose epaulets brightened, dulled, or remained the same between years x and $x+1$ did not vary significantly among the four quartiles of year x RE scores (4 X 3 contingency table, χ^2 = 3.65, P = 0.7). This result is not surprising given that we found no relationship between RE and initiation of breeding the following year.

CORRELATION OF RE SCORES BETWEEN YEARS

Pearson's correlation coefficients for RE scores of individual females between successive years were not significant (females breeding in the study area for their first and second years [excluding yearlings], r = 0.05, n = 318, P = 0.34; for their second and third years, r = 0.11, n = 167, P = 0.17; third and fourth years, r = 0.14, n = 95, P = 0.18; fourth and fifth years, r = 0.22, n = 48, P = 0.12). The prediction of a significant negative correlation between a female's RE scores in consecutive years was not supported; in fact, correlation coefficients, although not significant, were positive.

DISCUSSION: HOW MUCH EFFORT TO INVEST

Our analyses of RE scores provide no evidence that a female's reproductive effort in one breeding season strongly affects her ability to invest in reproduction the next year. Neither the time of the start of breeding the next year nor the total amount of energy invested the next year were correlated with investment the previous year. Also, whereas we predicted that females expending greater amounts of energy for reproductive activities in one year would have a lower probability of survival to the next year than females that expended lesser amounts, our analysis showed the opposite. However, our definition of "survival" is "returning to breed in the study area the next year and being detected by us." Therefore, our results could be biased if many females with low RE scores were unsuccessful breeders that, in response, were more likely to leave the study area. Such females would be counted in our analyses as "nonsurvivors." Support for this possibility is that if females' last nests in year x were successful, then they returned in $x+1$ to the same marshes 83.9% of the time, but if their last nests were unsuccessful, they returned to same marshes only 72.5% of the time, a significantly lower rate (Beletsky and Orians 1991). Thus, there is some "leakage" of females from the study area in response to nest failure.

Another way to test this possibility is to determine whether females who left our study area had below average RE scores before they moved. One group of females whom we strongly suspect moved from the study area are "skippers"—females with gaps of one or more years in their breeding records. Presumably they bred elsewhere but then returned to the study area in subsequent years. (A few females included as "skippers" probably attempted to breed on the study area without our identifying them with a nest.) Confining our analysis to females at least two years old, we found that the mean year x RE score for 109 females that skipped breeding for a single year (i.e., they nested in year x, were absent in $x+1$, and bred again in the study area in $x+2$) was significantly less than the mean "year x" (first nonyearling year breeding) score for 1,294 females with uninterrupted breeding histories (mean RE scores = 1541 ± 37 and 1682 ± 51, respectively; t = -2.97, 1-tailed P = 0.002). This result suggests that females are more likely to leave the study area following a poor than a good RS year. Therefore, many of the "nonsurvivor" females with low year x RE scores may have actually survived to $x+1$, but bred elsewhere, out of our range of detection.

Although our analyses failed to detect a between-season cost of RE, our results are not decisive because the methods we employed have several sources of potential error.

1. Energy scores for each reproductive activity were estimates obtained from investigations of other passerines breeding in different habitat types and/or under different environmental conditions. In particular, we did not account for uniparental care and, contrary to our intuitions, we did not scale effort on number of nestlings. Nonetheless, if we had substituted higher values for females feeding larger broods, we probably would not have appreciably changed the nature of our results.

2. Temperature is probably the most important environmental condition that may alter a female's reproductive energy output for a given day, because the net cost of all physiological activity is temperature-dependent. For example, foraging costs less on a cold day than on a warm one (Webster and Weathers 1990). We did not adjust our estimates in relation to temperature, either daily or seasonally. However, temperature-related variation in costs should generate random noise in the data. We doubt that such variation introduced a consistent bias in our estimates.

3. Because we estimated durations of incubation and feeding using a "halfway" rule, our calculations are imprecise. Nonetheless, because we applied the rule consistently, the imprecisions should not introduce a bias that favors any particular outcome.

4. Our scoring of RE assumes that all individuals are equally efficient. However, some females, for example, may be better foragers than others, and thus could acquire the same amount of food as other females at less cost (Stearns 1992). Such individual differences could have introduced systematic bias into our data.

5. Our data were nonexperimental. We have no information on the effects of manipulating female RE on future RE and survival. Such

experiments provide better evidence for reproductive trade-offs than do correlational studies in which individuals are allowed to choose their own level of effort.

Nonetheless, our results are informative because several of the imprecisions should make it difficult to detect trends but should not favor particular relationships. Further, errors in our assignments of the energetic costs of various activities are consistent throughout the data set. With better estimates of the relative value of each female's annual effort, the results of our analyses would probably be little changed. Moreover, if the trade-off between present and future reproductive effort is weak, as it appears to be, not much insight derives from greater precision in estimating minor influences. Even though our RE scores were rather crudely determined, they *were* sufficiently precise to detect the expected difference in breeding effort between yearling and mature females.

Our results indicate either that no matter how much effort females make in reproduction within a breeding season, they are able to recover their physiological condition prior to winter, or that they are able to adjust their within-season efforts so that they do not pay any between-season costs.

WHEN AND WHY FEMALES TERMINATE NESTING

In chapter 3 we explored in detail factors influencing when and why female redwings begin nesting each year. But birds capable of renesting must also decide when it is "too late" to begin again, i.e., when to terminate nesting for the year. It is generally considered that through natural selection birds have adjusted their breeding periods to the times that yield the highest annual fledging success and the highest survival of young to independence and beyond. Thus, female redwings should stop nesting when further efforts, on average, do not increase their LRS. Factors that could result in no fitness increments from continued breeding include poor fledging success, low survival of young fledged late in the season, and poor survival of females who continue breeding late in the season.

CNWR females start nesting about 1 April, and the final nests of each year are usually initiated in mid-June (fig. 3.6). The timing of initiation of final (or only) nests each year varies greatly, but there is a precipitous drop-off after week 22 (the end of May), and very few females begin new nests after week 24 (10–16 June) (fig. 5.1). (Females whose final nests began during weeks 13 to 15 [n = 110] include some whose first and only nests were successful [n = 78], and also some for

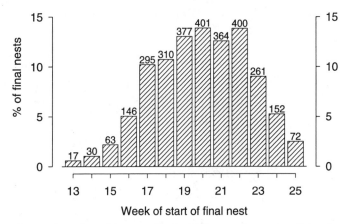

Fig. 5.1. Start dates (date of first egg) for the final nest each year for all females, 1977 through 1992. The analysis used nests of known, banded females and nests assigned to them by the HAREMSIZE program. Values above bars are total sample sizes.

whom we detected first but not subsequent nests.) Many females having a successful nest that started between weeks 13 to 17 later renested, but few did so after starting a successful nest during week 18 or later (fig. 5.2).

We can test five nonmutually exclusive hypotheses that could explain the annual termination of nesting at CNWR at the end of spring.

Hypothesis 1: Food supplies are inadequate to support summer breeding.

This hypothesis can be rejected. Orians (1980) monitored emergence traps at CNWR and found that odonates, the main food of nestling redwings, continued to emerge at high rates at least through July and early August. In fact, some of the highest odonate emergence rates occurred at the end of June, just as redwings usually cease breeding.

Hypothesis 2: Nest predation rates become too high late in the breeding season to make continuing worthwhile.

If an unacceptably high level of nest predation is the primary reason that females cease renesting, then predation rates should be increasing and highest when females stop their nesting efforts. Instead, predation rates peaked for nests *started* between weeks 18 and 20 and decreased thereafter (fig. 5.3), but females continue to renest at high rates through week 23 (cf. fig. 5.1). The depredation of eggs and nestlings in nests started during weeks 18 to 20 was spread over weeks 18 to 24, but females continued to start new nests throughout that period. A significant positive linear regression exists between nest-start date and

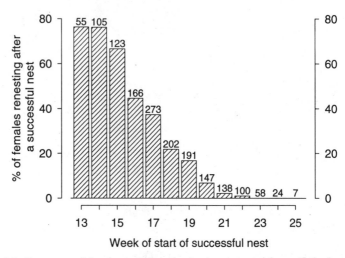

Fig. 5.2. Percentage of females renesting after having a successful nest (fledged ≥ 1) as a function of week of start of the successful nest. The analysis used nests of known, banded females and nests assigned to them by the HAREMSIZE program. Values above bars are total sample sizes.

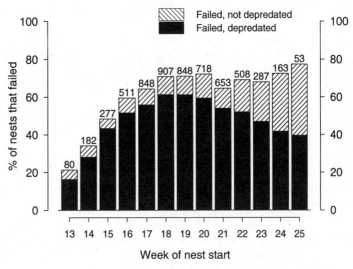

Fig. 5.3. Percentages of nests that failed because of depredation or for other reasons, 1977 through 1992, by week of nest start. Values above bars are total sample sizes.

probability of failure due to predation, but the test is clearly biased by the almost linear relationship between the two during weeks 13 to 18 ($r = 0.0009$, $P = 0.01$). The percentage of nests started each week that failed for reasons other than predation (desertion, starvation, weather or other physical effects on nests, interactions with Yellow-headed Blackbirds or Brown-headed Cowbirds) did increase during the final weeks of breeding, but the overall nest failure rate did not change appreciably between weeks 18 to 25 (fig. 5.3). Thus, nest failure rates did not increase enough during final weeks of breeding to give support for the nest predation hypothesis.

Hypothesis 3: Offspring fledged very late in the breeding season have a low probability of becoming breeders, either because they have less time to prepare for migration and winter, or because they are less competitive as adults.

If late-fledged offspring survive poorly we should observe (1) a negative correlation between the probability of gaining a territory to become a breeder and date of fledging among males, and (2) a negative correlation between survival to breeding age and fledging date for females. Our information on survival and recruitment to breeding of locally born redwings is limited by the small proportion of nestlings that return to the study area and are detected by us. We must also assume that natal dispersal distance does not vary as a function of fledging date. The 135 locally born males that acquired territories in the study area during the years 1977 to 1988 fledged fairly evenly throughout the breeding season—roughly 2% to 4% of clutches started during any ten-day period during nesting produced a territory owner (Beletsky and Orians 1993). Between 1978 and 1992 we captured 96 yearling or mature females that had been banded in the study area as nestlings. We have breeding records for only about half of these females, but all females probably attempt to breed each year. Females that fledged during the final third of the breeding season had the highest probability of returning to breed (fig. 5.4). Neither prediction is supported; the hypothesis is rejected.

Hypothesis 4: Continuing to breed exhausts females and reduces their overwinter survival.

First, none of the analyses we discussed earlier in this chapter suggests that females tire themselves during breeding to the point of negatively influencing their subsequent-year survival or breeding. Thus, we have no evidence that females stop early in a season to protect future efforts. A within-year prediction of the female-tiredness hypothesis would be that females should expend less energy on second nests, which

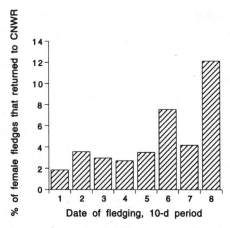

Fig. 5.4. Percentages of locally born females known to have returned to breed at CNWR (n = 96), as a function of their date of fledging; ten-day fledging period 1 = 21–30 April; 2 = 1–10 May; 3 = 11–20 May; 4 = 21–30 May; 5 = 31 May–9 June; 6 = 10–19 June; 7 = 20–29 June; 8 = 30 June–9 July. Total number of females fledged was estimated as half of all nestlings banded during each ten-day period, 1977 through 1990.

should have lower fledging success than first nests of other females started at the same time. We tested this prediction in chapter 3 and found no support for it (see fig. 3.9). Thus, we have no evidence that females stop breeding because they are exhausted.

Hypothesis 5: Females stop to preserve an adequate interval—at least two months—for energy accumulation and molt, prior to migration.

To test this hypothesis, we predicted that female survival in year $x+1$ would be negatively associated with the date of termination of their final year x nests, regardless of their total RE during the season. We looked at females whose last (or only) nests of a season were successful in year x (n = 1273) and regressed their probability of surviving to a future year on their nest termination (fledging) date; there was no significant relationship (logistic regression, $r \ll 0.01$, $P = 0.61$), indicating that females did not incur a survival cost by seasonally finishing later rather than earlier. This, however, is a weak test because all females stop nesting when they have at least a two-month period of high food availability during which they accumulate energy and molt before the onset of cooler weather.

DISCUSSION: WHY FEMALES STOP BREEDING

Our results do not provide any strong insights as to why the redwing breeding season terminates when it does. Food for breeding redwings and their young in eastern Washington is plentiful when nesting stops and continues to be for at least several weeks afterwards. The region's intense heat in July and August might unduly stress nestlings, leading females to refrain from nesting; but nestlings do not appear to be thermally stressed during May and June heat waves.

Nest predation rates and rates of failure due to other reasons *are* high when nesting stops, but those rates are similarly high for many weeks prior to the cessation of renesting. However, elevated nest-predation rates have been implicated as being responsible for terminating redwing breeding elsewhere. Three studies have reported that egg mortality rates were positively associated with date of nest initiation (Young 1963; Dolbeer 1976; Caccamise 1978). Caccamise (1978) also found that late nests had the highest nestling predation rates. Further, Ewald and Rohwer (1982), who "enriched" some territories with supplemental food to test whether they could advance breeding, provided some experimental support for a causal relationship between predation rates and seasonal nesting termination—"enriched" experimental territories had higher nestling mortality rates late in the breeding season than did control territories, and nesting apparently also terminated earlier on experimental territories.

We cannot clearly explain the differences in seasonal patterns of nest failure rates between other studies and our own, in which we found that the proportion of nests started each week that failed rose to about 70% by the end of April and remained at approximately that level during May and June (fig. 5.3). One plausible explanation, however, is that different populations are exposed to different predators, which depredate their nests at different rates and schedules. Nest predation rates at CNWR, for example, in most years are apparently closely tied to the breeding schedule of the Black-billed Magpie, the main nest predator.

All of our efforts to relate annual RE to future reproduction, and to determine whether females tire from one nesting attempt to the next, have been unsuccessful. Thus, RE, as we calculate it, does not closely scale on PI; and therefore, terminating nesting must be due to reasons other than reproductive "burnout."

Although we have no evidence for it, the rejection of our first four hypotheses leads us to believe that we should strongly consider the fifth: that females cease nesting before conditions for breeding worsen simply because to proceed longer would interfere with molt and energy recovery before winter. This means that females manage the trade-off by terminating breeding in sufficient time to molt and prepare for migration. We have no direct evidence for this trade-off, but molt and breeding generally do not co-occur in Temperate Zone songbirds, including redwings (Payne 1965). It has long been suspected that these two energy-demanding activities are segregated temporally to avoid exhaustion (Lack 1954; Pitelka 1958; King and Farner 1961). The scenario fits our population because adult redwings complete postnuptial molts in sixty to seventy days (Payne 1965). At CNWR, where most breeding terminates at the end of June, females would complete their annual molt in early September, shortly before they migrate and temperatures drop rapidly.

Part Three

MALE
DECISIONS

M ale redwings attempting to breed face one hurdle that is far more important than all others: they must acquire a territory, and getting a territory requires competition with other males. Male redwings at CNWR, and at every other location at which they have been studied, cannot reproduce unless they have a territory. Female redwings, as we have seen, face no comparable hurdle. They make several important decisions, all of which strongly influence their annual reproductive success, but none of them is highly constrained by strong intraspecific competition. All reproductively mature females apparently breed and are able to choose their nesting sites relatively unconstrained by social interactions. Many males, on the other hand, are unable to gain territories and therefore cannot make most subsequent decisions, such as when to switch from advertising to parental care behavior or which nests to defend more vigorously. Females copulate with their "mates," the males on whose territories they nest, as well as with adjacent territory owners. DNA tests in several populations (in Ontario, New York, Kentucky, and at CNWR) confirm that nearly all young are sired either by putative mates or by neighboring territory owners (Gibbs et al. 1990; Westneat 1993; Gray 1996a; D. Westneat, personal communication). In addition, our LRS data show that the lifetime number of fledged offspring per male territory owner accumulates, on average, almost linearly with the number of territory-owning years. Because behaviors that influence successful territory acquisition and retention clearly have strong effects on fitness, methods of territory acquisition and retention are the focus of this section.

In chapter 6 we discuss current hypotheses of territory acquisition and retention and develop some new hypotheses and predictions. Chapter 7 updates some of our previously published analyses of territory acquisition and brings new information to bear from our long-term data base, including demographic data, capture data, individual territorial histories, behavioral observations, and experiments. We examine the histories of territory owners by looking at natal dispersal, and the behavior of yearling and adult floaters. We then consider several correlational and experimental tests of hypotheses of territory acquisition. Chapter 8 takes a detailed look at site fidelity and territory movements. We consider proposed explanations of site fidelity as they relate to male redwings, and also explore why some males change territories.

Six

How to Acquire a Territory: Theoretical Considerations

INTRODUCTION

Territoriality, the maintenance of a defended area by one or more individuals within which activities are centered and to which access by most other individuals is prevented, is widespread among birds (Hinde 1956; Lack 1966). A territorial individual restricts most or all of its behavior for some period of time to a specific area. Within this area the individual advertises its ownership and defends against intruders, especially potential usurpers. An established owner is normally successful in defending its area against challengers. Such behavioral dominance ("site dominance") can override substantial size differences among individuals and can be established in short time periods. Defense of space in general is believed to evolve when the costs of defense are less than the benefits (Brown 1964), that is, when territories are economically defendable (Gill and Wolf 1975; Pyke 1979; Davies 1980).

Although biologists have long been aware of the widespread occurrence of territoriality and the dominance of owners over challengers, the mechanisms of behavioral dominance, and the processes by which individuals of many species actually acquire their territories, are still poorly understood. The most important recent advances in the theory of territorial behavior have come from the application of game-theoretic models to animal conflicts, of which territorial conflicts are a special case. A game-theoretic approach provides precise means for evaluating costs and benefits of territorial behavior and for analyzing situations in which the payoff from a behavior depends upon how other individuals in the population act and the relative proportions of individuals adopting different tactics. In addition, game theory lends itself well to models based upon selection at the level of the individual rather than the group selection approach characteristic of most earlier theorizing about animal conflicts (e.g., Lorenz 1966; Lewontin 1970). The goal of a game-theory model is to search for the existence of an evolutionarily stable strategy (ESS), a behavior pattern that, when employed by members of a population, cannot be invaded by a rare mutant employing an alternative pattern. That is, the fitness of individuals employing any alternative strategy is lower than the fitness of those using the prevailing strategy.

The first game-theoretic model of animal conflicts acting entirely at the level of the individual was that of Maynard Smith and Price (1973). They concluded that, in a species capable of seriously injuring an opponent, the ESS for individuals is to adopt a ritualized level of fighting but to escalate their defense if the opponent escalates its challenge ("retaliatory strategy"). This result was based on the assumption that an individual that escalates fighting too readily is more likely to get seriously injured than typical members of the population. This conclusion applied to situations in which individuals could use ritualized displays to assess the capabilities of their opponents. However, if the contest consists of displays that provide little or no information about which of the contestants would win if the struggle were escalated, persistence is favored, the winner being the last one to quit.

Parker (1974) first explored the nature of the information transmitted during conflicts and its influence on outcomes. He observed that once a retaliatory strategy had stabilized as an ESS, any mutant individual able to compare its own fighting ability—its resource-holding potential (RHP)—with that of its opponent would have a selective advantage because it could withdraw without being injured when the RHP of its opponent exceeded its own by some critical amount. Parker also noted that selection would favor exaggeration of those cues used to assess RHP, leading in turn to the evolution of new assessment mechanisms based on traits less subject to this type of "evolutionary cheating." Direct trials of strength can provide reliable estimates of RHP, as can displays that advertise features that cannot be exaggerated without incurring significant costs, such as loudness of vocalizations or vigor and frequency of performance of energy-demanding displays.

Parker (1974) also discussed some sources of asymmetries in animal conflicts. He identified asymmetries arising from intrinsic differences among individuals in RHP, those arising from differences in RHP due to the holding of the resource itself, and those arising because the value of the objects of the conflict may differ for the two contestants. Parker noted that the latter form of asymmetry should be common among territorial conflicts because resources may increase in value with duration of occupancy.

Game-theoretic models of animal conflicts also provide a basis for explaining the coevolution of *value* and *motivation*, and, hence, for predicting those situations in which an individual is expected to accept a subordinate status. For example, when a territory holder's loss in fitness from being evicted from its territory exceeds the attacker's gain from taking over the territory, the attacker should be less strongly motivated than the defender to continue the conflict. Thus, the basic postulate of game-theoretic models is that the motivational state of an individual in a conflict changes in concert with the "fitness change effect" achieved by shifting from one motivational state to another. The contribution of game-theoretic models to the study of animal social behavior in general, and for territorial dominance in particular, has been great. These models provide credible reasons why animals that must possess a territory in order to reproduce do not perpetually conduct escalated, bloody contests for ownership. The models also yield testable predictions that have guided observational and experimental work on animal contests.

Our objectives in this chapter are to review current models of animal contest behavior, and to extend the ones that are applicable to avian territoriality by developing predictions based on specific knowledge of avian natural history.

CURRENT MODELS OF ANIMAL CONTEST BEHAVIOR

Three major models have emerged from the game-theoretic work of Maynard Smith and Price (1973), Parker (1974), Maynard Smith and Parker (1976), Parker and Rubinstein (1981), and Hammerstein (1981). In their pure forms the models differ strikingly in their assumptions and predictions, but because they are not mutually exclusive, they may interact in ways that blur the distinctions. The resource-holding potential hypothesis (RHP) states that individuals gain and hold territories because they are bigger, stronger, or better proportioned than their opponents. As a result they are better fighters. Genetic, experiential, and situational factors may all contribute to the RHP of an individual.

The value asymmetry hypothesis (VA) asserts that owners win contests for their territories because the territories have greater value to them than to challengers. The value of the resources may be higher to owners because, for instance, they know the location of resources and escape routes or have stable relationships with neighbors. They may also have genetic investments—eggs or offspring—in the territory. The theory predicts that the winner of a contest is the individual to whom the resource has the greater value because that individual is willing to escalate the contest further than its opponent. The theory predicts that a challenger should assess the probable value of the territory to its owner and leave without fighting if its assessment indicates that the territory has greater value to its owner than to the challenger.

The arbitrary rule hypothesis (AR) suggests that contests are settled by simple, arbitrary rules, e.g., "the resident always wins" or "first to attack wins." AR is most likely to apply when the supply of contested resources exceeds demands or when the cost of fighting is high relative to the value of the resource under dispute (Krebs 1982). In the case of animals competing for breeding territories, AR might function where territories are short-lived and there is a surplus of suitable breeding habitat.

However, if territories are held for long periods, are in limited supply, and are necessary for reproduction, an "owner always wins" convention, i.e., an *arbitrary* rule, even if based on differential expected payoffs (VA), fails as an ESS (Grafen 1987) because the rule "owner always wins" is "divisive"—it creates a class of inevitable losers. For such individuals desperate attempts to acquire territories must have higher potential fitness payoffs than remaining for their entire life on the losing side of an arbitrary asymmetry. Thus, when floaters can breed only after acquiring territories, they should act like "desperados," always escalating contests, and even fighting to the death, if necessary, to acquire them (Grafen 1987). Because such behavior is rarely observed, we can reject a priori an arbitrary rule asymmetry, such as "owner always wins," as a viable explanation of dominance of territory owners over challengers in most species of birds. Therefore, we direct our attention to asymmetries that create owners and floaters without being divisive.

Although RHP and VA make predictions about how avian territorial contests may be settled—won, respectively, by the superior individual or the one who values the territory more highly—they do not unambiguously predict how territories are first acquired. RHP makes the clearest prediction about initial acquisition: the best individuals should get the best territories, perhaps even evicting lesser individuals to do so. VA predicts that individuals more familiar with an area are more likely to gain a territory there than individuals unfamiliar with the area. However, a third possible acquisition strategy—chance—exists (Eckert and Weatherhead 1987c; Beletsky and Orians 1989a, 1993). Searcy and Yasukawa (1995) name this type of territorial acquisition system a "lottery" model, because individuals that happen to be in the right places at the right times gain territories. By itself, however, the lottery model cannot explain the site dominance exhibited by territorial owners because, even if chance determines who initially establishes a territory, those individuals must be able to maintain their territories in the face of challenges. Therefore, a lottery model, whatever its role in initial territory acquisition, must be supplemented by some components of RHP and VA theories if the continuing dominance of territory owners is to be explained.

RESOURCE-HOLDING POTENTIAL: SOURCES AND DYNAMICS

Asymmetries in RHP among contestants arise because individuals differ in their ability and their motivation to fight. Ability and motivation may be influenced by genetic differences, developmental history, age, and current physiological condition. In combination these factors have the potential to generate a rich array of asymmetries that are not divisive.

GENETIC DIFFERENCES. Fighting ability is influenced by the sizes and shapes of an individual's internal and external structures and the functional properties of its organ systems. Motivation to fight is influenced by the structure and functioning of an animal's nervous system. Variability in all of these features has a heritable component that is not eliminated by consistent directional selection because those traits influence performance of many other activities in addition to fighting ability. Individuals differ in the situations they encounter and, hence, in the significance of their morphology and physiology for dealing with other contingencies.

DEVELOPMENTAL HISTORY. A nestling bird begins life as a member of a brood. Its condition at fledging is influenced by when it hatched in relation to its nest mates, its sex, and ecological conditions when it grows. The last-to-hatch nestling being fed by parents during a time of food scarcity may enter adulthood at a smaller size, with a different shape, and in much poorer condition than the first-to-hatch nestling fed by parents during a time of food abundance. In species with significant sexual dimorphism in size, the relative number of males and females among its nest mates may influence the amount of food an individual receives. The condition of an individual when it reaches maturity may also be influenced by the number of its nest mates (if and when they die before fledging), whether its nest is brood-parasitized, weather, and the experience and physiological condition of its parents. Variability in these factors is universal. In combination, they influence subsequent survival, the performance of individuals for the rest of their lives, and, hence, their fighting abilities. Developmental factors do not generate divisive asymmetries because chance events strongly influence the conditions to which individuals are subjected. There are no inevitable losers.

AGE. Up to a point, fighting ability generally improves with age and practice. In many birds, older individuals return to the breeding grounds or initiate territorial behavior earlier in the spring than younger individuals do. Therefore, owners are, on average, older than floaters, and they may win contests because they are more experienced than the floaters that challenge them. Age does not produce a divisive asymmetry because all young individuals become older and eventually may dominate younger individuals.

PHYSIOLOGICAL CONDITION. The physiological condition of an individual is influenced by physical and behavioral stresses to which it has been exposed, by past and recent injuries, by its ability to find enough high-quality food, and by past and current diseases. All of these factors influence both fighting ability and motivation to fight. Variations in physiological condition do not generate divisive asymmetries because chance largely determines the conditions to which individuals are exposed. Also, individuals can recover from injuries and diseases and can put on weight when foraging conditions improve. Thus, an individual's physiological condition is not fixed and there are no permanent losers.

HISTORICAL FACTORS. The universality of differences in genetic constitution, developmental history, age, and physiological condition guarantee the existence of considerable variation in RHP among individuals in all populations. How differences in RHP influence which individuals gain territories depends upon the intrinsic characteristics of a species and the type of environment in which it lives. An important intrinsic factor (perhaps the key factor in some species) is the quality of the weaponry of the competing individuals, which strongly determines the probability that escalated combat will result in debilitating injuries (Rohwer 1982). The higher the probability of injury in contests, the greater the relative value of waiting for vacancies to arise. Even minor injuries may permanently lower an individual's RHP and its long-term survival rate. Although dangerous weaponry may discourage fights, it does not produce divisive asymmetries because RHP differences are still important even if winning by the superior fighter is probabilistic.

In combination these effects could influence the outcomes of lottery competition because individuals in better physiological condition may be able to devote more time to prospecting than individuals in poorer condition. Therefore, they might have a higher probability of being the first to detect a vacancy created by the death or debilitation of a territory owner. In addition, if both lottery and RHP interact to determine success in gaining a territory, which seems likely, individuals with reduced RHP as a result of injury may succeed only if no other floaters discover the vacancy at about the same time.

In species for which fighting carries low risks of injury, and in which food is readily available away from defended territories, the penalties to floaters of escalating territorial contests may be relatively low. If these conditions are met, floaters should readily escalate territorial contests whenever they perceive that odds of winning are in their favor. These conditions should favor a strategy in which floaters search wide areas and challenge a large number of owners. Detailed information about the territories owners occupy matters relatively little because success requires the floater to find an owner with a lower RHP than its own.

In many species, effective protection against weapons cannot evolve because of design or cost constraints (Rohwer 1982). The necessity of streamlining and weight minimization for efficient flight mean that birds cannot easily evolve armor that could adequately protect individuals from heavy blows from beaks and talons. As a result, floaters may be reluctant to challenge owners even when the odds of winning appear to be in their favor (Rohwer 1982), provided that owners never relinquish their territories without a fight and that vacancies are created regularly by disappearance of owners for reasons unrelated to fighting. Under these conditions, floaters should either search widely, looking for vacancies, or establish restricted searching areas about which they are well informed. Payoffs from these strategies depend upon the value to floaters of different kinds of information, a topic we will address in the next section.

The strength of the correlation between territory quality and the fighting ability of owners should be a function of the relative importance of risk of injury, feeding opportunities for floaters, and vacancy rates. If the risk of injury is very low and food is readily available away from defended areas, floaters should initiate enough escalated contests to test most owners. Under these conditions there should be a strong correlation between territory quality and fighting ability, and the role of the lottery should be very small. If, however, the risk of injury is high, owners should be rarely challenged, and the role of the lottery should be more important and longer lasting. Redwings have sharp, powerful beaks and are quite capable of injuring each other during fights (Rohwer 1982; Freeman 1987; Beletsky et al. 1995). Their breeding territories, however, typically cover only a small portion of the general environment, so floaters usually can feed unchallenged in high-quality areas close to the territories they are attempting to acquire. Under these conditions, the correlation between territory quality and fighting ability should be low.

The minimum resource-holding potential an individual needs in order to acquire a territory depends in part on the ratio of floaters to territory owners. The larger the number of floaters, the more floaters with high RHP, and the higher the RHP needed to gain a territory. Therefore, in an "RHP world," the probability that a male with a particular RHP obtains a territory is a function of the size of the population in relation to the number of suitable territories. The greater the "contender pressure" (Stamps 1990), the lower the probability of gaining a territory.

VALUE ASYMMETRIES: SOURCES AND DYNAMICS

The value to an owner of a territory and the resources it contains may increase with time as the owner gains information about the territory, loses information about other places, and invests genetically in offspring in the area. The VA theory postulates that willingness to escalate a contest is correlated with the value of the territory and that a territory normally has more value to its owner than to a challenger.

SOURCES OF VALUE ASYMMETRIES

Knowledge of the temporal and spatial availability of food and experience in its exploitation (Davies and Houston 1981), knowledge of habits of local predators and of the locations of hiding places, and knowledge of protected nest sites should improve both the survival rate and reproductive success of the owner.

Knowledge also influences social interactions. A resident is likely to develop stable relationships with his neighbors, leading to reduced hostilities (Falls 1982) and perhaps even cooperative defense of the area—the so-called "dear enemy" phenomenon (Getty 1987, 1989; Ydenberg et al. 1988; Temeles 1994). A victorious challenger would have to devote time and energy to establishing comparable stable relationships (Krebs 1982; Falls 1982), while risking injury when fighting over new boundaries. Therefore, were a challenger to win an escalated contest, the territory would have less value to him than to the resident he replaced. Thus, the knowledge an owner acquires about his territory and neighbors makes a direct and an indirect contribution to fitness, both of which increase the value of the territory to the owner relative to its value to a challenger.

Another likely component of information asymmetry between owners and challengers arises from the fact that owners, as they gain knowledge of one area, forfeit gaining or maintaining knowledge of other areas. When an individual acquires a territory, its memory of extraterritorial information fades, and what it does remember becomes increasingly inaccurate. Loss of value of extraterritorial information proceeds slowly, and it probably does not contribute to value asymmetries between *new* owners and challengers. However, a long-established owner in a territorial contest is likely to know relatively little about other options, whereas the challenger is likely to have current and relatively extensive information about the surrounding area. Therefore, if a defender loses his territory, he is thrown into an environment about which he is very ignorant. The loss of a contest, then, has greater fitness consequences for the defender than for the better-informed challenger.

The value of a territory to its owner also increases once the owner has attracted a mate and sired offspring that are not yet independent. The degree to which this creates a value asymmetry between an owner and a challenger depends upon the number of offspring produced and the reduction in their survival that would result were the owner to lose a contest. If the victorious challenger provides no parental care to already-sired offspring or engages in infanticide, as reported for a number of mammals (Hrdy 1977a,b; Hausfater and Hrdy 1984; Labov et al. 1985) and a few birds (Hausfater and Hrdy 1984; Emlen et al. 1989; Veiga 1990; Kermott et al. 1991), the cost to the former owner of a defeat is great. If, on the other hand, the survival of already-sired offspring is relatively independent of the identity of the owner, previous reproductive investment may contribute little to value asymmetries (Rohwer 1986).

TIME SCALES AND THE DEVELOPMENT OF VALUE ASYMMETRIES

Knowledge (and, hence, value) of a territory increases as some function of the time it has been occupied, but there is no reason to expect the quantity of useful knowledge to increase uniformly or at the same rate for all types of information. Some types of information are readily acquired rapidly early during occupation of an area; other types are acquired more slowly. The kinds of information gathered and the ease with which they can be acquired also vary greatly with the habitat and type of territory.

Information Acquirable within the First Hour

Several kinds of information of potential value can be obtained during the first few minutes of occupancy. For example, whether an unoccupied territory is truly vacant or its owner is only temporarily absent usually can be determined quickly because owners in many species rarely leave their territories for long periods during breeding seasons. This determination greatly affects subsequent behavior because if an owner fails to appear, challengers quickly establish ownership themselves (e.g., Hansen and Rohwer 1986).

Knowledge of the size and boundaries of a territory also may be acquired relatively rapidly. Valuable information about gross vegetation structure, profitable foraging patches, and good hiding areas can also be acquired rapidly. Observations of nests or nesting activity by females could indicate quickly to new owners the status of breeding efforts already under way on the focal and nearby territories.

Information Acquirable over Several Hours or Days

A new owner is likely to gain increasingly complex information about a territory during the first several days of occupancy. Some knowledge of the spatial and temporal food-producing capacity of a new territory can be acquired within a few days. Additional roosting sites and potential escape routes from predators can be identified as familiarity with the territory's fine vegetational structure increases. RHP of neighbors and other local residents, if not already known, can be assessed during the first days of ownership but may take longer if fighting is dangerous (Freeman 1987).

The rate of intrusion pressure by floaters, and thus information about prospective territory maintenance costs, would become apparent to new owners during several days of occupancy. Intrusion pressure might also provide information on the quality of the territory because floaters should try harder to obtain better territories than poorer ones. By gaining familiarity with his territory and surroundings, a new owner could make an initial informed judgment about its overall quality and its potential for breeding success.

Information Acquirable Slowly

Some important types of information can be acquired only during many weeks or even months of occupancy. Long-term information about foraging opportunities and resource predictability may become available only after months or even several breeding seasons of occupancy. The frequency and extent of predation in the local area can be assessed only on a similar time frame. Familiarity with other individuals in the area also increases slowly. Because cooperation is most likely to evolve in long-lived animals where individuals have long associations (Emlen 1984), long-term familiarity could facilitate the operation of predator detection and mobbing systems that lead to increased survival and enhanced breeding success (Beletsky et al. 1986; Beletsky and Orians 1989b). Over time, owners can obtain information about reproductive success on their own territories and neighboring territories. Because several studies have demonstrated that birds may desert or change territories following poor breeding success (Greenwood and Harvey 1982; Shields 1982; Beletsky and Orians 1987a, 1994), comparative information on reproductive success may strongly influence the relative value a male places on his territory. If two or more males arrive simultaneously on the breeding grounds before nesting has begun and compete for the same territory, the area should have more value to a former owner, if there is one, because of knowledge he gained during previous years.

CHANGES IN TERRITORY VALUE DURING A BREEDING SEASON

The time during the breeding season when a territory is taken over affects its value to the new owner (Rohwer 1985, 1986). The earlier a territory is acquired, the greater the potential for reproductive success during that breeding season. A territory obtained near the conclusion of a breeding season may be of little value, unless information gained at that time increases the probability of success in maintaining dominance there the following year. However, information gained during even brief occupancy may be of use in establishing a future territory elsewhere (Yasukawa 1979; Zack and Stutchbury 1992).

SPATIAL ASPECTS OF VALUE ASYMMETRIES

The knowledge that generates value asymmetries between contestants for territories is site-specific, both because ecologically valuable information has a strong site-specific character and because individuals are able to acquire information about only a limited number of sites. Because movements of territory owners are highly constrained compared with those of floaters, individual members of the two groups possess qualitatively different knowledge. Empirical studies of territorial birds have shown that absences from territories are generally too short to allow them to acquire much information about qualities of territories more than a few kilometers away (Schartz and Zimmerman 1971; Nolan 1978; Hansen and Rohwer 1986; Beletsky and Orians 1987a). Therefore, territory owners probably possess detailed knowledge of their own territories, good information about adjacent territories and surrounding areas, and decreasing amounts of information about territories at increasing distances from their own. We call this the "information/distance hypothesis" (IDH).

The IDH provides an explanation for the strong site fidelity characteristic of many bird species (Greenwood and Harvey 1982) and for observations that individuals changing territories usually move only short distances (Nolan 1978; Greenwood and Harvey 1982; Beletsky and Orians 1987a). A resident is likely to know about changes in the physical condition of neighbors and when neighbors are absent from their territories for unusually long time periods. Thus, adjacent and other nearby neighbors should often be the first individuals to occupy vacancies or challenge sick or injured owners. With increasing distance from home, territorial individuals are less likely to detect vacancies and should know less about the quality of those areas when they do discover vacancies. The probability that a neighboring territory is better than the one already owned can be assessed by observing the activities of the owner, his mate or mates, and other residents, and by occasional trespass. Judging whether a more distant territory is better than the one already possessed would have to be based on much less complete information.

INFORMATION ACQUIRABLE BY FLOATERS

Information necessary for survival without a territory, such as locations of extraterritorial foraging areas and roosting sites and knowledge of site-related behavior patterns that minimize predation risks, can be acquired by floaters. Information of value to males attempting to become territory owners include locations of areas suitable for breeding, past success of residents of those areas, identities and characteristics of territorial and nonterritorial individuals in their neighborhood, and knowledge of specific locations where, because of social or environmental disturbances, better-than-average chances exist for acquiring new territories. Regional information possessed by floaters could influence value asymmetries because an informed floater may know which of many territories are of highest quality and, hence, most worth fighting for. A territory owner probably has comparative knowledge of only a few territories and therefore does not know the value of his territory relative to most others in the region.

The ease with which floaters can acquire information about territories is influenced by the sizes of territories, the complexity of the vegetation, the existence of high-quality neutral foraging areas, the length of the breeding season, and the methods by which owners advertise and the honesty of their signals. If territories are small, vegetation is of low stature, good foraging areas are available, and the breeding season is extended, floaters can readily gather information about many territories. On the other hand, if territories are large and situated in structurally complex vegetation, and few or no good neutral foraging areas exist, floaters can learn about many territories only with great difficulty. Owners can behave in ways that make it difficult for challengers to probe (i.e., to observe or enter territories in order to gather information about them or their owners) for even brief time periods. They also may be able to mislead floaters about boundaries and number of occupants (e.g., Krebs 1977).

Whatever the difficulty for floaters of information gathering, the amount of information they possess about individual territories should be inversely proportional to the number being monitored. The more a floater knows about a territory whose owner he challenges, the less the value asymmetry between himself and the owner, and the higher the probability that he can prevail in a contest. Also, the fewer the number of territories a floater monitors, the sooner he is likely to detect a vacancy in any one of them.

The larger the number of territories under surveillance by a floater, the longer the average time before he will detect a *particular* vacancy, but the greater the likelihood that he will discover *some* vacancy. The nature of the trade-off function should influence the searching strategies of floaters. If VA strongly determines territorial dominance, floaters attempting to acquire territories should adopt a "beat" in an area containing a moderate number of territories rather than roaming widely and gathering only limited information about many scattered locations. On the other hand, if a lottery dominates territorial acquisition, floaters should survey a large area containing many territories. In both lottery and VA worlds, the probability that a male gains a territory is a function of the ratio of owners to floaters, but any floater male can become an owner if he happens to be at the right place at the right time.

If a territory is taken over by a floater who already has considerable knowledge of the local area, the new territory should rapidly acquire a higher value than it would if the new resident began with no knowledge of the area. In addition, neighbors would be likely to recognize the new resident and to realize that he already places a high value on the territory. This should help reduce pressures from neighbors attempting to expand into the vacant area. The new resident might also possess information about former boundary locations, thereby reducing the intensity of, and potential for injury during, preliminary boundary skirmishes. For the same reasons, neighbors may be less antagonistic toward a new resident whom they recognize as a long-term floater with knowledge of the area than they would be toward a stranger.

In some avian species, floaters live secretively on the territories of breeders (Smith 1978; Arcese 1987) or as "satellite" males in suboptimal habitat directly adjacent to breeding territories. These "resident floaters" acquire detailed information about territories in which they live and about the health and vulnerabilities of the owners (Arcese 1987). They are first in line for uncontested opportunities for replacing owners (Smith 1978) and they are the first to detect decreases in the RHP of owners that favor initiating a challenge (Arcese 1987). Because such floaters gain territorial information that rivals that of the owner, value asymmetries may be small, and territory owners may gain by driving the floaters from their territories and adjacent areas, if they are able.

BEHAVIORS PREDICTED BY MODELS
OF ANIMAL CONTESTS

Models of animal contests combined with knowledge of avian natural history and territoriality lead to a number of predictions, some of which we will test in chapters 7 and 8. We outline them in general form here, leaving the redwing-specific predictions until we are ready to test them.

SITE-DEPENDENT DOMINANCE

The VA hypothesis predicts that dominance should be site-dependent. Owners should dominate all other conspecifics on their territories, but they are not expected to dominate other individuals when they are away from their territories. For example, although owners may dominate floaters on their territories, they may be subordinate to the same individuals elsewhere. IDH predicts that males should be less aggressive or dominant the farther they are from their territories. In contrast, RHP predicts a strong correlation between a male's level of dominance on and off his territory because an individual's RHP is not site-specific.

DOMINANCE DURING REMOVAL EXPERIMENTS

Removal experiments are one method of testing hypotheses to explain territorial dominance. In a removal experiment, a territorial male is captured and held in captivity for some period of time during which a replacement male occupies his territory. The original owner is then released, interactions between the two males who claim the territory are observed, and the eventual winner is determined. The experimental variable is the length of time the male is held in captivity. Removal experiments are informative because RHP and VA hypotheses make different predictions about the outcomes.

VA assumes that the value of a territory to a new owner increases as he gains familiarity with it. Therefore, the value of a vacant territory to a replacement male should increase with the time he occupies it. Accordingly, he should be increasingly harder to displace the longer his occupancy. Our view of the rate of knowledge accrual suggests that the initial rate of acquisition of useful information is rapid, leading to significant value asymmetries fairly rapidly. Therefore, new owners should be able to gain dominance over floaters quickly, but over former owners more slowly. In contrast, RHP predicts that removed owners should always be able to regain their territories when released unless their RHP was reduced as a result of being confined.

TERRITORIAL PROBING BY FLOATERS

VA predicts different patterns of probing by floaters than does RHP. Under VA, floaters can gain useful knowledge of territories if they are not detected by the owners or when the owners are absent. Therefore, floater trespassers are predicted to be furtive and to concentrate their probings while owners are absent. RHP, in contrast, predicts that probing when owners are absent is of little value because the RHP of the owner, the only relevant information, can be assessed only when the owner is present. VA also predicts that floaters should preferentially probe at times when the most valuable information can be obtained. Thus, probing to gain information should be concentrated (a) early in the breeding season to detect vacancies resulting from nonreturn of owners, and (b) during late nesting stages, to determine breeding success in various locations, information of value for the following year. However, vacancies can occur at any time; thus, some probing should occur throughout breeding seasons.

VA predicts that floaters, when they probe in their quests for territories, should establish relatively small beats that they follow regularly. In contrast, RHP predicts wider-ranging probing, because the more territories investigated, the greater the likelihood of finding an owner with lower RHP. In a pure lottery system, floaters are likely to benefit from searching a wide area, but they should not attempt to learn about the

characteristics of territories. The only relevant information is the presence or absence of an owner.

VA also predicts where floaters attempt to acquire information. Some
information about a territory can be gathered from outside its boundaries, particularly if neutral areas are adjacent to occupied territories.
Other information that generates value asymmetries, such as knowledge
of good foraging patches, hiding places, nest sites, and on-site predators,
can be gathered only by entering a territory and closely inspecting it.
Thus, VA predicts regular intrusive probing or trepassing. RHP predicts
that floaters will learn about owners by directly challenging them and
by observing the owner's interactions with other males (Freeman 1987).

FLOATER ASSESSMENT OF THE TENURE OF TERRITORY OWNERS

If VA dominates territorial contests, floaters benefit if they can distinguish between new and old territory owners. Under RHP, the length
of time a male has held his territory is irrelevant. How could floaters
detect new owners? Floaters with small beats may quickly recognize
that an old owner is gone and a new owner, perhaps known to them,
has taken over. The behavior of a new owner may also reveal his recently acquired status, even to floaters unfamiliar with the area's immediate past history. However, if floaters try to assess the amount of
time males have owned territories, new residents would benefit if they
behaved, as much as possible, as if they were long-term owners (Hansen
and Rohwer 1986; Beletsky 1992). Nonetheless, increased levels of interactions with new neighbors may be unavoidable, thereby revealing
the short tenure of any newly settled male. Therefore, VA predicts a
higher turnover of newer than of older territory owners. RHP predicts
no change in rates of territory turnover as a function of length of time
of occupancy.

FLOATER ASSESSMENT OF THE VIGOR OF TERRITORY OWNERS

The length of time an individual has held a territory, and hence its
current value to him, may be difficult to determine, but the current
vigor of an owner may be evident from cursory examination. Sickness
and injuries are generally readily detectable. RHP predicts that floaters
should regularly visit territories to assess the vigor of owners and should
challenge any owner in a weakened condition. All but the most rigid
VA hypotheses predict a similar behavior because even though an owner
might be willing to escalate a contest further than a challenger, an
owner's physical condition might indicate his inability to do so. A lottery hypothesis would not predict attacks under those conditions unless

it were modified to state that "occupied territories are ignored unless the owner is clearly debilitated."

PATTERNS OF ABSENCES FROM TERRITORIES

Owners of all-purpose territories may be able to remain on their territories at all times, but the territories of many species, including those of redwings, provide only some of the resources needed to support individuals and their breeding activities. Owners also may leave their territories to seek extrapair copulations or to gather information about nearby areas. VA predicts that owners should not leave their territories for long periods because the longer they are absent, the longer floaters can occupy and learn more about the areas. The longer the occupancy, the smaller the value asymmetry between the owner and the recent settler, and the less important other factors need to be to tip the dominance balance. In contrast, because an individual's RHP should not be influenced by the length of time he is away from his territory, a territory owner under RHP rules does not risk losing his territory by long absences. However, he may pay other prices, such as being cuckolded or failing to attract additional mates, that favor shorter absences. Under a strict lottery model, an owner should avoid leaving his territory, even to gain extrapair copulations, because any floater that arrives during his absence can take over and maintain the territory.

CORRELATION BETWEEN MALE QUALITY AND TERRITORY QUALITY

Under RHP there should be a strong correlation between male quality and territory quality. A male should be able to move to a better-quality territory when his RHP improves or when he observes a decline in vigor of a male holding a better territory; that is, better territories may be taken by force. However, if fighting is dangerous, the correlation between male quality and territory quality is weakened provided that individuals are reluctant to challenge owners, even if they believe themselves to be better fighters. Under VA, the correlation between male quality and territory quality should be relatively low because chance exerts a major influence on when and where males get territories and because the value of a territory to an owner relative to all challengers increases rapidly after a male settles. Under VA, a male may be able to move to a higher-quality territory, but he does so only by being the first to detect a vacancy, not because he is better able to defend that territory. Under a lottery model, there should be no correlation between male quality and territory quality.

COMBINATIONS OF MODELS

RHP, VA, and lottery are not mutually exclusive; none of them is likely to provide a complete explanation of patterns of acquisition *and* maintenance of territories. We have already shown that a pure lottery model can account for only the stage of initial acquisition of a territory, not for its maintenance. There is, however, no compelling theoretical reason why either VA or RHP could not provide a complete explanation of territorial behavior. There is equally no theoretical reason why both could not influence territorial behavior, their relative importance varying with the characteristics of species and the environments in which they breed. A rather substantial literature on redwings already shows that both hypotheses must be invoked in order to explain redwing territorial behavior, but their relative roles are as yet unclear. Our task, therefore, is to determine how, to what degree, and why VA, RHP, and lotteries influence territory acquisition and retention in redwings. Fortunately, because the models make a number of different testable predictions, we have been able to assemble a wide array of evidence to assess which components of territorial behavior are most strongly influenced by them.

Seven

Territory Acquisition
by Male Redwings:
When, Where, and How

INTRODUCTION

In the previous chapter we analyzed major current models to explain animal contest behavior as they apply to avian territoriality. In this chapter we adapt these models to territory acquisition by male redwings and make predictions specific to our study population. We test these predictions with extensive demographic data collected during our long-term study, supplemented by experimental removal of territorial males and limited information on movements of radio-tagged floaters. By their very nature, none of our tests is decisive; most are open to multiple interpretations even though one conclusion may appear more probable than others. However, an assemblage of weak tests can generate strong support for a particular hypothesis or for some combination of hypotheses.

Because male redwings in the CNWR population cannot reproduce without holding a territory, much of our effort was designed to gather demographic and experimental data that could reveal when, where, and how males gain territories and the consequences of their doing so in particular ways. To set the stage for male territory acquisition, we first describe several important ecological features of the study population and its environment. We then, in separate sections, consider when, where, and how males acquire territories. In each section we first make predictions from value asymmetry (VA), resource-holding potential (RHP), and lottery (L) hypotheses, and then test those predictions for which we have information. When, where, and how males get territories are not necessarily independent traits, but treating them separately allows us to consider clearly their contributions to territory acquisition.

THE SETTING: HABITAT AND COMPETITION

Our study site, and the Columbia National Wildlife Refuge (CNWR) as a whole, consist of highly productive marshes surrounded by broad expanses of dry, sagebrush-dominated uplands. Thus, only a very small fraction of the entire area is suitable redwing breeding habitat. On the other hand, these upland areas provide extensive undefended areas where floaters can feed unmolested and from which they can observe activities on the territories. The openness of the terrain and the presence of cliffs near most of the marshes offer excellent opportunities for non-territorial individuals to detect vacancies, injuries, or illnesses among territory owners, and to monitor the activities of females. Thus, they can probably learn a great deal without having to invade the territories. This situation, which characterizes most other redwing populations as well, contrasts with that typical of many passerines in which territories are situated in structurally complex vegetation and undefended foraging areas are not found close to territories (e.g., Krebs 1971, 1982).

Throughout our investigations there were many more male redwings in the study area than could acquire territories. Although we cannot estimate precisely the size of the floater population, the number of nonterritorial individuals probably exceeds the number of territory owners during most years. There are two types of floaters: adults that have not yet gained territories (plus a small number that previously held territories), and subadults, most of which do not acquire territories. As a result, competition for territories during the main period of the study (1977 to 1992) was always intense; groups of floaters regularly patrolled the study marshes during the breeding season. Floaters often entered territories, particularly during social disturbances, and they sometimes challenged residents for ownership. Many males that initially settled on or near our study marshes failed to establish territories. When we removed owners, they were quickly replaced by floaters (Beletsky and Orians 1989a). A sizable male floater population has been reported in every other investigation of redwing breeding and territoriality in North America (Nero 1956b; Orians 1961; Laux 1970; Peek 1971; Holm 1973; Wittenberger 1976; Yasukawa 1979; Rohwer 1982; Shutler and Weatherhead 1991b).

SUBADULT MALES

One-year-old males—subadults—have a different plumage than adults and average about 95% of adult body mass (Beletsky et al. 1989; Shutler and Weatherhead 1991b; Beletsky 1996). Although they are reproductively mature and produce viable sperm (Payne 1965; Wiley and Hartnett 1976), they only occasionally acquire territories and attract mates, and genetic analyses reveal that subadult floaters very rarely sire offspring via EPFs. If they hold territories, it is usually in marginal habitat (Greenwood 1985; Eckert and Weatherhead 1987a). Subadults usually acquire territories in prime habitat only when all adults—owners and floaters—are removed (e.g., Laux 1970; Shutler and Weatherhead 1991b). At CNWR, a few subadults managed to hold territories on our prime breeding marshes, where competition from adults is intense (see below), but we do not know whether all subadults at CNWR, even if they found vacant, uncontested territories, would choose to—or be able to—assume ownership and defend their terrain.

The behavior of floating subadults during the breeding season varies. Some trespass on territories singly or in small groups, chase females, and act like adult floaters. Others apparently spend the season in small flocks composed solely of subadults and do not attempt territory takeovers. Because the reproductive decison-making of adult and subadult floaters apparently differs, we treat them separately. Why subadults are reproductively mature but of different morphology than breeders is a separate evolutionary question, treated in detail by others (Rohwer et al. 1980; Rohwer and Butcher 1988).

HYPOTHESIS-INDEPENDENT PREDICTIONS

VA, RHP, and L hypotheses predict differences in only some components of the behaviors that influence territory acquisition. Some tactics should be favored by natural selection under all models of animal contests. In particular, lifetime reproductive success of a male redwing should be maximized, other things being equal, if a male begins to reproduce as soon as he is able and continues to do so for the remainder of his life. The fact that acquisition of adult plumage is delayed in male redwings requires analyses that lie outside the predictions of any of the hypotheses developed to explain territorial dominance.

WHEN TO GET A TERRITORY

When males get territories needs to be analyzed at two different temporal "scales": at what age and at what time of year it occurs. At both scales, most predictions are the same under all major hypotheses governing territory acquisition tactics.

AGE AT WHICH TERRITORIES ARE FIRST ACQUIRED

Lifetime reproductive success of male redwings on our study area is positively correlated with the number of years they hold territories (Orians and Beletsky 1989). Although extrapair copulations and extrapair fertilizations are frequent, nearly all EPFs are achieved by other territorial males (Gray 1996a). Therefore natural selection should favor obtaining a territory as soon as possible and maintaining it annually thereafter, unless there is an unusually high cost of territory acquisition and maintenance among young males. In our population, the number of years an adult male held his territory was independent of the age at which he first acquired it (Beletsky and Orians 1993). The age-independence of territory tenure, combined with a 35 to 40% annual adult mortality (Orians and Beletsky 1989), suggests that under any hypothesis of contest behavior, males should attempt to obtain territories as soon as they are able to.

If a male's RHP were genetically determined and fixed for life, nearly all males who get territories should do so as soon as they acquire adult plumage and mass—age two. High RHP two-year-olds should either find and successfully defend high-quality vacancies or, if none are available, evict lower-RHP males. VA and L also predict that males should obtain territories as soon as they find a vacancy after acquiring adult plumage, but because a certain number will not find vacancies, some proportion should not obtain territories until later ages. In other words, RHP predicts an earlier assumption of territorial status than VA and L, both of which predict more variation in age of first breeding. In the real world, however, RHP is not absolute and fixed; it varies within individuals over time, as a function of age and physiological condition. The range of RHP among territorial males also varies, with the result that a male floater with a given RHP might find no male of lower RHP defending a territory in one year but encounter others with lower RHP the following year. Thus, the prediction that most males should get territories as soon as they are mature, but some will not get them until they are older, fits all three hypotheses.

To examine the age at which males at CNWR obtained their territories, we analyzed males who acquired their first territories on our core marshes from 1983 through 1992. We knew the year of birth of about 60% of these males because they were initially banded as nestlings or subadults. We assumed that the remaining males, who were in adult plumage when first captured and banded, were two years old that year (Beletsky and Orians 1993), but a few of them were probably older. Approximately 64% of new owners during this period acquired territories by the time they were two years old, but the remainder did so when they were three or older (table 7.1). The percentages are similar when calculated using only males with known ages or when estimated-age males are included. Therefore, although most males get territories by age two, a third of them do not do so until they are older, a pattern that is consistent with all three models.

TABLE 7.1. Ages at which males first obtained territories in the core study area at CNWR, 1983–92

Age	Known-age males only		All males	
	n	%	n	%
1	10	7.4	10	4.3
2	77	56.6	144	62.3
3	36	26.5	49	21.2
4	9	6.6	18	7.8
5	2	1.5	6	2.6
6	2	1.5	4	1.7
Totals	136		231	

TERRITORY ACQUISITION BY SUBADULTS

Under VA and L, subadults should have the same chances as adults of discovering vacancies and assuming ownership. That they do not is evidence that adult plumage and body mass are important for establishing and maintaining territories.

The few subadults in the study area that do establish territories on our core marshes are presumably of very high RHP (Weatherhead and Robertson 1981). If RHP contributes to territorial success, subadult males able to secure high-quality territories ought to hold them longer and achieve greater LRS than males first establishing their territories when they are older.

Only 15 subadults obtained territories from 1977 through 1990 and held them sufficiently long to be included in our sample (8 were inserters, 7 replacers; see below). These males bred, on average, significantly fewer years than males that obtained territories at two years of age (known- and estimated-age two-year-olds; table 7.2). They also had significantly lower average annual harem sizes, average annual fledging success, and LRS (table 7.2). Thus, contrary to the RHP prediction, males that first gained territories as subadults had lower rather than higher RS—"super" subadults did not become "super" adults. Whether these males had higher or lower RHP than the average cannot be assessed because the costs of territory maintenance may be greater for younger males than for older males.

TIME OF YEAR

All three hypotheses predict that prospecting males should, at the beginning of a breeding season, quickly assert ownership of any vacancies they detect. Occupying a vacancy is relatively cost-free, and no

TABLE 7.2. Territory tenure and breeding success for male redwings who first obtained their territories on core marshes at one and at two years of age

Male age	n	Total no. of years with territory ($\overline{X} \pm SD$)	First year ($\overline{X} \pm SD$)		Average annual ($\overline{X} \pm SD$)		Lifetime no. of fledged young ($\overline{X} \pm SD$)
			Harem size	No. of fledged young	Harem size	No. of fledged young	
1	15	2.1 ± 1.2	1.8 ± 1.0	1.4 ± 2.1	2.7 ± 1.0	2.2 ± 2.2	5.9 ± 8.5
2	130	2.8 ± 1.9	3.3 ± 2.2	3.1 ± 4.3	3.6 ± 1.8	3.4 ± 3.4	11.1 ± 13.1
t value		-2.08	-4.55	-2.60	-3.03	-1.88	-2.12
1-tailed P		0.02	0.000	0.007	0.002	0.04	0.02

Note: Fifteen subadult males that first held territories on core marshes from 1977 to 1990 are compared to 130 two-year-olds that first held territories from 1983 to 1990; breeding information through 1992 is included for both groups.

TABLE 7.3. Periods during the year when males at CNWR established their first territories, 1983–92

Period	Known-age 2-year-olds		All males	
	n	%	n	%
July to February	10	13.0	22	9.5
1 to 15 March	15	19.5	60	26.0
16 to 31 March	16	20.8	66	28.6
1 to 15 April	20	26.0	41	17.7
16 to 30 April	11	14.3	22	9.5
1 to 15 May	4	5.2	13	5.6
15 to 31 May	0	0	4	1.7
1 to 30 June	1	1.3	3	1.3
Totals	77		231	

Note: Another 32 males that established territories on core marshes during this period, but that had previously held territories elsewhere, are not included.

advantage can accrue from forfeiting a good opportunity. The earlier in the season a male comes to a breeding area and attempts to find a territory, the greater the number of vacancies that are available.

Early occupancy of a territory results, on average, in siring more offspring. A male that gains a territory prior to the end of March does so before any females have begun nesting and any copulations have occurred. The later a male gains a territory, the larger the number of offspring on the territory that have been sired by the previous occupant. Because male redwings do not engage in nest destruction or infanticide (Rohwer 1986), opportunities to sire offspring on a territory do not exist until females renest after nest destruction or fledging of their first broods.

Male redwings at CNWR abandon their territories at the end of the spring breeding season, and they visit them only occasionally during the autumn and winter. Our sporadic observations of the study marshes during the autumn and early winter reveal that some, perhaps all, males roost on their territories at least occasionally during the nonbreeding season. By mid-March, when we have completed our first territory maps of the season, all territories are occupied and vacancies due to overwinter deaths or desertions have been filled.

Although early occupancy is clearly desirable, males acquired territories throughout the spring. The 35.5% of new owners first listed on our mid-March maps could have established their territories anytime between the previous July (when we terminated monitoring) and mid-March (table 7.3). Including all males that acquired territories prior to the end of March, when nesting begins, 64.1% of males got territories before any offspring had been sired. Of the males that acquired their territories later during the season, 27.2% did so during April and 8.6% did so in May or June. Nearly 47% of known-age two-year-olds that established territories during the nesting season did so from April through June (table 7.3). Because both VA and L predict a broader spread of timing of territory acquisition than does RHP, it might be argued that these data favor VA or L rather than RHP. However, the situation is not clear because the RHP of owners may change during the breeding season as a result of exhaustion, injury, or disease. Throughout a breeding season, therefore, some floaters can expect to find owners whose RHP has dropped below theirs. We cannot estimate the rate at which males do or are likely to decline in RHP during a breeding season, so we are unable to judge whether the proportion of males that acquire territories during April and May is higher than that compatible with an RHP view of the world.

One tactic to obtain a territory under VA rules would be to assume ownership of a territory late in the breeding season after the owner has finished breeding and departed. Males could acquire extensive information on the territory at this time, of potential use in contests with the previous owner during the subsequent breeding season. Also, should the previous owner die during winter, a male that had occupied his territory for a week or more at the end of the past breeding season might have an advantage there the next year. At Yellowwood Lake, Indiana, 19% (7 of 37) of new owners on a marsh during a nine-year period had occupied their year x territories briefly at the very end of year $x-1$, after previous owners disappeared (Yasukawa 1979). This was not, however, a regular tactic at CNWR. We made territory maps and identified all owners through mid-June, by which time late-season take-overs would have occurred. Of 231 males that first established territories in the core area between 1983 and 1992, only 7, or 3%, first acquired their territories between 15 May and 30 June (table 7.3). Four of the 7 retained the territory during the subsequent breeding season, 1 moved to another marsh the next year, and 2 were not detected again. The fact that late-season takeovers that resulted in permanent ownership were rare argues against VA and for RHP.

An alternative explanation for the failure of males to occupy vacant territories late in the season at CNWR, that such behavior is not pursued because it is very costly to males, is unlikely to be correct. Food is very abundant during June and the males have not yet begun to molt. The opportunity costs of spending time on a territory then are probably very low because males spend most of their time in flocks, much of it resting.

WHERE TO GET A TERRITORY: GENERAL LOCATION

The three hypotheses (RHP, VA, and L) predict different methods by which a male should select a general area in which to search for and establish a territory. Unless kinship or social relationships influence where redwings get their territories, which is unlikely in our outbred population, a pure RHP strategy predicts that males should acquire territories anywhere in the area to which their phenotypes are suited. A male should be no more likely to acquire a territory at his natal site or in the area he frequented during his subadult year than elsewhere. Also, RHP predicts that within a given locale, the highest RHP males should be able to obtain territories at the best sites—those that, on average, produce the most surviving offspring.

Under VA, familiarity with specific areas could serve both to hasten finding of vacancies and to decrease the difference in value of specific sites to owners and prospectors. Thus, VA predicts that males should obtain territories predominantly in areas in which they have spent much time. Useful information could be acquired during the natal year, and additional information could be obtained during the subadult year. Territories under VA, therefore, should be established in natal or subadult areas. Given the great interannual variability in the physical characteristics and biological productivity of our study marshes, information from previous years is of less value than current information; nevertheless, such information should increase the value of a territory to an individual.

As does RHP, L predicts that territory acquisition should not be influenced by location, provided the site is within the region to which the individual is phenotypically adapted and individuals have sufficient knowledge of their searching areas so that they can find food and sheltered roosts.

NATAL DISPERSAL AND TERRITORY OWNERSHIP

We believe that most males that held territories on our core marshes were probably born within 4 or 5 km of our core study area because: (1) the mean dispersal distance between natal and breeding territories for locally born males that later obtained territories within the study area was 1420 ± 1350 m (n = 127; median = 1000 m, range = 20 to 7200 m); (2) an average of 20% of males that owned territories each

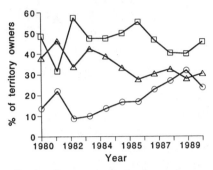

Fig. 7.1. Proportions of male redwings initially banded as nestlings ("locals"—circles), subadults ("second-year males"—triangles), and adults ("after-second-year males"—squares) holding territories on core marshes, 1980 through 1990 (from Beletsky and Orians 1993).

year on our core marshes were born on the core (fig. 7.1); and (3) there are about two hundred territories within a 2 km radius and at least four hundred more territories within a 5 km radius of our core area (Beletsky and Orians 1987a), more than enough to supply the territory owners on the core that immigrate from elsewhere. Given the known dispersal distances of marked nestlings and the large pool of males born on surrounding marshes that probably disperse for roughly the same distances, there is no reason to assume that more than a very small fraction of core territory owners were born more than 5 km away (Beletsky and Orians 1993).

SUBADULT DISPERSAL, SITE FIDELITY, AND TERRITORY OWNERSHIP

Thirty to 40% of males holding territories on the core marshes each year were initially banded in the area as subadults (fig. 7.1). Thus, at least 50% of males who held territories each year in the core were born there or spent time there as yearlings. Almost all the territory owners probably fall into one of those two groups. Therefore, most males at CNWR probably obtain territories in areas with which they have long-term familiarity, a pattern that supports VA but not RHP or L.

HABITAT TYPE

Habitat quality may also influence where males establish territories. The RHP hypothesis, in particular, predicts that males with superior fighting abilities should obtain the best territories, i.e., there should be a positive correlation between male quality and territory quality, an "ideal dominance distribution" (Fretwell and Lucas 1970). We have no data with which to assess possible relationships between RHP and territory quality at CNWR, but Eckert and Weatherhead (1987c) tested the prediction that redwings in Ontario that establish territories in marshes, where their RS is high, should be dominant in aviaries to males that establish territories at upland sites, where RS is lower. They removed territory owners from both habitat types, measured their sizes, placed them in the same cages, and monitored dominance interactions. Upland males, in contrast to the prediction, were, on average, larger than marsh males and usually dominated them. This result appears contrary to RHP. However, a possible explanation for Eckert and Weatherhead's results is that territory owners in the higher-quality marshes are more energetically stressed than upland owners because they spend more time on their territories defending them from floaters and so less time feeding (S. Rohwer, personal communication).

HOW TO GET A TERRITORY

Several aspects of how redwings actually search for and establish their territories may yield insights into whether they are operating under VA, RHP, and/or L rules. We first make general predictions based on the information a bird would need to obtain a territory under the respective hypotheses. We then consider several factors that influence territory prospecting and establishment and use them to assess VA, RHP, and L predictions. We examine (1) the influence of birth year and date on territory acquisition; (2) the proximate tactics of territory establishment—replacing dead or absent owners, inserting between owners, or evicting owners; and (3) floater searching behavior. Specific predictions are made in each section.

GENERAL CONSIDERATIONS AND PREDICTIONS

From the point of view of animal contest theory, the *timing* of takeovers matters greatly. During late winter or early spring, when many vacancies typically exist, all three hypotheses predict that males should make rapid surveys of breeding areas with which they are familiar, searching for vacancies. Occupying a vacant area is the easiest, least stressful, most danger-free path to territory ownership. Once all territories are occupied, however, vacancies are rare and those that arise are often quickly taken by expanding neighbors. Therefore, the three hypotheses diverge in their predictions of how floaters should behave to maximize their chances of obtaining territories after the initial settlement period. The kinds of information that individuals need to acquire to assess their options, the difficulty of acquiring that information, and how it can best be gained differ under RHP, VA, and L theories. General predictions of floater behavior just before or during the nesting period are these:

RHP: Under RHP rules, the essential information needed by floaters is the RHP levels of territory owners relative to their own. Floaters, therefore, should concentrate on evaluating the RHPs of territory owners relative to their own. Such information can be gathered only when the owners are present on their territories. Presumably a male redwing can assess his own RHP only by challenging owners, but he can evaluate the relative RHPs of territory owners either by challenging them directly on their territories or by observing from outside the territory their behavior and interactions with other males. Because it takes some time to evaluate a territory owner's RHP by either method, a single individual cannot evaluate many owners. Thus, floaters should restrict themselves to a relatively small "beat," the size set by the number of owner RHP evaluations they can remember or by the time required for the assessments.

During much of the breeding season owners are usually present and most active on their territories during the early morning and late afternoon. Therefore, because the essential information needed by floaters seeking to establish territories under RHP rules is the RHP of owners, floaters should concentrate their observing and probing at those times of day.

VA: Floaters operating under VA rules familiarize themselves not with the attributes of male owners—which are irrelevant—but with those of the territories themselves. A floater must accumulate sufficient information about a particular territory so that the site is as valuable to him as it is to its current owner. The more he learns, the smaller the difference between the value of the territory to him and to its owner. When a floater values the territory at least as highly as its current occupant, he should challenge the owner. The RHPs of the two individuals do not matter because the relative value of the area to the contestants determines the outcome.

Some information can be gathered about a territory from a distance, but gaining enough information to eliminate the VA differential probably requires detailed inspection of the area from within. Floaters can gather VA information at any time of day, but because it is difficult or dangerous to gather information within a territory while the owner is present, territorial probing should be concentrated during times when owners are absent. Therefore, under the VA hypothesis, floaters should enter territories primarily during midday and late in the season, when owners are absent for longer periods than they are during the peak of the season.

Sufficient information to reduce substantially or eliminate value differences takes time to acquire. Thus, beats for floaters under VA should be confined to the maximum number of territories with which individuals can achieve and maintain a high level of familiarity, probably a smaller number than the number of territory owners floaters might assess for RHP.

L: Males seeking territories under pure lottery rules need only ascertain whether an unoccupied territory is really vacant, which they can probably determine within half an hour by watching during times of day when owners are usually present. Floaters should maximize their chances of finding a vacancy, therefore, by visiting many territories during peak occupancy hours but spending no more than half an hour in any one location or territory. Accordingly, they should explore larger areas than either RHP or VA males; the larger the area searched, the greater the probability of finding a vacancy. They do not need to enter a territory in order to assess occupancy. Nevertheless, the surest way to determine quickly whether a territory is taken is to land in it; verification, if positive, will soon arrive. Being the first to occupy a vacant territory should also increase the probability of keeping it.

INFLUENCE OF BIRTH YEAR

RHP: Birth year could influence the probability that an individual acquires a territory in at least two ways. First, different year cohorts could vary significantly in average physiological condition because they were raised under qualitatively different environmental conditions, such as unusually warm or cold breeding seasons or in particularly low or high insect-production years (Beletsky and Orians 1993). Second, because fledgling production and survival vary among years, birth year influences the number of males with which each male floater must compete. If the number of territories each year is relatively constant, a male maturing following two or three years of unusually high fledgling production and survival faces stiffer competition and has a lower probability of obtaining a territory than a male born in a period of low fledging success of one year or longer.

VA and *L:* These hypotheses also predict that the probability of gaining a territory should vary with birth year, but only as a function of variation in the size of floater populations. A male's RHP is irrelevant, but the probability that he is the first to discover a newly created territorial vacancy must vary with the number of searching floaters.

Table 7.4 shows the natal years of known-age males that acquired territories on the core study marshes over sixteen years. Some years—1978, 1979, 1981, 1983, 1986, 1987—contributed relatively large numbers of territory owners, whereas others contributed few. The eruption of Mount St Helens in May 1980 was probably responsible for the very low number of owners born that year. Although a fair number of young fledged that year, the several centimeters of volcanic ash that blanketed the study area probably severely reduced fledgling survival (Orians 1985; Beletsky and Orians 1993). The volcano, by destroying a cohort, enhanced the chances of acquisition by males born in years surrounding 1980. However, because all three hypotheses predict that the year a male is born should influence his chance of gaining a territory, and because we have no estimates of RHP of males in different cohorts, the results are consistent with all three hypotheses.

INFLUENCE OF BIRTH DATE

The time during a breeding season at which a male is born could strongly affect his ability to get a territory because a male born early in the season has a longer period in which to mature prior to migration or winter than a later-born individual (Garnett 1981; Ydenberg 1989; Harris et al. 1992). Late-fledged young of several North Temperate Zone passerines are much less likely to survive to the next year than are early-fledged young (Murphy 1986; Drilling and Thompson 1988; Stutchbury and Robertson 1988; Perrins and McCleery 1989; Hochachka 1990).

RHP: This hypothesis predicts that males fledged early in a breeding season should have a higher probability of gaining a territory than males fledged later in the season.

VA and *L:* These hypotheses both predict no relationship between date of fledging and probability of obtaining a territory, provided the individual survives, because only locating vacancies or gathering information about territories matters; relative robustness does not.

Table 7.5 gives the distribution of fledging dates for males born at the study site, the percentage known to have survived to subadult and adult ages, and the number that obtained territories on core or peripheral marshes. Contrary to the RHP prediction, males that fledged early during the season did not have a higher probability of survival or of acquiring a territory than males fledged later during the season. In fact, slightly higher percentages of males fledged in June obtained territories

TABLE 7.4. Natal years of all known-age male redwings that obtained territories on core-area marshes from 1977 through 1992

First year on territory	Natal year																	Totals
	'74	'75	'76	'77	'78	'79	'80	'81	'82	'83	'84	'85	'86	'87	'88	'89	'90	
1977	5	7																12
1978	1	1	8															10
1979			1	4														5
1980			4	3	13	2												22
1981				3	9	20												32
1982					1	4	1	2										8
1983					1	4	1	13	1									20
1984					1			7	4	5								17
1985						1		1	4	11								17
1986										3	5	1						9
1987										3	7	11	1					22
1988											2	3	13	2				20
1989													6	10	1			17
1990												1		5	1			7
1991														4		2	1	7
1992														1	2	1	6	11
Totals	6	8	13	10	25	31	2	23	9	22	14	16	21	22	4	3	7	236

Note: Includes males banded first as nestlings or subadults.

TABLE 7.5. Fledging dates for male redwings born at the CNWR study site between 1977 and 1990 that were known to have survived to second-year status, to adulthood, and that obtained territories there between 1978 and 1992

Fledging dates	No. of males fledged[a]	Percentage that survived[b]		Those that got territories		% that later got territories	
		To sub-adulthood	To adult-hood	No.	%	Sub-adults	Adults
Before May 1	123	9.8	6.5	4	3.3	33.3	50.0
1–10 May	266	7.9	4.5	7	2.6	33.3	58.3
11–20 May	403	14.1	9.7	21	5.2	36.8	53.8
21–30 May	490	12.7	10.0	25	5.1	39.7	51.0
31 May–9 June	437	15.1	9.2	30	6.9	45.5	75.0
10–19 June	328	26.5	19.8	41	12.5	47.1	63.1
20–29 June	289	15.2	10.7	21	7.3	47.7	67.7
After 29 June	175	14.9	11.4	8	4.6	30.8	40.0
Totals	2,511			157			

[a]Total number of fledged young divided by 2.
[b]Estimated using our capture, banding, and territory owner records.

than did males fledged in May. Thus, our data on birth dates do not support an RHP argument for territory acquisition. They are consistent with VA or L, but do not constitute strong support for them.

METHODS OF TERRITORY ESTABLISHMENT:
INSERTING VERSUS REPLACING

Male redwings establish territories in one of three ways. They may take over a space vacated by the death or departure of the previous owner. Alternatively, they may insert themselves between occupied territories and displace established residents from parts of their territories (Nero 1956b; Yasukawa 1979). Finally, they may challenge and evict the current owner. Because a vacant area can be taken with little or no fighting with neighbors or other males, a high RHP is not a prerequisite for doing so. However, males that insert between other territory owners or evict an owner must fight, or at least endure lengthy periods of challenges (sometimes lasting several days) from the males they displace (Nero 1956b; Yasukawa 1979; personal observations). Neither existing theory nor empirical evidence suggests that territory owners should ever cede all or parts of their territories to nonrelatives without attempting to defend their holdings, although peripheral areas may be less vigorously defended than core areas.

RHP, VA, and L all predict rapid occupation of empty space, but

RHP and VA/L make different predictions concerning methods of establishment. RHP predicts that males should regularly gain territories by inserting themselves between two occupied territories, partially displacing the owners, and also by evicting owners. VA predicts insertions in only what must be the relatively few instances in which floaters' knowledge of particular territories approaches or equals that of the owners. Under VA, inserting and evicting should occur only rarely during breeding seasons because current owners are never away from their territories long enough for new males to acquire dominance. They could happen only if a male occupied a territory temporarily vacated by its current owner long enough to eliminate the value asymmetry. L predicts that all males obtain territories by occupying vacancies, that is, as replacements.

ANALYSIS. To determine how males acquired territories, we used our biweekly territory maps for each core marsh, from 1982 to 1992. For each new territory owner from 1983 to 1990 we determined when he first obtained his territory and whether he acquired it through replacement or insertion. Males known to have previously held territories elsewhere, either on core or peripheral marshes, and subadult owners were not included in the analysis.

Males first appearing on our mid-March maps could have acquired territories at any time from July of the previous year up to 15 March. These males were all considered to have obtained territories *between* breeding seasons. Those obtaining territories each year between 15 March and 15 June (when our final maps were prepared) were categorized as obtaining territories *within* breeding seasons. We included males in the analysis only if they held territories for at least one month and succeeded in attracting at least one female. We excluded males that held territories for only a few days or weeks because they did not establish themselves securely.

We define as inserters males that took parts of territories from already-established residents, either within or between breeding seasons. We can identify inserters because *all adjacent territorial males are still present after the insertion.* Most inserters first occupied a territory boundary between two established residents and then expanded in both directions. This process, which we have observed many times, is probably also how insertions happen between breeding seasons. However, because we monitored few insertions in detail, we do not know how much fighting or effort was required on average for inserters to establish themselves.

We define a replacement male as one that obtained a territory by acquiring approximately the same space as a previous, *but no longer present*, resident or residents. Because we actually witnessed events associated with few within-breeding-season and no between-season replacements, some "replacements" actually may have evicted an established owner. However, forced evictions of this sort rarely occur in redwings. Yasukawa (1979) reported only one such case over several years in his intensive studies at Yellowwood Lake, Indiana. Picman (1987) observed no cases in a five-year study in British Columbia, and we observed very few natural evictions at CNWR. The great majority of replacers, therefore, probably obtained their territories when previous residents died or left, especially during the nonbreeding months.

Most males (69%) obtained territories by replacing others, but 31% inserted (table 7.6). This frequency of insertions is consistent with RHP but not with VA and L. On the other hand, evictions appear to be rare among redwings, although under a pure RHP system they should be common. However, if the RHP hypothesis is modified by assuming that fighting for a territory is dangerous because of the risk of injury, then RHP also predicts that evictions should be relatively rare. Therefore, our data on territory acquisition are consistent with predictions from RHP.

Inserting provides indirect evidence of high RHP because inserters must overcome established owners. If inserting males have high RHP, they should hold territories longer than males that acquired their territories by occupying vacancies. To test this prediction, we divided territory acquisitions into those taking place between and within breeding seasons. Insertions and replacements are possible during both periods, so we have four acquisition categories. Because territory owners are only occasionally present and agonistic interactions are not intense outside the breeding season, acquiring a territory then should require less effort than during breeding, when owners are almost always present. Because inserting is probably always more difficult than replacing, we a priori ranked acquisition methods, in order of decreasing average difficulty, as (A) inserting during breeding seasons, (B) inserting between breeding seasons, (C) replacing within breeding seasons, and (D) replacing between seasons. If high RHP confers longevity and high RS, then the average territory tenure and RS of these groups should be A>B>C>D.

For this analysis we calculated annual reproductive success as described in chapter 2, but for males who gained territories while nesting was under way, we subtracted from their RS all offspring fledged from nests initiated on their territories before their takeovers. The fact that

TABLE 7.6. Method of territory establishment, territory tenure, and reproductive success for male redwings that acquired their first territories in core CNWR marshes between 1983 and 1990

Method	n (%)	Total no. of years with territory, 1983–92 ($\overline{X} \pm$ SD)	First year ($\overline{X} \pm$ SD)		Average annual ($\overline{X} \pm$ SD)		Lifetime no. of fledged young ($\overline{X} \pm$ SD)
			Harem size	No. of fledged young	Harem size	No. of fledged young	
Replace another male(s)							
Between breeding seasons	109 (52.7)	2.8 ± 1.8	3.5 ± 2.4	3.9 ± 5.5	3.7 ± 2.0	4.0 ± 4.6	11.4 ± 14.1
Within a breeding season	34 (16.4)	2.5 ± 2.0	2.6 ± 1.7	2.5 ± 3.7	3.0 ± 1.8	2.3 ± 2.6	9.2 ± 14.7
Insert between males							
Between breeding seasons	25 (12.1)	2.8 ± 2.2	3.4 ± 2.4	3.2 ± 4.3	3.5 ± 2.2	4.1 ± 4.5	11.4 ± 13.5
Within a breeding season	39 (18.8)	2.2 ± 1.4	3.3 ± 2.5	3.5 ± 5.3	3.6 ± 2.1	3.2 ± 4.4	7.1 ± 7.8
Total	207						
$\overline{X} \pm$ SD		2.6 ± 1.8	3.3 ± 2.3	3.5 ± 5.1	3.6 ± 2.0	3.6 ± 4.3	10.2 ± 13.2
Kruskal-Wallis ANOVA, X^2		3.51	2.76	3.49	2.55	6.06	5.91
P value		0.32	0.43	0.32	0.47	0.11	0.12

many broods contain young sired by multiple males (Gibbs et al. 1990; Westneat 1993; Gray 1996a) does not affect our analyses because all young are sired either by the putative father or by his territorial neighbors (Gray 1996a,b); and our prediction that a male's RHP and the number of young fledged from his territory should be positively correlated still holds.

RESULTS. From 1983 through 1992, 227 adult males established their first territories in the core study area. Annual return rates ranged from 50% to 65%. Males that first obtained their territories from 1983 through 1990 (n = 207) bred for an average of 2.6 years, through 1992, a slight underestimate of average lifetime tenure because a few of these males continued to own territories after 1992. There was no significant difference in territory tenure among males acquiring territories as inserters or replacers, either within or between years (table 7.6). However, males that established territories within breeding seasons tended to hold them fewer years than males that gained territories between seasons. Inserters within seasons had the lowest average tenure. There were no significant differences in our measures of reproductive success among the four groups, although within-season inserters had relatively low average lifetime fledging success (table 7.6).

DISCUSSION. Contrary to our predictions, males inserting on territories within years did not maintain territories for longer periods or produce more fledglings than males that acquired territories by other means. In fact, they tended to perform more poorly than replacers. Possible reasons for this outcome include the following: (1) we incorrectly assigned the relative difficulty levels of gaining a territory by various methods, i.e., our RHP rankings were incorrect; (2) our postulated association between RHP and RS was incorrect; (3) RHP is *not* a prime determinant of territory acquisition; and (4) insertion is so energetically costly that it results in lowered LRS.

Our chief assumption for ranking territory acquisition methods is that inserting is more difficult than replacing and, thus, inserters must have, on average, higher RHP. But because we did not witness how males actually obtained territories, our evidence is circumstantial. We assumed that owners always fight to prevent loss of all or part of their holdings; however, a territorial male may tolerate loss of part of his territory more readily than the loss of his entire territory, especially of lower-quality peripheral areas. Also, inserters may seek out places where territorial boundaries are in flux and ownership is contested (Beletsky 1992). Inserting in these situations might be easier than we assumed. Another possibility is that inserters displace males of unusually low average RHP. However, because inserters usually take portions of territories from more than one male, and insert themselves on both low- and high-quality marshes, we reject this possibility. Given the intense competition in the study area for territories, any male that attained territorial status on our core marshes probably had high RHP relative to those individuals that never got territories.

We postulated a positive relationship between RHP and RS because, if males of high RHP are better able to establish territories because of their superior physical attributes, they should also be able to maintain their territories for long periods. Because the number of years breeding is the key component of LRS in the population, high RHP should positively affect breeding success. Arguments for a positive relationship between RHP and RS assume that RHP is static, but an individual's RHP may vary over time. Therefore, the territory acquisition groups we identified as having high RHP may have been better males at the time they established territories, but their body mass, hormone levels, motivation, or energy levels could have deteriorated subsequently. Inserters may have been temporarily powerful and dominant, which allowed them to evict one or more owners from parts of their holdings. Such bursts of RHP could explain why within-season inserters did not already own territories at the beginning of the breeding season.

The act of gaining a territory in the face of considerable opposition may stress individuals sufficiently to lower their RHP and negatively influence their survivorship. Such an effect could explain why males that obtained territories by inserting within breeding seasons, the most difficult and stressful method, also had the lowest average lifetime territory tenure and LRS. Therefore, one of the reasons floaters seldom strongly challenge owners may be that even when they are successful at inserting or even at evicting a resident, they may pay a significant price for doing so.

FLOATER BEHAVIOR AND TACTICS

Our knowledge of the behavior of floaters is limited because they are difficult to monitor. They move often. Even if they are banded, it is difficult to read their color combinations because they rarely sit in exposed situations for more than a few minutes. However, we have ascertained much information by indirect methods. Marked floaters that subsequently become territorial, for instance, provide us with information concerning the duration males that eventually gain territories spend floating (table 7.1). For assessing floater behavior relevant to predictions of searching and probing strategies from RHP, VA, and L, we need to know, among other things, (1) how large an area they search, (2) how far they get territories from sites they frequent as floaters, (3) the times of day they search, and (4) whether and how often they enter territories to gather information. In this section we analyze our extensive trapping records of color-banded males, data on the movements of radio-tagged adult floaters, and information on floaters from our territorial male removal experiments. In all of our analyses we define adult floaters as *adult males trapped in a year in which they were not associated with a territory.*

As outlined earlier, an RHP model predicts that floaters should establish a beat of limited size within which they monitor RHPs of territory owners and assess weaknesses. Such information gathering, which can occur only when owners are on their territories and active, can be accomplished either by trespassing on territories and challenging owners or by remaining outside and observing owners interacting with other males. VA predicts even smaller beats because VA floaters need to become familiar with real estate, which is more complex information to gather and to retain than is information on male fighting abilities; floaters can probably maintain good familiarity with only a small number of territories. Floaters using a VA strategy should be able to gather information on territories at any time of day, but it should be easier and safer to do so when owners are absent or inactive; most information would need to be collected from inside territories. Lottery floaters should have either no beats or very large beats because they look only for vacancies. Identifying potential vacancies could be accomplished either from within or without, but it is easiest at times of day when owners typically occupy their territories.

Longevity and General Beat Size of Floaters

We have two main sources of information about floater longevity and beat size. One is our censuses of the entire study area, conducted from 1985 through 1992, in which we identified all color-banded males that held territories. Because we are confident that we located almost all color-banded territory owners in the study area (see chapter 2), banded males not found holding territories were almost certainly floaters. Another data set consists of capture records—each time we trapped a male judged to be a floater we recorded his identity, body mass, and trap location.

To analyze movements and beat sizes we measured all distances with reference to 52 locations. Three of these were our large, stationary traps (see below). The other 49 were the central points of each of the marshes in the study area on which we censused territory owners. We trapped extensively at the eight core-area marshes (11 general trap locations), occasionally at a few of the peripheral marshes, and not at all at most peripheral marshes. Most traps were in the uplands near marshes. Occasionally, males were caught during experiments with small traps placed within territories.

From 1977 through 1992 we caught 2,577 different adult males a total of 13,857 times, about five times each during their adult lifetimes (mean = 5.4 ± 8.4 times). During the same period we caught 2,895 different subadults a total of 4,596 times, about 1.5 times each in their subadult year (mean = 1.6 ± 1.5 times). We recaptured 27.3% of the 2,895 subadults as adults, and 30.7% of all adults were first captured as subadults.

The accuracy of our information on the distances over which floaters move, within and between years, is limited by several factors.

1. Our trapping records from 1977 through 1984 cannot be used to assess adult floater behavior because we did not conduct area-wide territory censuses during those years. Therefore, many color-banded males could have held territories outside the core study area. Although nearly all subadults captured during those years were almost certainly floaters, for consistency we present in some analyses only data on subadults from 1985 through 1992.

2. We have only limited information on the distances between where subadults were trapped (usually in the core) and where they later obtained territories as adults because we gave subadults either only a numbered FWS band or a numbered band and a year-coded colored band. These males were not individually identifiable when they later obtained territories unless we had subsequently trapped them as adult floaters and given them unique color-band combinations. Although we knew the year they obtained their subadult band colors, we did not know their precise banding locations. Therefore, we can determine the distances from the core at which subadults later got territories only for subadults who were trapped in the core that returned to the core as adults, were trapped again to receive new bands, and then obtained a territory (or obtained a territory first and then were trapped and given adult bands). This biases the observed distribution in favor of short-distance dispersal.

3. Our conclusions concerning male movements are derived primarily from males captured in our large, fixed-position traps. Fully 82% of the 18,453 captures occurred at the three large traps. The Ranch trap (R), situated in the northern half of the core (fig. 2.2), accounted for 5,813 captures from 1977 through 1990 (5,600 of them from 1977 through 1985). The Morgan Road trap, on the southern half of the core, accounted for 6,596 captures from 1977 through 1982. In 1983 the trap was moved a short distance across the road to the refuge subheadquarters (SH), where, from 1983 to 1992, it accounted for another 2,713 captures. Males captured in the large traps may not be a random sample of all floaters. Most of the remaining 3,331 captures (18%) took place around individual breeding marshes in the core area, but some males were captured at peripheral marshes during experiments.

4. We trapped males primarily where they foraged, not where they searched for territories. Foraging ranges and territory-monitoring beats may not coincide, but to use our data to assess the latter we must assume that males forage primarily within the area they monitor for territorial opportunities.

Temporal Aspects of Being a Floater. We caught floaters throughout the breeding season (fig. 7.2). They constituted about 30% of the adult males caught in late February and early March, about 20% from mid-March to early May, and between 10% and 15% from mid-May through June. We do not know the size of the adult male floater population, but during most years of the study it was probably at least equal in size to the population of territory owners. The evidence for this assertion is that we observed many floaters—banded and un-banded—trespassing on territories, we often saw groups of nonterritorial males, and floaters often rapidly replaced territory owners during removal experiments. The entire floater pool of subadults and adults must, for demographic reasons, have been larger than the territorial population, because subadults are, on average, the largest single age-class of males and many older floaters are also present.

Although the resident floater population was probably at least as large as the size of the owner population, we caught floaters less often than owners (fig. 7.2). The main reason may be that, unlike owners, which are tied to territories and probably under pressure when they leave to return quickly, floaters can wander farther than owners in search of food and can be more selective in their decisions about when and whether to enter traps. Supporting this possibility is the observation that individual territory owners, although often caught in our large

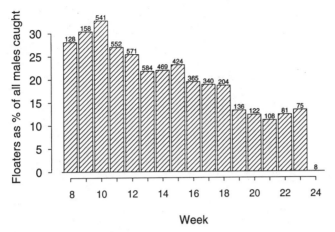

Fig. 7.2. Proportion of adult males trapped each week of the breeding season that were floaters, 1985 through 1992 pooled. All other adult males captured were identified as territory owners. Each individual was counted only once per week within a year, but could have been included several times in the distribution, in different years and in different weeks within years. Values above bars are the numbers of different adult males, regardless of territorial status, trapped each week. Total n = 4,866 captures; n floater captures = 1,119. Week 8 = 19–25 February; week 24 = 10–16 June.

traps in years before they owned territories, were rarely caught in those traps once they owned territories if their territories were more than 1,600 m away (Beletsky and Orians 1987a). Also, when we finished trapping for the day, we opened traps so that birds could eat seeds without being caught. We know some males waited for this opportunity because we watched them. Floaters, under no time constraints to return to territories, may have waited more often that did owners to enter traps to feed "for free." Furthermore, although the great majority of males that we caught from mid-April through June already wore color bands, we know that unbanded floaters were in the area because we occasionally caught them later in the season and they often took territories during territory owner removals or were observed trespassing on territories during other experiments.

Figure 7.3 shows the distributions of the longest within-year interval between trapping dates for all floaters caught at least twice during a season, i.e., the minimal intervals that individual floaters remained within the study area within breeding seasons. The average interval for adult floaters was 24.5 ± 24.6 d (n = 270); for subadults, it was 24.4 ± 21.3 d (n = 79). Adult floaters we trapped at least twice that eventually obtained territories floated for an average of 1.1 ± 0.5 y (n = 209);

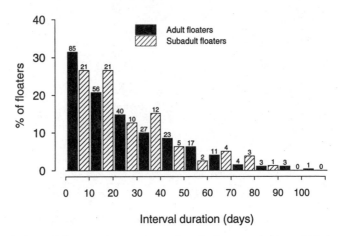

Fig. 7.3. Intervals between the two capture dates farthest apart in time within breeding seasons for adult and subadult floaters. Individuals could be counted in more than one breeding season. Values above bars are sample sizes.

those that never obtained territories floated for an average of 1.5 ± 1.1 y (n = 109).

GENERAL BEAT SIZES. To estimate typical distances over which adult floaters moved around the study area, we determined the maximum distance between capture locations for all adult floaters that were trapped at least twice within a year. The distribution is plotted in figure 7.4, together with the distribution obtained from randomly selected pairs of captures from any of our trap locations. That the two distributions are similar tells us that the numbers are strongly influenced by our trap locations, but they also demonstrate that adult floaters are commonly caught within a year in traps located at least 2.0 to 2.5 km apart. The distribution of distances for subadult floaters closely resembles the one for adults. This information does not provide data on patterns of floater space use within the area, but it shows that floaters commonly roam over distances up to at least 2.0 to 2.5 km.

Floater Reconnaissance of Eventual Territory Sites

We estimated the sizes of floater beats by determining the distances at which floaters eventually obtained territories from first capture sites or from a common, fixed point, either the SH or the R trap. We also determined the proportion of males that were trapped as floaters either at the marsh on which they later obtained territories, or nearby.

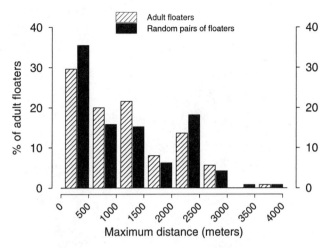

Fig. 7.4. Maximum distances between two capture sites within years for all adult floaters trapped between 1985 and 1992 that were caught more than once (mean = 1,130 m, n = 125). Only one interval per male per year is included. Also shown is the distribution of 125 distances between two capture locations randomly drawn from the 52 possible trapping/marsh locations, also as a percentage of males caught more than once.

SUBADULT FLOATERS. From 1977 through 1991, we trapped 428 subadult floaters that acquired territories at least one year later. Figure 7.5 shows the distribution of distances between the locations where they were first trapped as subadults and where they established territories. The average distance was 1,740 ± 1,254 m; most males acquired territories within 2.5 km of their initial trapping location (usually the R or SH trap). There is a sharp decline after that distance. The distribution for 1985 through 1992 only (not displayed) is almost identical in shape (average distance = 1,816 ± 1,301 m, n = 193). As we mentioned previously, these means are underestimates because all of the males in the sample had to either remain in or return to the core area as adults to obtain adult color bands. The many subadult floaters trapped in the core area that later got territories, especially those that did so far from their initial capture sites, but which we could not identify because we never caught them as adults, are not in the sample.

ADULT FLOATERS. Our information is much better for adult floaters because we gave all adults full color-band combinations when we captured them. Figure 7.6 shows the distribution of distances from the SH trap, for adult floaters caught there, to their first territories. The figure also includes the distribution of the number of available redwing territo-

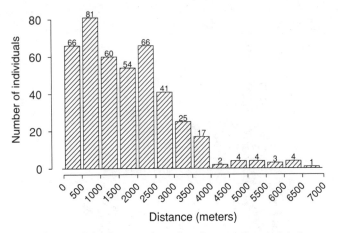

Fig. 7.5. Distribution of the distances from their first or only subadult floater capture locations at which males obtained territories as adults, 1978–92 (mean = 1,740 ± 1254 m, n = 428).

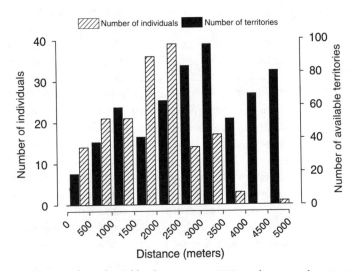

Fig. 7.6. Distances from the Subheadquarters trap (SH) to the eventual territories of adult floaters caught at SH that established territories in later years, 1985 through 1992 (mean distance = 1954 ± 1165 m, n = 174). Also shown is the distribution of available redwing territories at 500 m intervals from the SH trap. Neither distribution is cumulative.

ries at 500 m intervals from the SH trap (determined by drawing concentric circles at 500 m radii on a map of the study area, with SH at center, and summing the numbers of territories located within each ring during 1990, a typical year). Adult floaters acquired territories in direct proportion to the number available at increasing distance from the SH trap, until about 2.5 km. The hypothesis that there is an association between the number of available territories at 500 m intervals, through 2.5 km, and the number of acquisitions in each interval cannot be rejected (Pearson $\chi^2 = 7.59$, df $= 4$, P $= 0.11$). Beyond 2.5 km, however, although the number of territories available per concentric ring increased or remained fairly constant, the number of banded floaters establishing territories sharply declined. We replicated this analysis using floaters caught at the R trap (located 2.4 km north of SH) and found the same pattern (distributions not displayed). Many redwing territories were available at marshes beyond 2.5 km from our traps, but few floaters we marked in our study area obtained territories there.

Another indirect method to assess floater monitoring of territories is to determine the proportion of territory owners that were trapped as floaters in previous years at the marshes where they acquired territories. Of 126 males that first established territories in the core at age $3+$ from 1986 through 1992, only 5 (4%) were trapped as adult floaters one or more years beforehand at the marsh where they eventually gained territories. Six others (4.8%) were trapped within 500 m of their eventual territorial marshes. However, if we include subadult captures, we find that 12 males (9.5%) were trapped as floaters one or more years beforehand at the marshes on which they obtained territories, and another 14 (11.1%) were trapped within 500 m. Fifty-six, or 44.4%, of the 126 territory owners were trapped either on their eventual marshes or within 2,000 m of them during their subadult and/or adult floater years.

DISCUSSION OF FLOATER BEATS AND RECONNAISSANCE OF TERRITORY SITES. Our information on marked floaters shows that they spend one or more breeding seasons either entirely within the study area or at least visiting it occasionally. Our data on the maximum intervals between trapping dates within a breeding season and on geographic pattern of territory acquisitions, as well as the fact that many breeding males are trapped as floaters on or near their eventual marshes one or more years before becoming territory owners, suggest that redwing floaters in our study area, both subadults and adults, confine their activities to a restricted area during the breeding season. This information is inconsistent with a pure interpretation of the lottery hypothesis, which predicts wide-ranging beats as males search for vacancies.

The patterns of floater fidelity, limited movements, and territory acquisitions could be artifacts of our trapping if, by providing a regular food source at a particular location, e.g., the SH trap, we caused floaters that would otherwise have roamed far and wide to restrict their wanderings to within a few kilometers of the site. Some males did appear to use the agricultural fields and undefended shore areas on Morgan Lake near the SH trap as a feeding and loafing place. Nonetheless, rich feeding sites occur naturally and redwings typically forage at them frequently. Also, even if our SH trap had not been operating, large numbers of redwings would still have fed in the nearby agricultural fields because flocks of redwings were observed daily in the SH area before we initiated trapping. In fact, we placed the trap there initially because the birds frequented the area so regularly. Therefore, we do not believe that trapping seriously altered the beats of floaters.

Our evidence indicates that adult floaters used regular beats that ranged up to about 2.5 km from the SH area. The fact that few banded floaters acquired territories more than 2.5 km from where they were trapped—even though many territories were available beyond that distance—strongly suggests that searching beats are seldom larger than that. The fact that many males acquired their territories more than 1.5 km from their trapping sites indicates that their beats were commonly that large.

That floaters move frequently over distances of 2.5 km or more to search for and acquire territories is not consistent with the VA prediction that they should concentrate their attention on a few territories about which they learn a great deal. A floater centering his search at the SH or R trap and following a 2.5 km radius beat would have encountered between 200 and 250 territories, a number that is more consistent with our interpretation of an RHP strategy or a limited lottery.

Subadult floaters were clearly strongly faithful to the study area. We recaptured 27% of banded subadults as adults. Because 35 to 40% of them die between breeding seasons and because we do not trap floaters as often as residents, this percentage shows that floaters were highly likely to return to the same area they had frequented the previous year. High between-year fidelity to the same area where they possess long-term information on real estate and on individuals is more consistent with VA or RHP than with L.

Telemetry and Beats

To gather more information on activity patterns of the difficult-to-observe floaters we glued tiny ($\leq$ 4 g) microtransmitters to the back feathers of thirteen long-term floaters in March of 1989 and 1990. These were males caught at our SH trap that had been color-banded in previous years and that we knew (after a thorough census of territory owners in the study area during early March) did not then hold territories. Transmitter battery life was about four weeks. Ground-to-ground "pick-up" distance for the transmitters was between 1.0 and 1.5 km. We searched for the males each day with a hand-held antenna and radio receiver, first trying to pick up signals near the SH trap and then at our core and many peripheral marshes. We continued searching for and tracking the floaters until (1) we found the transmitter on the ground (they were designed to fall off the birds in three to four weeks), (2) we trapped the bird again after three weeks and removed the transmitter, or (3) four weeks had passed and the batteries had expired.

Our specific aims during the telemetry study were to determine (1) whether floaters visited the marshes at which they later got territories; (2) the distances covered and numbers of marshes and territories visited (beat size); and (3) daily activities, such as times of the day they searched for territories and whether they observed territories for long periods undetected by territory owners. We had hoped to locate radio-tagged males at marshes and follow their movements and interactions with territory owners. However, we managed to locate these males at breeding marshes only a few times, even though during the two years we searched for their signals with either one or two radio receivers for four or more hours during 62 days (133 transmitter-male-days, the minimum number of days males were known to carry active transmitters and be in the general area).

Many of the floaters spent most of each day in small feeding flocks in the agricultural fields that surround the SH trap (table 7.7). For example, floater no. 2 was detected on 5 April in a flock of about 100 female and 50 male redwings and 25 male yellowheads that foraged all day in the fields and occasionally rested on the south side of McMannamon Lake. Some of the radio-tagged floaters could be found in these fields almost any day at any time; on average, each of the 13 males was located there during 61% of the days they were still known to be in the general area. However, even the males whose signals we detected in the fields most days were absent some days, indicating that they

TABLE 7.7. Detections and subsequent histories of thirteen radio-tagged floaters caught at the subheadquarters trap (SH)

Male	Date radio on	Last date known in SH area	No. of days detected in SH area	Maximum distance detected from SH (km)	Did male get a territory and if so, how far from SH? (km)	Subsequent history
1989						
1	11 Mar	27 Mar	14	2.0	Yes, 2.0	Territory in 1989 on Hays Creek; no records after June 1989
2	11 Mar	8 Apr	18	—	No	Trapped as a floater in 1990
3	15 Mar	18 Mar[a]	3	—	No	No records after June 1989
4	19 Mar	12 Apr	20	—	No	No records after April 1989
5	23 Mar	28 Mar	3	—	No	No records after April 1989
1990						
6	15 Mar	19 Mar[a]	1	—	Yes, 1.4	Territory in 1990 through 1994 on Juvenile Pocket
7	16 Mar	28 Mar	1	—	No	No records after March 1990
8	16 Mar	4 Apr	10	—	No	No records after April 1990
9	17 Mar	29 Mar	4	1.2	No	No records after April 1990
10	17 Mar	—	0	—	Yes, 2.2	Territory in 1990 on Lake Marie and in 1991 and 1992 on Juvenile Pocket
11	18 Mar	30 Mar	7	2.9	No	No records after June 1990
12	18 Mar	20 Mar	2	—	No	Territory in 1992 and 1993 on Hays Creek
13[b]	19 Mar	—	—	—	Yes, 0.7	Territory in 1990 through 1992 on Crab Creek

[a]Transmitter fell off bird on this date.
[b]This male was caught and radio-tagged at the Ranch trap (fig. 2.2) and later obtained a territory 0.7 km from that location.

temporarily left the area. We detected the signals of only 3 of 13 floaters at a breeding marsh (other than the ones bordering the agricultural fields), on a total of five occasions. The marshes were 1.2, 2.0, and 2.9 km from the SH trap. Of these 3 floaters, only 1 eventually acquired a territory, and he did so at the marsh, 2 km away, at which he had been detected twice. Four of the floaters got territories during the year they wore transmitters (table 7.7); none of the other 9 got territories then or in future years.

Our limited telemetry sample provides some insight into floater behavior. Most floaters apparently remain during the early part of the breeding season in small flocks in rich food areas, leaving only occasionally. The data suggest that if floaters have searching beats, they have radii of at least 2 to 3 km (which, if the SH trap was at the center of the beat, would include between 150 and 300 territories). Both RHP and VA hypotheses predict that floaters remain within relatively small areas, gathering information about males or their territories of use in future takeover attempts, and our telemetry data are consistent with this prediction. The lottery hypothesis, which is not supported by telemetry data, predicts that floaters search for territories over wide areas.

Timing of Probing

RHP, VA, and L hypotheses predict that floaters prospect for territories and probe for information or vacancies at different times of day. VA predicts that gathering information about particular sites can be accomplished at any time of day but the safest and most efficient time should be when male owners are most likely to be off territory or inactive. In March, owners are usually absent from their territories between 1000 and 1500, or they are present but inactive, often hidden in the vegetation. Later, during the nesting season, owners also are relatively inactive and are absent from their territories longer at midday. Because males searching for territories under RHP or L rules need to know, respectively, about the vigor of territory owners or whether they still occupy their territories, probing under these rules should occur primarily during the early morning and the late afternoon, when owners are nearly always on their territories.

OBSERVATIONS OF PROBING. We observed probing by floaters— defined as trespassing on the territories of owners—almost exclusively during mornings and late afternoons, coinciding with the periods when owners spend most of their time on their territories advertising from elevated, high-visibility perches. Although owners are away or inactive in the late morning and the early afternoon, probing by floaters rarely occurs at this time. If it did, presumably owners would need to respond defensively by being more visible and active then.

EXPERIMENTAL SIMULATION OF INTRUDING MALES. To test responses of owners to intruders, we attached papier-mâché models of male redwings high in the cattail vegetation in the centers of redwing territories, in early mornings (0600 to 0830) during March (one presentation each to twenty-five owners; Beletsky 1992). The models were black with red shoulder epaulets, life-sized but not exact replicas of real birds. All territory owners noticed the model immediately and approached to within one meter of it, with a mean latency of 22 ± 15 s. Almost all (96%) hit the model, and they did so within 70 s of its placement (average latency to hit = 38 ± 14 s, n = 24). Detection of and aggressive response by owners to intruding floaters during the early morning, therefore, is quick and decisive.

In April during midday (1300 to 1500), we attached the model to the top of the cattail vegetation after a male left his territory. The average latency to detection during sixteen trials was 8.8 ± 9.9 min, range 1 to 32 min. Thus, floaters, if they entered territories at midday immediately after owners left, would have much more time to gather information before they were detected and evicted.

The fact that territory probing by floaters takes place when owners are present and active is consistent with both RHP and L. It is contrary to VA, however, which strongly predicts a peak of probing to collect information at midday. Territory owners very quickly approach and attack intruding floaters even in March, when females are not yet present or are not yet copulating. Therefore, the owners' behavior could function to prevent floaters from gathering information, which is consistent with RHP and VA interpretations. If floaters gain territories only under lottery rules, i.e., by detecting and filling vacancies, territory owners should have no need to confront floaters or evict them; their simple presence would be sufficient defense.

Information from Removal Experiments

We conducted several removal experiments in which territory owners were captured, held in cages for several days, and then released. Most of these removals were parts of experiments to test hypotheses of territorial dominance (detailed in chapter 8). Floaters that occupied the vacant territories were quickly trapped and banded if they did not already carry bands. After one to nine days in captivity, the original owners

TABLE 7.8. The temporal pattern of floaters filling empty marshes in March, following removal of original owners

Year	Marsh	No. of males removed	No. of days held	No. of new males on the removal marsh by end of:						
				1d	2d	3d	4d	5d	6d	8d
1986	Unit 3	18	7	7	14	15	15	15	16	
1987	Frog Lake	10	7	6	7	7	10	10	10	
1988	Lower Hays	11	7	5	9	12				
1993	Juvenile Pocket	10	9	6	6	6	7	7	7	7
1993	McMannamon Lake	6	9	0	2	2	2	3	3	3
1994	Upper Hays	10	9	2	3	4	5	5	5	5

were released. Almost all returned to their territories and fought their replacements for ownership. Depending on a number of factors (see chapter 8), the original owner either evicted his replacement and regained his territorial status, failed to evict him and rejoined the floater pool, or regained part of his territory. Replacements either kept all or part of their new holdings, or returned to floater status. These manipulations provide a wealth of information on floater tactics.

PATTERN OF FILLING OF MULTIPLE VACANCIES. All three hypotheses predict that floaters should opportunistically occupy vacancies, but the rapidity with which vacancies are found tells us something about floater behavior. Because both VA and RHP predict that floaters monitor a fairly small number of territories or marshes, they also predict a rapid discovery and filling of vacancies. Lottery strategy predicts floater movements over wide areas, with particular marshes not necessarily monitored daily. However, if the floater population is very large, vacancies are predicted to be occupied rapidly by floaters under all three hypotheses.

We conducted several experiments during March in which we removed nearly simultaneously all territorial males on marshes that had no adjacent or surrounding territory owners who could quickly annex the vacant real estate. Table 7.8 presents the chronological patterns of territory filling on these initially empty marshes. By the end of the first day, the marsh typically had less than half the number of new owners than the number of males removed. It then took several days for the number of territories to return to or approach preremoval levels. The CNWR redwing population was low in 1993 and 1994 (chapter 8), perhaps accounting for the fact that the numbers of replacements during those years never approached preremoval territory numbers (table 7.8).

These data suggest that some vacancies are immediately detected and taken by floaters, but that the replacement process is often gradual. Clearly, each marsh (or small group of marshes) does not have its own population of floaters that stay just outside defended areas, watching constantly and waiting to take vacancies or challenge weak owners. We have never observed such resident floaters and also, if they were present, they would have immediately filled all the vacancies on removal marshes. Rather, the slow replacement process suggests either that the beats are so large that it takes a floater several days to make the rounds to every marsh he monitors or that floaters do not spend much time each day prospecting. The latter interpretation is consistent with our telemetry data. A slow process of discovering vacancies suggests that floaters do not visit the same territories or marshes every day, as might be the case under VA or RHP rules. The gradual pattern of territory filling is more consistent with the lottery prediction of floaters roaming wide areas as they search for chance vacancies.

Another aspect of floater searching behavior made clear by these removals is that most floaters prospect for territories as single individuals. The ones we observed arriving and taking territories immediately after our removals did so one at a time. In a few instances, however, we arrived at removal sites shortly after dawn to find a group of males that had not been there during the early evening of the previous day, fighting among themselves and previous arrivals for space. Usually several of the new males were evicted by the end of the morning. The simultaneous appearance on the marshes of several males in these cases suggests that they arrived together.

IDENTITIES OF REPLACEMENTS. If most floaters that we banded in the core (where most trapping occurred) and close peripheral study marshes (where most removals occurred) have small beats, a large fraction of replacement males during our removal experiments should have already been banded. On the other hand, if floaters have large beats, a smaller fraction of them would be expected to have already been banded because they would have spent less time in the vicinity of our traps. During all of our removals (including those from 1983 through 1989 and 1992 through 1994), of 74 floaters that became replacements, 42 (56.8%) were unbanded males. The remaining 32 (43.2%) wore single FWS bands (10.8%; at least 6 of the 8 were born on our core marshes), subadult band combinations (7, 9.4%), or adult color-band combinations

(17, 23.0%). Of the latter, 4 (5.4%) were banded floaters who had never, to our knowledge, held territories previously; each had been an adult floater for one to five years before becoming a replacement. Thirteen (17.6%) were banded floaters who held territories in previous years, 9 of them on the same marshes on which they claimed replacement territories.

The high percentage of replacements who had been banded in past years (43.2%) strongly suggests that many floaters reside in the study area and have small beats that overlap substantially between years, which is consistent with either VA or RHP. Replacement males who had owned territories previously on the same marsh provide particularly strong support for VA. When they rejoined the floater population, they clearly remained close enough to their former holdings to detect vacancies quickly. *Of the three hypotheses, only VA predicts that a male that loses his territory has his best chance of regaining a territory at the same site*, where he has prior knowledge that reduces the value asymmetry of the territory between him and the new owner or other contenders.

REPLACEMENTS THAT WON CONTESTS WITH ORIGINAL OWNERS. Some floater replacements prevailed in their contests with original owners, permanently retaining all or part of the territory. RHP predicts that, because these males did not already hold territories at the start of the breeding season, they had low RHP and thus should hold their new territories for shorter-than-average durations. Under VA and L, any territory acquired, regardless of method, should be held for the usual duration. The distribution of number of years holding territories for 42 replacement winners was 17 males, 1 year; 9 males, 2 years; 8, 3 years; 3, 4 years; 1, 5 years; 3, 7 years; and 1, 10 years, for a mean duration of 2.6 ± 2.1 years. This mean, which is close to the population mean for our core-area males, 2.4 ± 1.8 years (n = 461), provides no support for RHP but is consistent with VA or L.

ORIGINAL OWNERS THAT LOST TO REPLACEMENTS. RHP theory says that because original owners had acquired a territory naturally, they must have had high RHP at that time. Even if their RHP declined in captivity, it should be regained after their release. Therefore, RHP predicts that these males should have a high probability of gaining another territory in the same or following year but not necessarily on the same marsh, because knowledge of a particular marsh is not necessary to gain an advantage. VA says that previous owners have advan-

TABLE 7.9. Subsequent histories of males who lost territorial contests during removal experiments conducted from 1984 through 1988, and in 1992

| | Number of males that lost territories | |
Subsequent history	Original owners	Replacements
Never detected again	15	6
Known to be a floater in a future year	3	0
Acquired another territory:		
Same year, same or nearby marsh	11	0
Same year, marsh ≥ 500 m away	1	1
Future year, same or nearby marsh	14	5
Future year, marsh ≥ 500 m away	10	1
Totals	54	13

tages only on their former territories and adjacent areas. It thus predicts that these males should have a high probability of regaining a territory only on their former territories or nearby. The lottery hypothesis predicts that floaters who previously owned territories should have no special advantages anywhere and, thus, if they regain a territory, its location should be random with respect to their former location. Most former owners, 36 of 54 (66.7%), that were forced back into the floater pool eventually established new territories (table 7.9). Twenty-five of the 36 (69.4%) obtained territories on the same marsh as their original territories or less than 500 m away, a result strongly consistent with the VA prediction.

REPLACEMENTS THAT LOST TO ORIGINAL OWNERS. RHP suggests that replacements are actually inferior males, able to get territories only because we created artificial openings. Thus, RHP predicts that those evicted by the original owners should have a low probability of acquiring other territories; if they do, it should not necessarily be at the same marsh. The VA prediction is that, because the replacement males held territories for only short periods, they still have relatively little territory knowledge and so should have a low probability of acquiring another territory. However, if they do, their new territories should be at the same marsh or nearby because they have some knowledge of the area. The lottery hypothesis suggests no special advantage or disadvantage for these males in acquiring future territories; in fact, the proportion that get new territories should be the same as the proportion of "losing" original owners that later reestablished territories. Our sample is small, but 7 of 13 evicted replacements later acquired other territories, 5 of the 7 at the same marsh or nearby (table 7.9), a result that supports the VA prediction.

HOW WINNERS REGARD LOSERS. Most subadult and adult floaters that trespass into a male's territory are quickly approached, chased, and evicted. The chase normally ends at the territory boundary, but some floaters are not tolerated anywhere within sight of the territory. Our male removals permitted us to identify these special floaters as former territory owners from the same marsh. We observed many times that banded males who had lost a territory, whether they were original owners or replacements, were not tolerated near the marsh but were chased far away by the current owners of their former territories. These floaters did not even have to trespass; the owners left their territories to chase them whenever they were spotted in the general area. Clearly, these floaters are perceived by the owners as special threats to their territory ownership and are treated more aggressively than other float-ers. That current owners treat former owners differently than they treat "stranger" floaters is predicted by both VA and RHP. The lottery hypothesis predicts that owners should ignore all floaters, regardless of their histories.

CONCLUSIONS: RELATIVE CONTRIBUTIONS
OF RHP, VA, AND L

How do male redwings in the CNWR population obtain their territories? Our observations and experiments suggest that most of them search for and acquire their territories within five kilometers of their birthplace. Most males do not gain territories during their subadult year, but during that year they apparently select the area which they will monitor and within which, if they are successful, they will probably acquire a terri-tory. Although a few subadult males do acquire territories, our evidence indicates that subadult males are much less vigorous in their attempts to get territories than older males; many probably do not occupy vacancies potentially available to them.

Most males establish their first territories when they are two years old. Survival rates of territorial males during the breeding season are very high, but 30 to 40% of males disappear between consecutive breed-ing seasons. As a result, most males probably acquire their first territo-ries during late winter, but because we have few observational data at those times, we cannot exclude the possibility that they have identified potential vacancies during the autumn and early winter. Because we never again see the majority of the males whose territories are occupied by newcomers, we believe, but cannot prove, that most males gain their territories without a contest by replacing others that die or desert. Nonetheless, about 30% of males acquire their territories by inserting between already-established owners, and they almost certainly had to engage in escalated contests to do so.

A large population of floater males is present in the study area throughout the breeding season. Most of them are subadult males, but many are adults, as indicated by our trapping records, observations, and the fact that about one-third of males on our study area were at least three years old when they first established a territory. Thus, a substantial number of adult males are excluded from breeding each year; many of them die without becoming breeders. Some of them acquire territories within breeding seasons as inserters or replacers. As floaters, adults apparently search for territories within an area less than 5 km in diameter. Even within this limited range, they could, in our study area, potentially monitor more than two hundred territories.

Our extensive observational and experimental data fail to yield an overwhelming preponderance of evidence in favor of any one of the three hypotheses to explain territorial dominance (table 7.10). This result is not surprising because the hypotheses are not mutually exclusive. All three could, on theoretical grounds, be expected to contribute to the patterns we observed.

All three hypotheses predict that males should search actively in late winter to locate vacancies because that is when the most opportunities exist to acquire a territory without fighting. Once all territories are occupied, which in our area happens by late February or early March, then a male must either challenge another male to gain a territory or wait until a vacancy is created by the death or departure of an owner.

Evidence in favor of the lottery hypothesis of territory acquisition includes the fact that males probe to detect vacancies primarily when owners are most likely to be present on their territories, and the temporal pattern of filling of multiple vacancies. Nonetheless, this evidence is weak because the resource-holding potential hypothesis predicts the same pattern of timing of probing. Contrary to the L model, which predicts no escalated contests, many males acquire territories by taking parts of occupied territories. In addition, the fact that floaters establish beats of limited size and that most of them acquire territories close to where they were previously trapped and observed is not consistent with the wide searching for vacancies predicted by L. Also, as we have argued on theoretical grounds, the L hypothesis is capable of explaining only

TABLE 7.10. Evidence for and against RHP, VA, and L hypotheses as they relate to territory acquisition in the CNWR redwing population, and degree of support for each

Tests	RHP Pro	RHP Con	VA Pro	VA Con	L Pro	L Con
When						
1. Age	0	0	0	0	0	0
2. Subadult acquisition		X				
3. Time of year						
a. General	0	0	0	0	0	0
b. Late-season acquisitions				X		
Where						
1. Natal dispersal			XX			
2. Subadult area			XX			
How						
1. Birth year	0	0	0	0	0	0
2. Birthdate		XX				
3. Method of establishment (insert vs. replace)	XXX		X			
4. Floater behavior						
a. Trapping beats	X			X		X
b. Telemetry beats	X		X			XX
c. Timing of probing	XX			XXX	XX	
d. Filling of multiple vacancies				X		
e. Identities of replacements	X		XXX			XX
f. Behavior of losers in removals			XXX			

Note: X = weak; XX = moderate; XXX = strong; 0 = theory-independent

initial acquisition and not long-term holding of a territory. Therefore, we conclude that of the three hypotheses we tested, lottery explains the least about initial territory acquisition in our redwing population.

The resource-holding potential hypothesis predicts that males should monitor a relatively small number of territories because they must acquire detailed information about the RHP of owners relative to their own. They should challenge when they perceive that the RHP of an owner has dropped so that it is lower than their own, which may be a time-consuming assessment. Our data offer some support for the RHP hypothesis because beats of floaters are small and because nearly one-third of males on our study area acquired their territories by inserting between returning territory owners. RHP is also supported by the fact that the probing behavior of floaters appears to be directed at learning about owners and not about their territories. Floaters concentrate their probing at times when territory owners are present and they do not take advantage of temporary absences of owners to learn about features of the territories.

The value asymmetry hypothesis predicts that floater males should concentrate their monitoring in a limited area within which they attempt to learn as much as possible about the territories, thereby raising the value of the areas to themselves. Under a pure VA model, when a floater has acquired enough information to equalize the value of the territory to him and its owner, he should initiate a challenge. Some information about territories can be acquired by observing them from adjacent areas, but other information can be acquired only by examining the territory from within. Therefore, VA predicts that floater males should take advantage of the absences of territory owners to occupy their areas in order to acquire information, retreating when the owners return.

The fact that floaters do not take advantage of opportunities to acquire information about territories when the owners are absent constitutes strong evidence against VA. On the other hand, support for VA is provided by the strong fidelity of males to their natal areas and to the area in which they establish their subadult beats. VA is also supported by the fact that all losers during removal experiments, whether they were original or replacement owners, if they obtain a territory in future years, usually regain their former territories or ones nearby.

We interpret the results of our observations and experiments as follows. Early in spring adult males who have not previously held a territory search all or most marshes in the area in which they established their previous year's beat. They occupy quickly any vacancy they detect and rapidly become dominant over most floaters (see chapter 8). The remaining floaters confine their activities to small areas within which they observe reproductive activities on the territories and monitor the vigor of owners. They also look for contested territory boundaries and areas with unstable ownership because they may be of high value to a male if he can insert there (Beletsky 1992). Males do enough probing to assess their own RHP so that they can determine when a vigorous challenge of an owner is likely to be profitable. We suspect that floaters usually wait for a significant decline in the RHP of an owner before challenging because contests are likely to escalate and injuries to one or both contestants are likely.

We believe that males concentrate their probing when owners are present because, even though valuable information can be acquired during short occupancy times, it is unlikely that a floater can acquire enough information about a territory to eliminate the value asymmetry in favor of the owner. Once breeding has begun and the owner has sired offspring, the territory is certain to have much greater value to its owner than to any floater no matter how much time the floater spends on the territory, because floaters do not sire offspring. However, if the VA is reduced by general information gained from observing from outside the territory, a floater may be motivated to challenge an owner whose RHP is closer to his own than he would if the territory had little value to him. Therefore, we believe that the information floaters gather about territories is valuable, both in determining when a challenge is likely to be successful and in knowing what to do if occupancy is achieved. In addition, a floater contesting for a territory against a male whose RHP has declined must contend not only with the owner but also with neighbors and other floaters who may attempt to take over the same territory. A floater that has acquired much information about a territory should be dominant over floaters with less information. Therefore, the information gathered by observing a territory may function primarily to enhance the dominance status of a male within the group of floaters whose beats include the local area. We suggest that floaters often travel solitarily because of the advantage of detecting a vacancy alone and establishing dominance on it before other floaters are aware of the vacancy.

Because of the great interannual variation in marsh conditions, gaining information about territories late in the breeding season is probably of insufficient value to favor much investment of time. The most useful information must be gathered during the breeding season and integrated with information about the status of the owner.

Thus, our data provide strong support for both RHP and VA hypotheses because floaters gather and use information about both territories and their owners. An alternative hypothesis is that males differ in their strategies, some being pure RHP tacticians, others pure VA tacticians. Although we have no direct data with which to test this hypothesis, we regard it as unlikely for several reasons. First, RHP is not a fixed, genetically determined attribute. The RHP of individuals, both owners and floaters, varies sufficiently that a pure strategy is unlikely to be as successful as a conditional strategy. In one year a floater may have high RHP relative to owners, whereas the same floater might have a low RHP relative to owners in another year or even later within the same year. Therefore, although RHP clearly influences territory-acquisition behavior of male redwings in the CNWR population, males also confine their monitoring activities to small areas in ways that indicate that information about territories and marshes is valuable to them. Nonetheless, males of high RHP may well employ an RHP-dominant mode of searching, whereas males of low RHP may employ a VA-dominant mode.

SUBADULT TERRITORY OWNERS. Although subadult males usually do not establish territories at CNWR, a few did so on our strongly contested core marshes. If RHP is a primary determinant of territory ownership, then these few subadults should have been individuals of extremely high RHP, demonstrable through superior breeding success or ability to hold territories for long periods. These predictions were not upheld, suggesting that RHP is not a major contributor to these males' precocious territorial abilities, that individual RHPs fluctuate, or that there is a high survival cost to becoming territorial at one year of age. The few subadults that manage to enter the breeding population probably differ from their peers in some way, but the differences that allow them to challenge successfully and gain territorial footholds may be transient. Hormone levels are unlikely to be the cause because our research suggests that higher-than-normal circulating androgen levels do not affect dominance relationships between territorial and nonterritorial redwings (Beletsky et al. 1990). However, twelve of the fifteen territorial subadults we measured had an average body mass, 74 ± 4 g, equivalent to that of adult males during the early part of the breeding season (Beletsky and Orians 1987a; Beletsky 1996) and 3 g heavier than average for subadults. The weight of these males may have been an important influence on their abilities to gain territories.

Defending a territory as a subadult against adult challengers, without some of the experience and size/mass of adults, could stress these males and result in low survival and RS. For example, the orange epaulet feathers of subadults, which contrast with the bright red of adults, may have a role in reducing aggression by adult males and could aid subadults during insertions. However, experiments have indicated that the bright red feathers of adults are important signals for repelling other males from territories (Smith 1972; Røskaft and Rohwer 1987), and, thus, the orange-epauleted subadults could have high rates of attacks from other males once they have gained territories.

SUBADULT RECONNAISSANCE OF BREEDING SITES. Recent studies suggest that juvenile migratory songbirds explore a finite area around their birth sites prior to their first migration and that their early wanderings determine the site to which they will return in spring and within which they will breed (Van Balen 1979; Morton et al. 1991). Although we are not sure whether CNWR subadult male redwings migrate, the presumption that most males obtain territories within 4 to 5 km of their birth sites and the observation that many subadult males are present during the breeding season within 2 to 3 km of their eventual territories suggest that they gather information within a limited range of their birth sites and return there as subadults and each breeding season thereafter. The distances involved in juvenile reconnaissance in other species are on the same order as the ones we identified for redwings, e.g., Pied Flycatcher juveniles explored around their birth sites areas within a 5 km radius (Van Balen 1979).

REDWINGS IN OTHER REGIONS. Investigators elsewhere have reached different conclusions about the behavior of floaters and the relative importance of RHP, VA, and L in territory acquisition by redwings. Shutler and Weatherhead (1994) concluded that redwings at their study site in Ontario acquired their territories using a lottery strategy in which they looked for vacancies over large areas. They reached this conclusion because they failed to resight the majority of floaters they banded and because some radio-tagged floaters (that had become short-term replacement owners) moved from their study area. The highly migratory redwings in that population may behave differently than CNWR redwings, but the apparent differences could also be explained if Shutler and Weatherhead included in their analysis many individuals that were trapped and banded while migrating to breeding grounds farther to the north. In addition, because Shutler and Weatherhead did not search for banded males in areas peripheral to their study areas, many of their males could have established territories within a few kilometers of where they were trapped and marked.

Eight

How to Continue as a
Breeder: Territorial Dominance
and Movements

INTRODUCTION AND PREDICTIONS

INTRODUCTION

To achieve reproductive success, male redwings not only must acquire territories, they must also maintain them long enough to attract and mate with females. If they survive, most males return to the same territory they held the previous breeding season, but some males change territories between seasons and a few change within a season. Males without territories rarely, if ever, sire offspring, and LRS, on average, rises linearly with number of years holding a territory. In this chapter we adapt models of animal contest behavior to territorial dominance and site fidelity, the main factors that influence ownership for extended periods. We test the models chiefly with information from our territory owner removal experiments and from long-term demographic data on territory ownership.

In this chapter we seek to explain two phenomena. One is territorial, or "site," dominance—that territory owners nearly always defeat conspecific males that challenge them for their territories. Because of the small size of most redwing territories, the low vegetation characteristic of most of them, and the fact that owners and floaters often remain at the top of vegetation or in exposed perches, there is little that is covert about floaters' trespassing in territories. Owners usually are immediately aware of an intrusion, and the intruders know they know. Generally challengers quickly leave territories when confronted and threatened by owners. If a floater intrudes into an occupied territory and does not depart immediately when approached by the owner, we define the encounter as a "challenge." A floater that stands his ground but departs after obvious threats—song spread and bill-up displays—constitutes a weak challenge. A trespasser failing to leave a territory despite being threatened and chased by an owner constitutes a moderate challenge. A strong challenge is one that escalates to physical combat. Floaters rarely strongly challenge owners, a phenomenon called "challenger inhibition." Therefore, territory owners rarely have to fight; when fights do occur, they are usually won by owners.

Territorial dominance could arise because territory owners are superior fighters or are more motivated to escalate contests and to fight, or because floaters are inferior or less motivated to fight, or because of a combination of these. Both RHP and VA hypotheses potentially could explain territorial dominance. The lottery hypothesis is inapplicable because its main prediction is that floaters should never challenge owners, but should simply look for and occupy vacancies. But floaters often trespass on territories and challenge owners, even if most challenges are weak or moderate. Thus, even if male redwings acquired initial territories under lottery rules, other rules must govern territorial dominance and floater inhibition.

We also wish to explain why owners occasionally abandon current territories and move to other sites. In our population, this occurs primarily between breeding seasons (Beletsky and Orians 1987a). One hypothesis to explain territory movements suggests that individuals disperse between breeding attempts in order to find better mates or better territories, because of social constraints, or because of genetic predispositions (Greenwood and Harvey 1982; Dobson and Jones 1985; Payne and Payne 1993). Male redwings are unlikely to move to find better mates. They are assured of multiple mates by remaining where they are; moving to find a better mate is more likely to benefit a female than a male. We know of no social constraints (other than direct competition with conspecifics) that compel a male to leave his territory voluntarily. We have no way to evaluate possible genetic propensities for territorial movements, but, given the high site fidelity of most males (Beletsky and Orians 1987a), we suspect they are weak. Thus, the most likely reason redwings move is to improve the quality of their territories and to increase the rate at which they accrue RS. They may be able to improve their RS by moving if they initially obtained a poor territory, if their territory declined in quality, or if clearly superior territories are nearby. RHP, VA, or L considerations may govern territorial movements.

GENERAL PREDICTIONS

Removal Experiments and Territorial Dominance

Several methods exist to test RHP and VA contributions to territorial dominance, among which are comparing the physical or behavioral attributes of owners versus floaters, and manipulating individuals' RHP levels or knowledge levels. The experimental method we chose was

territory owner removal. Removal experiments have a long history
in ornithology for exploring how territoriality influences breeding
density (Orians 1961; Watson 1967; Harris 1970; Krebs 1971;
Charles 1972; Knapton and Krebs 1974; Holcomb 1974; Hurly and
Robertson 1985), for elucidating sources of site dominance (Rohwer
1982; Krebs 1982), and for determining dominance or breeding hierar-
chies (Hannon et al. 1985; Smith 1987). In our experiments, we
captured territorial males on their territories, held them in cages for
varying periods, and then released them to challenge for ownership
the floaters who replaced them on their territories. Essentially, we
orchestrated fights, or escalated contests, between original and replacement owners, and we used patterns of contest outcomes to test the
sources of territorial dominance.

Removal experiments are an effective method for redwings because
floaters usually rapidly replace removed owners during the breeding
season. Indeed, there are enough adult floaters that replacement males
can be sequentially removed from the same area many times—up to
nine or more—and still be replaced by more floaters (Laux 1970;
Shutler and Weatherhead 1991b).

Removal experiments allow us to discriminate between RHP and
VA hypotheses, in the following manner. If RHP determines which
males get territories and which do not, then brief removal of owners
should not alter the dominance relationships. Therefore, when original
owners are released, they should be able to evict their replacements
and recover their territories and site dominance. But if dominance
relationships between original and replacement owners (recently
floaters) reverse over brief periods during which RHP should be
roughly constant, VA would be supported—changes over time in the
valuing of the territories by the original owners and/or replacements.
During our experiments we varied the amount of time owners were
held captive off their territories and the duration replacements owned
the territories. Because we controlled when the original owners were
released, we could observe the resulting strong territorial contests,
which are rarely witnessed under nonexperimental conditions. Nonetheless, there are two major drawbacks to these experiments. Males
in captivity sometimes lose weight, which could alter their RHP and
make results difficult to interpret. Also, removals create artificial
situations in which two individuals "believe" they own the same
territory, which may happen naturally only rarely. Therefore, removal results must be interpreted cautiously.

Morphological and Behavioral Correlates of Dominance

Another method of testing for an RHP contribution to territorial dominance is to compare the morphology and/or behavior of owners and floaters. The best way to accomplish this is to assess the RHP of a group of territory owners by measuring their aggression levels, their willingness to fight other males, or their morphology, then remove these males and perform identical assessments on the floaters that replace them. Such removals permit the researcher to control for the effects of territory quality. The RHP prediction is that the original owners' "measurements" should significantly exceed those of the floaters. If the prediction is correct, the presumption would be that the owners' superior attributes determined their territorial dominance. In these comparisons, VA has sometimes been accepted as the default alternative to RHP. We did not perform such experiments, but we will briefly summarize the experiments of other investigators. Also, we will present information on the body mass of owners versus floaters in our study area, which bears on RHP and on the behavior of owners and floaters.

Territory Fidelity and Movements

In general, strong site fidelity is predicted under RHP, VA, and L hypotheses. A male that maintains the same territory enjoys all the benefits of familiarity with the site and its inhabitants—knowledge of food resources, predator habits, hiding places, and mates and neighboring males—and incurs none of the costs and risks of moving. The costs of moving are expenditures of time and energy associated with searching for and assessing new territories and familiarization with them following acquisition. The main risk is that an attempted takeover at a new site could fail, by which time the male has lost his original territory. Special circumstances, such as dramatic deterioration of marsh vegetation between years, may favor abandonment even when knowledge of other areas is weak, but the risks remain high.

When males accept the risks and move voluntarily, their behavior should be governed by the information/distance hypothesis (chapter 6), which predicts that moves should be only to nearby territories where males have good familiarity with real estate, harem sizes, and/or information about other males, and that the frequency of such movements should decline with increasing distance from the males' original territories.

RHP, VA, and L hypotheses make similar predictions about males that voluntarily switch to new territories adjacent or nearly adjacent to their old ones. When vacancies occur on nearby territories that are significantly better than their own, males should quickly take the opportunity to move and assume ownership of the new site. The risk in such movements of losing territorial status is very low under any of the three hypotheses. A male who held his initial territory because of a superior RHP level will have the same relative advantage over other males on the new site. A male that held his initial territory because of his superior knowledge of the area (VA) will also likely have good familiarity with adjacent sites. Thus, value asymmetries between the mover and floaters on a new, adjacent territory should be in the mover's favor. Under lottery rules, simple occupancy of the new, adjacent site is decisive for holding it.

The three hypotheses, however, make different predictions concerning moves to other-than-nearby sites. The lottery hypothesis predicts that such moves should be very rare because, if chance is the sole route to territory ownership, then males, once established, should not voluntarily relinquish their holdings and try to move to other areas where occupancy statuses of territories are not known (unless their territories have seriously declined in quality). They would have no special advantage at a new site for securing a subsequent territory, and if they did not find a ready vacancy, they would again become floaters. In general, VA predicts shorter-distance moves than RHP. Males moving under VA rules should shift only to adjacent or nearby sites about which they already possess levels of information that rival the information they have on their own territory. Movements according to RHP rules could be anywhere within range of a male's regular daily activities where he has knowledge of another territory's relative superiority to his own and where he detects a weakened territory owner.

Some territory movements are undoubtedly involuntary ones by males that have been displaced from their territories but have been able to establish others. The rules governing the searching for new territories by these males would be the same as those for any floater trying to gain a territory.

We should be able to detect voluntary movements that are made to increase territory quality by comparing pre- and postmove RS. For example, the territories males switch to in year $x + 1$ should have, on average, fledged more young in year x (the year the males presumably compared breeding success on the territories) than did the males' original territories. Also, males that change territories should, on average, improve their RS from year x, before the move, to year $x+1$, after the move.

The following summarizes our predictions about site fidelity and territory movements in the population.

1. Between-year territory fidelity should be high.

2. Voluntary movements should occur only over short distances; long-distance moves should be rare and involuntary, the result of forced eviction by other males or of habitat deterioration.

3. Movements to adjacent territories can be explained by RHP, VA, or L hypotheses. Movements over short to intermediate distances could occur under RHP rules, but only short-distance moves are predicted under VA.

4. Short-distance moves should lead to improved RS; long-distance moves, because they are made involuntarily to sites about which males are relatively ignorant, should not lead to improved RS.

Territory Fidelity following Interactions with Yellow-headed Blackbirds

Red-winged and Yellow-headed Blackbirds are interspecifically territorial. Yellowheads colonized some of our core marshes during the study, although their numbers fluctuated widely over a period of only five years (Beletsky and Orians 1994). The migratory male yellowheads arrive in the study area more than a month after male redwings have already begun occupying their breeding territories. Some redwings are evicted by the larger yellowheads or leave, but some are only partially displaced, being squeezed into smaller, poorer areas near shore. Because yellowheads consistently occupied the same sites in successive years (Beletsky and Orians 1994) we can evaluate the site-fidelity decisions that redwings make in response to having their territories occupied by the yellowheads. Displaced redwings may know that yellowheads will return again the following year; thus, they may decide whether to move or to reoccupy the same territories.

Because moving is risky, RHP, VA, and L hypotheses predict that redwings who are only partially displaced by yellowheads should stay, even if each year they undergo the same reduction in territory size as a result of yellowhead invasion. When males are evicted by yellowheads, VA predicts that if they get territories again the next year, they will be the same ones or nearby on the same marsh; RHP predicts longer-distance moves, on average; and L predicts that evicted males are no more likely to obtain a new territory at the same marsh than they are anywhere else.

REMOVAL EXPERIMENTS AND
TERRITORIAL DOMINANCE

CNWR REMOVALS, 1983–88

In our initial series of removal experiments, conducted each spring from 1983 through 1988, we held original owners off their territories for one to seven days, released them to challenge their floater replacements for ownership, and monitored contest outcomes. If territorial dominance was due primarily to RHP differences, then the prediction was that original owners should always be able to recover their territories from replacements. Even if RHP declined slightly in captivity, upon release the males should quickly regain condition and then evict their lower-RHP replacements. If dominance was due primarily to VA, the probability that original owners recaptured territories should decline with time in captivity, because over time territories would gain in value to replacements, who would then be increasingly likely to escalate contests and win (Beletsky and Orians 1989a).

METHODS. We conducted removals on marshes outside the core area, where territory owners were banded but where we did not regularly monitor RS. Removals in 1983 through 1985 were conducted in March through early May. In these experiments (we consider each year's removals to be one experiment) we removed only one or two males at a time with seed-baited traps. As a result, neighboring territory owners annexed some of the vacancies we created before floaters could discover and occupy them. Experiments in 1986, 1987, and 1988 were conducted in March, before females arrived in the study area or, if present, before they nested. Thus, the removed males had no current reproductive investments to motivate them to recover their territories. In these experiments we removed all or most owners on a single marsh nearly simultaneously, usually within a three-hour morning period, thereby creating a large expanse of vacant real estate. Males that were not captured within a few hours with seed traps were caught in a decoy trap (Smith 1976). Because there were no remaining neighbors who could rapidly annex vacancies, almost all territories were claimed by new replacements, sometimes within 30 min of a removal, and often by dawn of the following day. Original owners either wore color bands before they were removed or were given bands when they were captured; replacements that did not already have bands were captured in seed traps and banded prior to the releases of original owners.

Males were held outdoors in cages (66 cm × 73 cm × 78 cm) within

800 m but out of sight of their home marshes. They were given water, sunflower seeds, cracked corn, and cereal ad libitum and mealworms each morning. Each male was weighed at the time of capture and at release. All males were released at their cages, except for a few in 1984 and 1985, who were released on or near their territories (see Beletsky and Orians 1987b).

RESULTS. When territory owners were held 1 or 2 d, they usually returned to their territories within 15 min of release. When they were held 6 to 7 d, it often took them from several hours to until dawn of the day following their release to return. But almost all returned eventually and fought their replacements. Some fights were brief, others were long, drawn-out contests, sometimes continuing intermittently for days, often with apparent dominance shifting several times (for details, see Beletsky and Orians 1987b).

During the 1983, 1984, and 1985 breeding seasons we held males off their territories for only 1 or 2 d to minimize weight and condition loss while in captivity. Although the birds were fed ad libitum, some still lost weight. In these experiments, 91% of 55 original males recovered their territories from floater replacements or from neighbors that annexed the vacant territories (table 8.1). This result was difficult to interpret because it is predicted by both RHP and VA. The RHP explanation is that the original owners had higher RHP than the replacements; the VA explanation is that because replacements had only 1 or 2 d of ownership, they did not yet value the territory sufficiently to defend it against strong challengers.

During the next two years we performed longer-term removals and obtained a different result. In 1986 we removed 18 males from a marsh, held them 7 d, and then released them to battle their 6-d to 7-d replacements. Only 11% (2 of 18) recovered their territories. The others were observed on and near the marsh on many occasions, challenging their replacements. They tried to regain their territories, sometimes repeatedly, but they could not. We replicated the experiment in 1987, removing 10 males and holding them 6 to 7 d. Seven of the 10 were replaced for 6 to 7 d, and only 28% of these (2 of 7) evicted their replacements and regained their territories. Three of the original 10 confronted replacements who had occupied their territories only 3 d because they did not take over the territories until 4 d after we removed males. Two of these males (67%) were able to recover their territories. Two males that we removed for 4 d, and whose replacements held the territories for 4 d, also recovered their territories (table 8.1).

TABLE 8.1. Results of territorial male removal experiments, 1983 through 1994

Year	Marsh	Date of removals	No. of males removed	Time held	X̄ weight loss in captivity (g)	(% of body weight)	n	Time replacements on territory at release	No. (%) of males that recovered territories
1983–85	varied[a]	varied[a]	55	7–49 h	1.0 ± 1.5	1.4 ± 1.9	43	3–48 h	50 (91)
1986	Unit 3	26 March	18	7 d	5.2 ± 2.5	6.9 ± 3.2	18	6–7 d	2 (11)
1987	Frog Lake	21 March	9	7 d	3.9 ± 1.5	5.3 ± 2.0	9	6 = 7 d 3 = 3 d	1 (17) 2 (67)
			1	6 d	2.0	2.9	1	6 d, 2 d[b]	1 (100)
			2	4 d	1.0 ± 1.4	1.3 ± 1.8	2	4 d	2 (100)
1988	Lower Hays Creek	19 March	8	7 d	3.7 ± 2.1	4.9 ± 2.7	11	1 = 1 d 7 = 2 d	8 (73)
			3	6 d				2 = 1 d 1 = 2 d	
1993	Juvenile Pocket	14 March	10	9 d	1.4 ± 1.2	1.9 ± 1.6	10	5 = 9 d 1 = 7 d 1 = 5 d	8 (80)
1993	McMannamon Lake	19 March	6	9 d	2.2 ± 1.5	3.0 ± 2.0	6	2 = 8 d 1 = 4 d	5 (83)
1994	Upper Hays Creek	18 March	10	9 d	2.1 ± 1.2	2.8 ± 1.6	10	1 = 9 d 2 = 8 d 1 = 7 d 1 = 6 d	9 (90)

[a]See Beletsky and Orians 1987b.
[b]Two males replaced this original owner, one inserting on the territory four days after the other.

Thus, males held in captivity 1 to 4 d generally recovered their territories, but males held 6 to 7 d did not. This pattern is most consistent with predictions of the VA hypothesis, because under RHP the original owners should always triumph. VA, on the other hand, predicts that who wins depends on how both contestants value the territory, and that the balance can shift. In a week a new owner could learn enough about a territory and its resources to increase its value sufficiently that he would be willing to engage in escalated contests (see chapter 6 for an explanation of how we expect learning about new territories to proceed).

However, these results do not entirely rule out RHP because a week in the cages could have reduced the RHP of males for some time. The clue to resolving the problem was provided by the 3 males removed for 7 d that confronted replacements who had occupied their territories for only 3 d. Two of these 3 males recovered their territories, as opposed to others held 6 to 7 d, who usually did not. *The difference was how long the replacements owned the territories, not how long the former owners had been held in captivity.* Therefore, we designed a double-removal experiment to eliminate the usual strong correlation between the length of time we held males and the length of time replacements held their territories. In 1988 we removed 11 males on another marsh and held them for 7 d. Replacements quickly took the vacant territories. Five days after the removals, we trapped and held the first set of replacements. A second set of replacements quickly took the territories. Thus, when we released the original males 2 d later, although they had been off their territories for 7 d, they faced replacements who had owned their territories for only 1 or 2 d.

We knew from our first removals that original owners typically evict replacement males that own the territories for only 1 or 2 d. Thus, in the double removal, if the original owners could not evict the replacements, who were present for only 1 or 2 d, this would suggest that the original males could not evict 7-d replacements or the double-removal 1- to 2-d replacements because they had lost condition (RHP) during the week of captivity. But if the original owners did recover their territories, it would suggest that the change occurring was not a reduction in the RHP of the original owners, but a change in the replacements. After 1 to 2 d of ownership they did not yet value the territory sufficiently to defend it against the persistent previous owner, but after 6 to 7 d they did. The result (table 8.1) was that 8 of 11 original owners (73%) recovered their territories, which supported the VA hypothesis. This result, together with the result of our previous removals, constitutes some of the best evidence available for birds that value asymmetries contribute to territorial dominance.

OTHER REMOVALS

Other researchers have also used removal experiments on redwings to test hypotheses of territorial dominance. Shutler and Weatherhead (1991b) removed territory owners and placed them in the same aviaries with the first, second, third, and subsequent replacement males from the same territories. If RHP determined territorial dominance, the original owners should have been able to dominate their replacements in the aviary setting. But in fights and supplanting each other at food trays, original owners were no more likely to dominate replacements than vice versa. Therefore, attributes that determine dominance in nonterritorial aggressive interactions did not explain which males owned territories. Shutler and Weatherhead rejected RHP as an explanation for territorial dominance and accepted VA as a default alternative.

MORPHOLOGICAL, BEHAVIORAL, AND PHYSIOLOGICAL CORRELATES
OF DOMINANCE

Several investigators have tested the role of RHP in redwing site dominance by examining its expected morphological and behavioral correlates. Rohwer (1982), 50 km from our study site, scored territorial redwings for fighting ability by the intensity of their attacks on a stuffed, mounted conspecific placed inside their territories. He then shot the owners and quickly scored the replacements in the same manner. The original owners, on average, attacked faster, approached closer, and caused more damage to the mount than the replacement males, supporting the RHP hypothesis. Rohwer's work is the only field study of redwings to support RHP as the explanation of territorial dominance. However, he found that some replacements scored higher in attacking the mount than the males they replaced. Also, our removal results, which showed that males do not exhibit complete territorial dominance until they have owned territories for more than 4 d, suggest that Rohwer's replacement males, regardless of their RHP, might not have vigorously attacked a mount during their first few days of occupancy because full site dominance had not yet been achieved. Also, because some banded replacements during our removals are actually former territory owners (see chapter 7), some of Rohwer's also may have been former owners. Males with previous territorial history, especially if at the same marsh, might be expected to respond more aggressively to a quick challenge to their new ownership than would a territorially naive floater.

In Ontario, Eckert and Weatherhead (1987b) compared the morphology of owners and their replacements during removal experiments. In that study, replacement males did not differ significantly from the original owners in body size or epaulet size. Eckert and Weatherhead concluded that morphological factors that may be associated with competitive ability (RHP) do not determine which males own territories. Shutler and Weatherhead (1991b) examined both morphological and behavioral attributes of owners versus floaters, also in Ontario. They found no significant differences between removed territory owners and their replacements in length of the red and yellow portions of the epaulet, wing length, tarsus length, bill length, bill depth, or body mass. Thus, RHP was rejected in both of these studies as an explanation of territorial dominance.

We compared the body mass of floaters and owners during the breeding season. All color-banded adult males not known to hold territories were considered to be floaters. Because in a pure RHP system, mass and size might determine which males own territories, we predicted that owners would be significantly heavier than floaters if RHP were operating. However, owners' masses may decline seasonally because the demands of territory defense and mate guarding compete with foraging time (Searcy 1979b). Floaters, because they occupy undefended uplands that during spring become increasingly rich in food, should not decrease in mass and might actually increase. If RHP determines outcomes of territorial contests, floaters might eventually be able to dominate owners whose RHP declines during the spring.

The actual body mass changes of owners and floaters differed from our expectations (fig. 8.1). Territory owners began the breeding season, in March (Julian dates 60 to 90), slightly heavier on average than floaters. Owners lost mass steadily throughout the breeding season, but floaters maintained about the same mass during March. Masses of owners and floaters converged and declined as nesting began, at the beginning of April, and continued declining at the same rate, on average, throughout April (days 91 to 120). During May to early June (days 121 to 160), masses of both owners and floaters continued to fall, that of owners at a faster rate (fig. 8.1). Owners and floaters lost, on average, 0.03 grams per day. Using only one randomly selected mass measurement per male per year, multiple regression with mass as the dependent variable revealed significant effects of both male status (owner vs. floater; $r = 3.32$, $t = 3.40$, $P = 0.0007$) and date ($r = -0.03$, $t = -4.83$, $P < 0.0001$). The interaction term of status X date was also significant ($r = -0.03$, $t = -3.10$, $P = 0.002$), indicating a significant change in the relative masses of owners and floaters as the season progressed. We ran the regression ten times, each run using a randomly

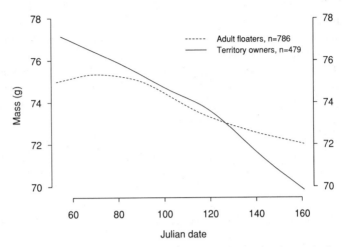

Fig. 8.1. Mean masses of adult male floaters and territory owners during the breeding season, 1985 through 1992 pooled. Individuals were included only once per year. Randomly drawn mass values were used for those individuals weighed more than once (see text). Cubic spline function (Wahba 1990) fitted to data. Julian dates: March, 60 to 90; April, 91 to 120; May, 121 to 151; June, 152+.

drawn mass for males that were weighed more than once per year; P-values, although they fluctuated between runs, were always significant, and regression coefficients varied very little between runs.

Although owners were slightly heavier than floaters in March and slightly lighter in May, the mean differences of 1 to 2 g probably were insufficient to determine dominance. We can only speculate as to why floaters decrease in mass during the breeding season. One explanation is that they spend increasing portions of their time *trying* to gain territories, with the result that their masses decrease, but challenges are not frequent enough to support that hypothesis. More likely, both owners and floaters maintain large energy reserves during winter and "slim down" during spring because the optimal winter mass is higher than the best mass for spring and summer. Evidence for this is provided by the fact that floaters maintained high mass in March, which usually is a cold month at CNWR, with overnight temperatures often below 0°C; but owners, who in March spend increasing amounts of time maintaining their territories, declined in mass (fig. 8.1).

A physiological attribute that might influence RHP is circulating testosterone levels. The sex steroid testosterone (T) influences aggressive behavior and social dominance in reproductive contexts. Circulating T levels in male songbirds are generally high during periods of breeding seasons when male-male aggressive interactions—such as those during territory establishment—are frequent (Wingfield et al. 1990). If high circulating T levels affect the abilities of males to engage in escalated, aggressive contests, then higher T levels should be advantageous to males seeking and maintaining territories.

Circulating T levels of free-ranging male redwings at CNWR during the 1987 breeding season were significantly higher in territory owners than in floaters during March and May, and there was a trend for higher T levels for territory owners in April (Beletsky et al. 1989). There are two possible explanations for the difference. One is an RHP explanation that only floaters with higher T levels are able to acquire and hold territories, whereas floaters with low T levels cannot. The other is that all floaters initially have relatively low circulating T levels, which rise only if they acquire territories, either in response to the agonistic interactions involved with territory ownership or simply as a physiological consequence of owning a territory.

To test the hypothesis that high T allows floaters to acquire territories via elevated aggression and strength of challenges, we caught twelve resident adult floaters at our SH trap early during the 1988 breeding season and implanted them with exogenous T. We confirmed that this procedure significantly raised circulating T levels by catching some of the floaters during the two weeks following the implants and taking blood samples for later analysis. Despite their high T levels, which were as high or higher, on average, than those of owners, only one of twelve implanted floaters obtained a territory. Because this rate of acquisition of territories was not above the natural, "background" rate for floaters, we concluded that high circulating T was not a physiological component of RHP that strongly influenced territory acquisition (Beletsky et al. 1990). If it were, floaters would be expected to manufacture more of the hormone, a trivial energetic cost, unless other costs of maintaining high T levels override the advantage of high circulating T. On the other hand, pharmacologically reducing the action of T in territory owners did impair their abilities to hold their territories (Beletsky et al. 1990), suggesting that normal circulating T levels are necessary for the expression of complete territorial dominance.

CNWR REMOVALS DURING 1993 AND 1994

In mid-March 1993 we initiated experiments on our core marshes, where we knew the complete territorial and reproductive histories of the males, in order to gain greater insight into the behavior of removed males than we had been able to obtain by removing peripheral-marsh males. We removed all the territory owners from Juvenile Pocket (JP) and McMannamon Lake (Mac) and held them long enough that, based on our earlier experiments, they should lose their territories to replacements. We hoped to produce a cohort of previously territorial, local floaters whose activities we could follow in detail to determine whether and how they acquired subsequent territories. Because we knew from our previous experiments (table 8.1) that males held off their territories for 7 d are usually unable to recover them, we held the 10 JP and 6 Mac males 9 d, expecting them to lose their territories to replacements. If they operated under VA rules, which our previous removal results suggested would be the case, we predicted that (1) they should remain in the local area as floaters, continuing to challenge for their territories or for others on the same marsh; (2) the following year they should regain their own territories or ones nearby, provided that they survive and their replacements die or leave.

Both of these predictions derive from the general VA prediction that, if these males were ever to regain teritorial status, their best chance was on their former territory or marsh—the area about which they possessed the best, most up-to-date information. We also predicted that, because JP and Mac were relatively high-quality breeding areas, (3) territory owners from lower-quality sites would abandon their territories and become replacements on the removal marshes. This kind of territory switch is predicted by RHP, VA, and L hypotheses because when opportunities occur to "trade up" territory quality with little or no risk, males should move quickly (see "Territory Fidelity and Movements" above).

The 1993 removals produced surprising results, which prevented us from testing predictions 1 and 2. In 1993 there were fewer male territories on all marshes in the study area during early March than in any recent previous year, and the overall adult male population in the study area was very low. There were 17 males on JP at the start of, and 15 at the termination of, the 1992 season, but only 10 males in 1993. On Mac, there were 13 territories in 1992, but only 7 in 1993 (see table 2.2 for the pattern of declining territory numbers in the core area that started in 1990).

Surprisingly, although we removed all males on each marsh within a few hours, replacement males settled slowly, and, contrary to our earlier results, the number of new owners never equaled or closely approached the number of originals (table 7.8). On JP, where we removed 10 males, only 6 had been replaced at the end of the removal day, and only 7 males owned territories there by the time we released the original owners 9 d later. At the end of the removal day on Mac, where we trapped 6 of the 7 owners, there were no replacements, an unprecedented result. The next day 2 new males had established territories, but when we released the original owners, after 9 d, there were only 4 males with territories on the lake—3 replacements and the original owner we had been unable to catch.

Another surprise was the identities of replacements. Most of them had been color-banded in previous years (only 1 replacement on JP and 1 on Mac were unbanded). Two were long-term floaters. A few were males who currently held territories on other, nearby, but generally poorer-quality marshes who moved quickly to the removal sites as soon as we provided vacancies. Some were males who had owned territories in the past on JP or Mac. On JP, 3 of 7 replacements had previously held territories there. That they were floaters in 1993 and not on their previous territories suggests that their physical abilities to hold territories (RHP) had decreased. However, under the condition we created—the absence of all current owners—and in a time of reduced competition from other floaters, these previous owners were able to recover their past holdings. One replacement on JP abandoned a low-quality territory located 400 m away. On Mac, the 3 replacements included 1 unbanded male, 1 banded at the SH trap a few days prior to the removals, and 1 who moved from a roadside ditch territory 500 m away.

Finally, in contrast to all of our previous findings, many original owners that were held for 9 d regained their territories. On JP, 7 of 10 did so (4 within 24 h, 3 more within a week), and another obtained a territory on another marsh. One regained his territory after a month but held it only three weeks, and 1 was not observed again after being spotted daily at JP during the first few days after he was released. On Mac, 5 of the 6 males regained their territories, all within 3 to 4 d of their release.

We replicated our 9-d removal experiments in 1994 on Upper Hays Creek (Hays). The section of Hays from which we removed males had 14 territories in 1992, 12 in 1993, and 10, from which we removed all owners, in 1994. Replacement again was very slow (table 7.8) and peaked at only 5 males. Three of the replacements were unbanded and 2 were banded former owners; 1 had a territory on Hays in 1992 and 1993 and 1 moved from Morgan Pocket, a distance of 1.6 km, within hours of the removals. Within 24 h of their releases, 9 of 10 original males had recovered their territories (1 of these subsequently lost his territory, but the tenth original owner eventually regained his, bringing the recovery rate back to 90%; table 8.1)

Thus, our 1993–94 removal experiments, conducted under conditions of low population density, yielded very different results than did our previous removals, which were conducted at higher population levels. We discuss possible explanations for these differences later in the chapter.

MARSH AND TERRITORY FIDELITY/MOVEMENTS

We determined the frequency with which territorial males switched marshes between breeding seasons and the distances they traversed with data from 1985 through 1994 on the core and peripheral marshes. Our previous estimates of fidelity and movements were based only on information from the core area (Beletsky and Orians 1987a). This biased our breeding dispersal estimates downwards because some males moved long distances that took them outside the core. We also use our information on breeding success to test the hypothesis that males switch territories within or between marshes to improve their RS.

The predictions about territory fidelity and movements we tested are:

1. Moves, especially between marshes, should be rare, because of the risk of moving (loss of site dominance) and the costs to individuals of familiarizing themselves with new areas and conspecifics.

2. Under RHP, VA, and L hypotheses, site fidelity should be high, with males changing territories voluntarily only when opportunities occur at adjacent or nearby sites, i.e., where a male can move quickly to occupy a new territory about which he already possesses information and that he can be reasonably certain is really vacant.

3. VA predicts movements only over short distances; RHP predicts moves over short to intermediate distances.

4. Short-distance moves should lead to improved RS; long-distance moves, which we assume are made involuntarily and to sites about which males are relatively ignorant, generally should not lead to improved RS.

MARSH FIDELITY

From 1985 through 1993, 576 color-banded males established their first territories in the study area and held them for at least two years. About 150 of these males (26.6%) changed marshes during consecutive years at least once during their breeding lifetimes (table 8.2). A small number of males (n = 23) that bred multiple years changed marshes in consecutive years more than once. Thus, although the majority of males showed high between-year fidelity to their marshes, generally supporting our prediction, a higher proportion than we expected moved.

The average distance that males moved between marshes was 1.7 ± 1.4 km (measured as distances between marsh centers). The pattern of distances moved supports the information/distance hypothesis: most moves were over short distances and the number of moves decreased rapidly with increasing distance (fig. 8.2). Only a few owners got new territories more than 3 km from their old territories. The distances are similar to those at which floaters obtained territories from our fixed trap sites (fig. 7.6), which suggests that current owners gathering informa-

TABLE 8.2. Consecutive-year movements between marshes, through 1994, for male redwings first holding territories from 1985 through 1993

| | No. of between-year, intermarsh moves | | | | |
No. of years with a territory	0	1	2	3	Sum
2	117	45	n.a.	n.a.	162
3	107	34	5	n.a.	146
4	63	20	10	1	94
5	53	17	4	0	74
6	22	10	2	1	35
7	15	4	0	0	19
Sum	377	130	21	2	530[a]

[a]Total of 530 males differs from value of 576 used in the text because 46 males that switched marshes with one or more intervening nonterritorial years are not included in the table.

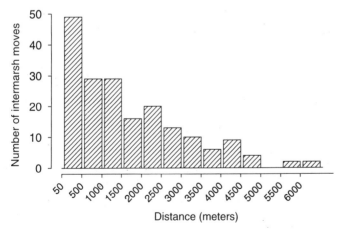

Fig. 8.2. Distances males with territories moved when they changed to a territory on a different marsh, 1985 through 1994 (n = 276).

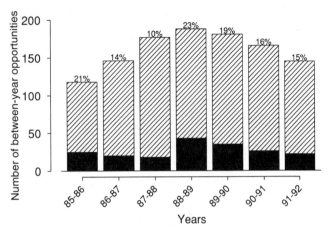

Fig. 8.3. Numbers of between-year opportunities males had to switch breeding marshes and the numbers of male territory owners each year that switched (solid bars). The percentage that switched is indicated above each bar.

tion about other areas travel over the same distances as do floaters prospecting for first territories. However, these distances are on average short enough to be consistent with either RHP or VA searching.

Figure 8.3 shows the number of between-year opportunities to move that male owners had from 1985 to 1992 (i.e., the number of males that held territories in both years of each two-year period and thus had opportunities to make between-year moves) and the proportion of opportunities acted upon. The percentage varied from 10 to 23% per year, with an annual mean of 16.9%. The fairly even distribution of movements among years suggests that moving between marshes is a regular feature of CNWR redwing biology and not a consequence of habitat degradation or fluctuating population densities.

DO MALES MOVE TO IMPROVE THEIR RS?

To test the hypothesis that males voluntarily change territories to improve their breeding success, we use our information on territory ownership on our core marshes from 1984 through 1991, which supplements information gathered from 1977 through 1984 that supported this hypothesis (Beletsky and Orians 1987a). From 1978 through 1984, 107 males obtained their first territories on our core marshes and held them for at least two consecutive years. Twenty-three of these males (21.5%) changed territories between years. Because some of them held territories for more than two years, these 107 males had, in total, 185 between-year opportunities to move; 23 (12.4%) were taken. From 1984 through

1991, 101 new males established territories on the core marshes and held them for two or more consecutive years. Thirty-nine of them (38.6%) moved. They had, in total, 235 between-year opportunities, of which 16.6% were acted upon. Therefore, because approximately 85% of between-year opportunities to move were not taken, interyear territory fidelity predominated, supporting predictions from RHP, VA, and L models. However, a nontrivial proportion of owners in the core did move. Most males that moved from 1978 through 1984 (73.9% of 23 males) and from 1984 through 1991 (71.8% of 39 males) did so after their first breeding season. These data suggest that some males may have initially acquired poor-quality territories that they vacated. With increasing time on and investment in a territory, males were less likely to change territories.

If males change territories to increase their RS, they must be able to compare RS in year x between their own and other territories and have an opportunity to switch. If so, on average, (1) movers should experience below-average RS the year before they move; (2) movers should increase their RS from year x, the year before the move, to year $x + 1$; and (3) territories to which males moved in year $x + 1$ should have had higher RS in year x than the movers' own year x territories.

All three predictions were supported. Movers had significantly lower RS the year before their moves than did nonmovers in both replicates (table 8.3). Because nonmovers do not have a "year x," defined as the breeding year before a move, and because most moves occur after first breeding years, we used nonmovers' first breeding years for comparison. Movers improved in RS after their moves (table 8.3; significant from 1977 through 1984 and almost significant from 1984 through 1991), whereas nonmovers did not improve their RS rate between their first and second breeding season (Beletsky and Orians 1987a). Finally, males that moved in year $x + 1$ changed to territories on which male RS in year x was higher than it was on their own territories (table 8.3; trend from 1977 through 1984 and significant from 1984 through 1991). Thus, we have strong evidence to support the hypothesis that males switch territories voluntarily in order to increase their production of offspring.

From 1977 through 1984, the average distance moved between core-area territories was 385 ± 642 m (n = 30; includes males moving from 1977 to 1978, which were excluded from other analyses because we did not know the territorial histories of males present on territories in 1977). A greater proportion of short-distance movers (n = 22), those traversing less than 200 m, increased their fledging success from year

TABLE 8.3. Predictions and tests of the hypothesis that male redwings switch territories to improve their reproductive success (RS)

	1977 through 1984			1984 through 1991		
	$\overline{X}$ ± SD no. young fledged/territory	n	P	$\overline{X}$ ± SD no. young fledged/territory	n	P
Prediction 1. Movers should have lower RS than nonmovers in year x.						
Movers	3.3 ± 4.6	23		2.2 ± 3.3	39	
Nonmovers	5.5 ± 6.4	81	0.05[a]	4.0 ± 4.4	62	0.009[a]
Prediction 2. Movers should improve their RS in year $x+1$.						
Year x	3.3 ± 4.6	23		2.0 ± 3.1	39	
Year $x+1$	5.4 ± 5.5	23	0.05[b]	3.4 ± 4.7	39	0.06[b]
Prediction 3. RS on movers' year x territories should be < RS on their year $x+1$ territories in year x.						
Year x territory in year x	2.6 ± 4.1	22		2.0 ± 3.1	39	
Year $x+1$ territory in year x	4.4 ± 4.6	22	0.09[b]	5.2 ± 6.9	39	0.04[b]

[a]Mann-Whitney U test.
[b]Wilcoxon matched-pairs test.

x to $x+1$ than did longer-distance movers (n = 8; Beletsky and Orians 1987a). From 1984 through 1991 the average distance moved in the core was only 178 ± 260 m (n = 39). Short-distance movers (n = 28) did not increase their RS more often in this sample than did long-distance movers (n = 11). In neither replicate was there a significant correlation between distance moved between territories and the change in males' fledging success before and after the moves.

TERRITORIAL RESPONSE
TO YELLOW-HEADED BLACKBIRDS

Because locating new territories is both difficult and risky, and a return to the floater pool is an unattractive option, we predicted that male redwings that were partially displaced from their territories by later-settling yellowheads would remain faithful to their territories between years, in spite of the high likelihood of the same displacements occurring during subsequent years. If they are evicted from their territories by the larger yellowheads, VA predicts that redwings, if they survive, should reoccupy the same territories or ones nearby the next year. RHP predicts that these males should reestablish nearby, but not neces-

TABLE 8.4. Responses of male redwing territory owners to partial or total displacement by Yellow-headed Blackbirds during their first breeding year (= year x)

| | n | % known to breed in year $x+1$ | % of year $x+1$ breeders on | | | Total no. of years breeding[a] ($\bar{X} \pm SD$) |
			Their year x territory	Another territory on their year x marsh	Another marsh	
Redwing males unaffected by yellowheads						
	40	62.5	80.0	4.0	16.0	2.6 ± 1.7
Redwing males displaced by yellowheads						
Partial						
displacement	18	61.1	72.7	9.1	18.2	2.8 ± 2.1
Total						
displacement	18	44.4	25.0	25.0	50.0	2.2 ± 1.2
Combined	36	52.8	52.6	15.8	31.6	2.4 ± 1.5

Note: Data are pooled from three marshes: North Juvenile, 1984 to 1989; McMannamon Lake, 1988 to 1991; and Morgan Pocket, 1985 to 1991.

[a]Through 1992.

sarily at the same location. Lottery predicts that once evicted, males should search for vacancies over wide areas; thus, they should be more likely to acquire territories elsewhere than at their original sites.

We analyzed male movements on three core marshes during years of high yellowhead settlement: North Juvenile from 1984 through 1989, McMannamon Lake from 1988 through 1991, and Morgan Pocket from 1985 through 1991. During these years, 76 redwings established territories for the first time on these marshes. From biweekly territory maps, we determined which males were partially displaced (defined as losing ≥ 50% of their pre-yellowhead area) or totally displaced (evicted) from their territories by yellowheads, and also which territories were unaffected by yellowheads. We also calculated the survival of the redwings and their subsequent territorial histories.

Redwings that were only partially displaced in year x, although each lost 50% or more of his territory, were highly faithful to their territories. About the same proportion owned the same site in year $x+1$ as males unaffected in year x by yellowheads (table 8.4). Males that were totally displaced had a lower return rate in year $x+1$ than either unaffected redwings or those that were partially displaced, either because they had lower survival or because some of them could not regain territorial status. Fifty percent of evicted redwings that reestablished territories in year $x + 1$ did so on the same territory they had held previously or on another one on the same marsh, providing support for VA or RHP, but negative support for L. The average number of years breeding for evicted redwings was somewhat less than that for either unaffected males or those partially displaced (table 8.4); evicted males may have suffered injury or high stress during their interactions with yellowheads, resulting, on average, in curtailed breeding lifetimes. These data show that male redwings holding territories where yellowheads regularly settle are equally faithful to them as are males holding territories where yellowheads do not settle.

CONCLUSIONS

REMOVAL EXPERIMENTS AND SITE DOMINANCE

The combined results of our series of removals from 1983 to 1988 and those of Eckert and Weatherhead (1987b) and Shutler and Weatherhead (1991b) provided support for the VA hypothesis rather than the RHP hypothesis as the likely explanation of territorial dominance in redwings. However, our main finding in support of VA, that territorial dominance relationships between owners and floaters reversed over as brief a time as six to seven days, was contradicted during our 1993–94 experiments. The more recent results provide additional insight into territory acquisition and dominance and the relationships between RHP and VA.

The redwing population in the study area declined steadily for several years before the 1993–94 removals. Both the number of territory owners on our core marshes and the number of adult floaters trapped declined from a peak in 1988 to lows from 1992 to 1994 (fig. 8.4). There were probably several reasons for the decline but an important one was the destruction of marsh vegetation by beavers (see chapter 2). The number of territories in the study area, even the number on marshes uninfluenced by beavers, such as JP in 1993 and Hays in 1994, was low. The floater population also appeared to be much lower than it had been during the earlier years of the study. The small population of floaters also explains the slow replacement rate on the vacant territories we created and the fact that fewer replacements occupied territories on the marshes than the number of males removed. Thus, all indications were that the number of adult floaters prospecting for territories at the core-area and nearby marshes was very low during the 1993–94 removals.

Our 1993–94 removal experiments provide evidence that RHP plays

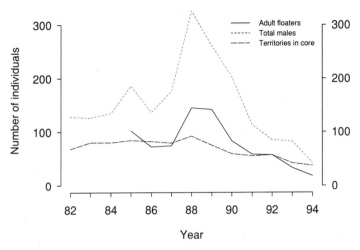

Fig. 8.4. Number of adult floaters and the total number of adult male individuals (floaters plus owners) trapped in the study area each year. Floaters were defined as those banded males trapped that were not known to hold territories within the study area. Also plotted is the number of territories on the core marshes each year.

a greater role in territory ownership than appeared to be the case during our earlier experiments. In 1993 and 1994, some of the replacements were former territorial males that reacquired territories at their former marshes. They did so only when we created vacancies, suggesting that they had such low RHP that even though the territorial population on the core was only half the size it was during times of peak population, they could not by themselves establish territories. Similarly, unbanded floaters that became replacements were not able to establish territories without our assistance, even though there were fewer males occupying territories on our undisturbed marshes.

Thus, the roles of RHP and VA in territorial dominance may vary together with population densities. When population levels are high, as they were during our 1983–88 experiments, adult floaters may include both low-RHP males who challenge owners infrequently or weakly and have little chance of acquisition except by finding a vacancy (lottery), and higher-RHP males who make moderate and strong challenges and occasionally gain territories by inserting or evicting. When owners with high RHP are challenged by floaters with high RHP, VA rules may predominate in determining contest outcomes. We believe that we created this type of contest during our initial series of removals. When population levels are very low, however, all males with moderate and high RHP have territories and all floaters are males with extremely low RHP. Under these conditions, RHP rules may govern most new acquisitions and also relegate low-RHP males to floater status.

A very low RHP of replacement males in 1993 and 1994 is also consistent with the fact that they were partially or totally displaced rapidly by the released original owners. Apparently, value asymmetries cannot overcome the gap between two males of radically different RHP.

The 1993–94 removals provided support for the prediction that males with low-quality territories will abandon those sites quickly to occupy superior territories that become vacant. One replacement on JP and one on Mac did so within a few hours from 400 m and 500 m away, respectively. A third male, who moved 1.6 km from Morgan Pocket to Hays, did so probably at dawn of the day after the removal. The section of Morgan Pocket held by the male before he moved was in an area that was occupied each year in early April by yellowheads; had he not moved, he would soon have been evicted from the site. We described previously how a male with a poor-quality strip territory abandoned it and switched within twenty-five minutes to a better, adjacent territory made vacant by a removal (Beletsky and Orians 1987a). Such behavior is expected because adjacent neighbors probably have extensive knowledge of each other's holdings and their relative values. But the moves during the 1993–94 removals suggest that male owners, particularly those on low-quality territories, assess other territories up to at least several hundred meters from their own. When opportunities to move arise, they can act quickly.

Shutler and Weatherhead (1992) tried to identify the value asymmetries that determined whether original or replacement owners in their removal experiments were able to keep territories, but they were unable to predict winners on the basis of any of three different payoff "currencies": replacement occupancy time, owner familiarity with neighbors, or owner reproductive investment. Although they rejected RHP as an explanation of their results, they suggested that any asymmetry between owners and floaters that produced site dominance was "uncorrelated" with actual values placed on territories by the birds. However, as is the case with measuring RHP of owners and floaters, it is possible that the investigators measured the wrong currencies, or that males use combinations of territorial strategies. Shutler and Weatherhead speculated that the arbitrary rule hypothesis (see chapter 6) may explain site dominance in redwings, i.e., an "uncorrelated" asymmetry, such as "owner always wins," may determine dominance. In their view, floaters would acquire territories only by lottery and quickly assume site dominance. However, as we have argued (chapter 6), the lottery model cannot explain site dominance and does not explain how floaters at CNWR search for territories.

CHALLENGER INHIBITION

Under natural conditions, owners are rarely strongly challenged for their territories. Factors influencing floaters' challenger inhibition may include the risks of fighting, the probabilities of locating vacancies or low-RHP owners soon, VA between owners and floaters, population density, and the stability of territory boundaries. In stable, high-density populations, challenger inhibition typically may result from a combination of four factors: (1) the potential for serious injury during fights; (2) the VA in favor of owners and, hence, differences in motivations to fight; (3) the high probability of locating future vacancies, which can be occupied with little or no fighting; and (4) the fact that most owners during periods of high population densities will have moderate to high RHP, rendering fighting particularly dangerous. At low population densities, both factor 3 and factor 4 change. Finding unoccupied territories, especially at low- to moderate-quality sites, is even more likely, and the proportion of owners having low RHP rises.

Although floaters usually do not seriously challenge owners, they do so occasionally. Some owners are targeted by floaters for persistent challenges, arguing against a fixed arbitrary rule that "resident always wins." Variation in floater behavior during challenges suggests that floaters evaluate each situation on its merits and quickly reach decisions about retreating, persisting, or escalating. The more information floaters have about the situation, the more likely they are to arrive at "correct" decisions about fighting or fleeing. The correct decision, on average, in cases where floaters have little or no current information about a particular situation, is probably to retreat.

TERRITORY FIDELITY AND MOVEMENTS

VA, RHP, and L models of territory acquisition all predict strong territory fidelity. In fact, redwing territory owners at CNWR should never voluntarily rejoin floater pools. They cannot achieve RS as floaters, and there is a high probability of never again acquiring a territory. Males should voluntarily abandon their territories only to move to better ones. Involuntary abandonments may follow eviction by other males or catastrophic habitat changes.

Territory fidelity predominates in the CNWR system. In fact, some males that held territories for five or more years never moved (e.g.,

Beletsky and Orians 1989b,c). However, we detected sufficient numbers of moves to be able to conclude that switching territories is not unusual and that some males, for unknown reasons, moved around frequently. (Male 64655, for example, first held a territory as a subadult on Crab Creek in 1986, moved 4.5 km in 1987 to take a territory on Halfmoon Lake, 1.2 km in 1988 to Upper Hays Creek, and 2.0 km in 1990 to Marsh Unit 3.)

Between-marsh moves averaged 1.7 km, which suggests that such moves are based in part on RHP or L considerations and not on VA. By moving more than 1 km, a male in the CNWR area typically passes up to one hundred or more territories about which he could not have detailed prior knowledge. However, a male might evaluate his RHP relative to that of other territorial males on many territories during foraging trips, and he might also notice vacancies on such trips. We suspect that many of these between-marsh moves, especially those made involuntarily, represent males who relocated by finding vacancies.

That males switch territories over distances of 2 + km indicates that studies of territory acquisition and survival in redwings need to monitor large areas. If a study area is small, male owners that move intermediate or long distances will simply disappear and be thought dead. Also, some new territory owners that will be presumed to have been to that point floaters, will have previously held territories elsewhere. Our conclusions would be very different had we monitored only one or two breeding marshes and had we not censused all breeding habitats within several kilometers of the core area.

Our comparisons of pre- and postmove fledging success for males that switched to nearby territories generally supported the hypothesis that they move voluntarily to better territories. Also, if males move voluntarily when neighbors or other nearby owners die or disappear, then movers should usually be replacers and not inserters. Our data support the prediction: 72% of males (18 of 25) that gained second territories between 1983 and 1990 on our core marshes did so as replacers. Although we found little between-year predictability in the proportion of successful nests on each of our core marshes (chapter 4), such predictability, on a smaller, territory-wide scale, must exist if males are to compare territories in year x and move to better ones in year $x+1$. In fact, this is the case. From 1977 through 1984, there was a significant positive correlation between fledging success on a territory in year x and on the same territory, regardless of its owner, in year $x+1$ (Beletsky and Orians 1987a). From 1984 through 1991, for males that did not move, there was a positive correlation between their first and second year's fledging success (first year mean success = 4.0 ± 4.4 fledged young, second year = 4.0 ± 0 4.8 fledged young; Spearman r = 0.23, P = 0.04, n = 62). Therefore, information on the relative breeding success on their own and nearby territories can be used by males to predict success the next year.

Finally, CNWR males show high between-year fidelity to their marshes once they own territories on them, even if yellowheads partially or totally displace them. They may do so because other options, such as returning to the floater pool, are even less attractive than repeat bouts with the yellowheads. However, several marshes at CNWR that were particularly favored by yellowheads were avoided by redwings. For example, redwings did not establish territories in the northern and western sections of Morgan Lake, although these areas were apparently highly suitable for redwing breeding and although redwings foraged, loafed, and roosted there before yellowheads arrived each year. This pattern indicates that redwings "know" that yellowheads colonize these areas in large numbers and decide to avoid them.

Part Four

CONCLUSIONS

Nine

On Being a Successful
Red-Winged Blackbird

In the preceding chapters we have explored decision-making by female and male Red-winged Blackbirds during the breeding season under the assumption that decision rules are key components of the design for fitness. We viewed the life history of an organism as a sequence of choices, each of which influences lifetime reproductive success (LRS) and, hence, fitness. We employed actor-based accounts to analyze the redwing social system because we believe that social systems are usefully viewed as the result of repeated decisions by the individuals comprising those systems. The richness and variability among individuals in the ways in which decisions are made strongly suggest that most decisions are not hard-wired. Rather, we believe that the influence of the genetic program expresses itself as conditional rules of the general form "If the environmental situation is x, then do y."

Many of the decisions we analyzed are strategic, that is, the consequences of the choices depend on the conditions under which they are used, the array of alternative behaviors found in the population, and the frequency with which individual actors use them. Of necessity, we took a decision-by-decision approach in our attempt to untangle the complex web of decisions and interindividual interactions that characterize a breeding population of redwings. The consequences of specific decisions depend, in part, on how individuals make other kinds of decisions, the order in which they make them, and the variable physical environment in which they are made. In this chapter we integrate our analyses and interpretations of specific breeding-season decisions to provide a more coherent picture of how behavior contributes to LRS among Red-winged Blackbirds in the Columbia National Wildlife Refuge (CNWR) population, and we explore the broader implications of our results for behavioral ecology.

Throughout our analyses we used the "phenotypic gambit" (Maynard Smith 1978; Grafen 1984), that is, we assumed a genetic basis for the behavior patterns we examined and the existence of sufficient genetic variability to provide a substrate upon which natural selection could act. We also assumed that natural selection favors traits with the highest fitness regardless of the specifics of inheritance. We used a variety of partial surrogates for fitness that were specific to the focal decisions, emphasizing ones that have consequences we could measure or estimate with our field data.

The consequences of some of the decisions we have examined are determined primarily by the physical environment. The consequences of others depend primarily on the behavior of individuals of other species (predators, parasites, competitors), or of conspecific individuals of the same or opposite sex.

LIFETIME REPRODUCTIVE SUCCESS

The most important determinant of LRS for redwings of both sexes is the number of years breeding. For both males and females, the lifetime number of fledged young per individual breeder increased, on average, almost linearly with the number of breeding years. Therefore, the decisions we have analyzed are usefully viewed in the context of how they influence the age at which individuals become breeders and the probability that they will continue to breed during subsequent years.

No significant socially imposed constraints to breeding by females appear to exist. Our evidence suggests that all females that are physiologically capable of breeding do so every year. Their decisions potentially influence the likelihood of success within any breeding season and the probability that they will survive to the next breeding season. However, we found no correlation between the investment of females in reproduction in a given season and their probability of survival to the next season. We searched for but did not find evidence to suggest that females experience higher mortality if they invest heavily in a given season or that they terminate reproduction early to avoid incurring a higher probability of dying between breeding seasons. This conclusion must be tempered, however, by the fact that our data are nonexperimental. Levels of investment and termination of breeding were controlled by the birds themselves, albeit modified by the weather and predators. Therefore, we cannot reject the hypothesis that there is a survival cost to high investment in a given year but that individual females adjust their investment level to their own physiological condition, with the result that females terminate breeding efforts during a season before they have invested enough to reduce their survival probabilities and abilities to invest in reproduction the next year.

It is somewhat surprising that females do not invest heavily enough in reproduction within breeding seasons to influence their survival because the probability of surviving to a subsequent breeding season averages only about 60%. Survivorship might, in fact, be higher if females invested substantially less in reproduction, but unless the marginal decrease in survivorship with increasing reproductive investment is great, females should invest more than they do within seasons. Our data do not permit us to estimate the marginal costs, but if the curve is steep, we should have detected some sign of it. We conclude that females manage the trade-off between reproductive investment and survival by terminating breeding in sufficient time to molt and prepare for migration while food supplies and weather conditions are still favorable, but we have no conclusive evidence for this belief.

Reproductive effort by males differs strikingly from that of females. Males invest most of their efforts in gaining and maintaining their territories, courting females, and seeking extrapair copulations. The level of a male's efforts is probably not strongly correlated with the size of his territory or the number of females he attracts because most investments are not female- or nest-specific. More males feed fledglings at the end of the breeding season than earlier (Beletsky and Orians 1990), presumably because the opportunity costs of feeding fledglings then are much lower than they are earlier during the breeding season, when other uses of time have potentially higher fitness payoffs. Continued defense of territories appears to have little value as the breeding season comes to a close. Floater males at CNWR rarely invade territories at that time, and occupancy of a territory late in the season appears not to increase the probability of gaining it in a subsequent breeding season. If occupying a territory at the end of the breeding season did substantially increase the probability that a floater male would be able to acquire that territory the following breeding season, we would expect floaters and territory owners to behave quite differently than they do.

THE CONTRASTING DECISIONS OF MALE
AND FEMALE REDWINGS

We organized this book around the sequential decisions that adult redwings make during the breeding season. Half the genes in the offspring produced during a breeding season come from females and half from males, no matter how the decisions are made. Nonetheless, the relative

TABLE 9.1. Contrasting decisions of male and female redwings

Type of decision	Made by Males	Made by Females
Location decisions		
Searching beat	Yes	No
Breeding marsh		
Territory	Yes	Yes
Nest site	0	Yes
Renesting site	0	Yes
Foraging areas	Yes	Yes
Aggressive decisions		
Defend space	Yes	No
Defend individuals		
Mates	Yes	No
Offspring	Yes	Yes
Defend nest	Yes	Yes
Delay other breeders	No	Yes?
Timing decisions		
Migrate	Yes	Yes
Begin and stop nesting	0	Yes
Start feeding offspring	Yes	No
Long-term fidelity		
Site	Yes	Yes
Mate	0	No
Copulation choices		
Intrapair	Yes	Yes
Extrapair	Yes	Yes

Note: Yes = makes choice; No = does not make choice (or behavior is invariate); 0 = not applicable

contributions of different individuals are influenced by their choices. Because the key choices confronting males and females differ so strikingly, we performed separate analyses of female and male decisions. For males, the major breeding-season decisions concern when, where, and how to gain and maintain a territory and when to change locations. For females, the major decisions are where and when to nest, with whom to breed, and how much effort to invest annually in reproductive activities (table 9.1).

THE FEMALE STRATEGY

The breeding environment presents a newly arriving female with a complex array of information about the quality of breeding sites and their surroundings, the features of the males that own specific territories, the identities of neighboring territory owners, and the number and identities of already-settled females. Because these conditions change during the breeding season, no two females confront the same situation, and females make their later decisions under circumstances that differ from those under which they made their earlier ones. The seasonal reproductive success (RS) of a female is determined by the initial site she selects, patterns of change in the vegetation on the site, weather, food abundance in the area, the activities of predators, and the behavior of other members of her species. At the time of settling, little can be inferred about the future states of many of these factors. Weather cannot be predicted more than a few days in advance (even with powerful computer models that birds probably lack), future food supplies are difficult to infer from conditions at settling time, the activities of predators are patchy in space and time, and how many other females will arrive and settle is unknown. Even if a female bred in the same environment the previous year, her memories of events that year are of limited use in the current year. In other words, the environment presents females with a wealth of information, most of which is of little value in assessing future conditions. Furthermore, females have little ability to manipulate most environmental conditions; rather, these are "givens" to which they must adapt.

Given this information-rich but value-poor environment, how do females make their key breeding-season decisions? Features necessary to stimulate settling include a male with a territory having at least some suitable nest sites. At CNWR, if she is a returnee from the previous year, a female is more likely to remain on the same territory if at least one neighboring male from the previous year also returned. Females tend to avoid places with poor nesting cover, but once a female has bred at a site, she exhibits strong site fidelity even if vegetative cover has deteriorated considerably. Although redwing nests survive well over winter, the presence of old nests does not influence female settling. The relative lack of attention females pay to features of vegetation may reflect the fact that marsh vegetation grows rapidly during the spring. Thus, support and cover for nests are usually much better when eggs and nestlings are in the nests than when settling decisions are made.

Within- and between-year site fidelity is relatively high among female redwings. More than 90% of CNWR females remained on the same marsh for their first and second nests even if their first nest failed. Between years, a female was more likely to change marshes if her last nest of the previous year failed than if it was successful, but the great majority of females nested on the same marsh in successive years regardless of their success. We believe that site fidelity is favored because, given the low predictive value of most environmental information, remaining in a known area is generally the best tactic.

Within a marsh a female can choose from among available territories. Choice of a particular territory also determines the female's rank in harem. Additional females may arrive, but how many and when they will do so is unknown. Thus, harem size is unknowable, but unless a female delays starting her first nest, her harem rank is established when she settles. At CNWR, rank in harem is not correlated with seasonal RS. As expected, females do not select territories to achieve particular ranks and their site fidelity is unrelated to their rank in harem. Females can settle anywhere within male territories, but most of the information available to them does not predict their likely future RS in specific places.

When a female selects a nesting site, she also selects her social mate, but she does not automatically select the father of all of her offspring. All females at CNWR copulate regularly with the male on whose territory they nest, but most, and perhaps all, of them solicit from and copulate with neighboring territorial males. At CNWR, 34% of offspring in nests on Juvenile Pocket were sired via EPCs over a three-year period (Gray 1996a). High incidences of EPFs also characterize populations of redwings in eastern North America (Ontario: Gibbs et al. 1990; New York: Westneat 1992a; Wisconsin: K. Yasukawa, personal communication), but females in those populations apparently do not solicit EPCs. Rather, they acquiesce in them. Female redwings at CNWR improve their seasonal RS by engaging in EPCs because the percentage of eggs that fail to hatch is lower among females known to have engaged in EPCs than among females not known to do so. Males are more likely to defend actively the nests of females with whom they have copulated and to permit them to forage on their territories (Gray 1996c), with the result that fledging success is higher among EPC females than among "faithful" females.

The timing of initiation of nest building is a function of when a female arrives on the breeding grounds and how long she delays after settling. At CNWR females arrive over a period of nearly two months, with older females arriving on average before yearlings. Early-arriving females delay nesting longer after they settle than do later-arriving females, which usually initiate nest construction soon after they settle. Early females may delay because they need to accumulate more energy reserves or because weather conditions do not favor quick starts. In contrast, most females renest within ten days of the destruction of their nest and continue to renest until late May. After that time most females terminate nesting following either failure or success of their previous nest. The decision rule is apparently "Initiate breeding as soon as internal and external conditions are favorable and continue to do so until such time as the payoff from future nesting attempts is less than the cost of doing so." We have found it very difficult, however, to determine what the costs are, much less estimate their magnitude. Nest initiations stop when food is abundant and will remain so for at least two months. Nest predation rates, although high, are no higher when renesting stops than they were during the previous month. Females apparently do not invest enough in reproduction during any season to affect their future survival, time of initiation of breeding, or reproductive success the next year.

Most of the factors influencing the decisions of female redwings also influence the decisions of females of many bird species. Site characteristics at the time of settling, changes in those characteristics during a breeding season, weather, resource availability, predators, and behavior of other conspecific individuals are universal or nearly universal environmental attributes to which female birds respond during a breeding season. Nonetheless, because the contexts in which females of other species evaluate these factors vary enormously, our specific results with redwings are unlikely to have broad applicability.

In many environments, especially those dominated by woody plants, the structure of the vegetation changes slowly over time and is relatively constant during a breeding season. The time of both budbreak of Temperate Zone trees and hatching of eggs of the insects whose larvae dominate the food delivered to nestlings of many passerine birds is determined by early spring weather (Lack 1966; Perrins 1970). Therefore, unlike female redwings, birds of some species in those environments do use early spring weather, even though it is unpredictable, to time their nesting activities (Perrins 1970; Immelmann 1973). Both temporal pattern of availability and quantity of food are probably generally more predictable to birds breeding in woody habitats than they are to birds breeding in marshes and other vegetation dominated by herbaceous plants. Information from year x may also be a better predictor of conditions in year $x + 1$ in those habitats than it is in marshes.

We have argued that site fidelity is favored in redwings, despite the low predictive value of much environmental information, because it is generally better to live in a place whose features the individual knows well than in an unfamiliar environment, especially during the familiarization period. In general, the nature of the correlation between site fidelity and predictability of environmental information may depend on how the environment varies. For example, site fidelity may be low in environments with high variation in features influencing RS, provided that the state of the environment can be assessed in a timely manner. Thus, high-latitude predators of microtine rodents and conifer cones are typically highly nomadic, congregating in areas temporarily having high densities of food. The density of those foods is readily assessable at the time of settling, and supplies typically last long enough to support a complete breeding cycle (e.g., Coombs-Hahn 1993). On the other hand, high site fidelity may characterize species living in environments having little variability, whether predictable or not.

Females of monogamous, territorial species may assess traits of potential mates and the resources they control, but rank in harem or number of probable future arriving females is not a relevant consideration. In species in which males are polyterritorial, females may benefit by finding out whether a potential mate is already bonded to a female on another territory, but the polyterritorial species so far studied breed in areas where even a short delay in initiating breeding by arriving females reduces average reproductive success so much that females do not spend much time in making that assessment (Harvey et al. 1985; Lundberg and Alatalo 1992).

The ability of females to separate at least partially their social and genetic mates appears to be widespread among birds (Birkhead and Møller 1992). The redwing is the only species for which factors yielding benefits to females from seeking extrapair copulations and fertilizations have been identified (Gray 1996c). Guarding against sperm depletion is most likely among polygynous species in which males copulate at high rates (Gray 1996d). Gaining access to resources on territories of males to which a female is not socially bonded is a potentially widespread benefit of EPCs. Many more extensive comparative data must be gathered before the detailed information now available for redwings can be evaluated and interpreted in a broad ecological context.

THE MALE STRATEGY

Compared with female tactics, male tactics are relatively simple: the game is to acquire and defend real estate, and copulate! To donate genes to a subsequent generation, a male redwing must obtain a territory and hold it long enough to attract females with whom he can mate. Various tactics may be employed in attempts to obtain a territory, but gaining RS via copulations as a floater is not an option for CNWR redwings. A female confines her extrapair sexual activities to males holding territories close to the one on which she is nesting (Gray 1996a).

Our extensive observational and experimental evidence shows that both the competitive vigor of a male redwing—his resource-holding potential (RHP)—and the value of a territory to him influence his probability of gaining and holding a territory. The simplest and probably most common method of obtaining a territory is to occupy a vacancy created by the death or departure of a territory owner. Vacancies are common because 30 to 40% of males disappear between breeding seasons. Occupying a vacant area is probably the least costly way to get a territory because no owner needs to be challenged or defeated. Outcomes of contests among floaters for vacancies may often depend initially on their relative RHPs because no individual has occupied an area long enough to have acquired much knowledge about it. Nevertheless, a floater with such knowledge should have the advantage, which may be why floaters confine their activities to relatively small areas. Our removal experiments reveal that the value of a territory to an owner rises rapidly, with the result that within a week a new owner usually is able to defend his territory against even the former owner.

Detecting vacancies early in the spring is best accomplished by establishing beats that are patrolled repeatedly. We do not know how large beats are in late winter, when most vacancies are filled, but in March and April floaters at CNWR patrol beats averaging about 2.5 km in length, within which, theoretically, they could monitor up to two hundred territories. The period of searching for and occupying vacancies in late winter is probably very short because floaters greatly outnumber the vacancies. Thereafter, options for occupying vacancies are greatly reduced, and floaters must search for rare vacancies and for opportunities to evict owners from all or parts of their territories.

As we have emphasized, two major, nonmutually exclusive hypotheses can explain the phenomenon of territorial dominance. The RHP hypothesis postulates that fights are rare and are usually won by owners when they do occur because owners actually have higher RHP than floaters. To win a contest, a floater must challenge an owner whose RHP is lower than his own. Because the owner gained his territory in the first place because he had high RHP, a challenge is likely to be successful only if the RHP of the owner has for some reason decreased significantly while that of the challenger did not, or if luck intervenes. To determine which owners have declined in RHP, floaters can monitor their behavior and interactions with other males, especially adjacent territory owners, supplementing this observation with direct challenges in which relative RHPs can be assessed. Therefore, the RHP model predicts that floaters should invade territories primarily at times of day when owners are most likely to be present.

In contrast, the value asymmetry (VA) hypothesis postulates that territorial contests are won by the individual for whom the territory has the highest value. Value is assumed to be positively correlated with knowledge of the territory and, eventually, with genetic investment in it. To increase the potential value of a territory to him, a floater must spend time observing it and, when possible, learn additional details by occupying it. Because territory owners leave their territories frequently for short periods during the day, many opportunities exist for floaters to occupy territories, to learn about them, and to solicit copulations from females.

The behavior of floaters suggests that RHP plays an important role in territory acquisition because floaters seldom occupy territories while owners are absent, and they concentrate their monitoring and probing at times of day when owners are nearly always present and are the most active. Also, floaters rarely occupy territories late in the breeding season, when owners abandon them, even though much could be learned about the areas by doing so. Short-term occupancy of a territory probably cannot completely eliminate the VA in favor of the owner, especially after females have begun nesting. Nonetheless, knowledge of the territory could reduce the difference in value of a territory to its owner and a challenger, thereby reducing the RHP differential necessary to trigger a serious challenge. Therefore, our evidence suggests that, once all late-winter vacancies have been occupied, both RHP and VA contribute to the probability of gaining a territory and that floaters both monitor the behavior of owners and attempt to learn something about their territories. Both types of information influence the probability that a floater challenges an owner and the likelihood that he is successful if he does. Also, prior knowledge of a territory should improve a new owner's chances of retaining the territory when challenged by floaters.

Given the speed with which value asymmetries develop and influence territorial dominance, the optimal tactic for a male when he first occupies a territory is to mimic the behavior of a longtime resident as soon as it is clear that the territory is really vacant. This determination can usually be made within half an hour, which is roughly the interval between when a male occupies a territory and when he begins to perform full-fledged territorial defense and advertising displays (Hansen and Rohwer 1986). Other floaters, however, may recognize him and continue to challenge for ownership, in which case relative RHPs among floaters with approximately equal knowledge of the territory should determine the outcome. Unfortunately, because we have been able to witness very few occupations of vacant territories by new owners, we lack empirical evidence of the extent of struggles among floaters for ownership of vacant territories early in the spring.

Once a male has established a territory, his success is determined by the number of females he attracts, their nesting success, and the number of EPFs he achieves. Males display vigorously to newly arriving females. The significance of these female-directed displays is uncertain because our evidence, and that from all other studies of redwings, indicates that females are little influenced by the owner of the territory when they make their settling decisions. Nonetheless, we may have underestimated the importance of traits of the territorial male because the frequent displays and vigorous sexual chases could influence both female settling decisions and the probability that a female solicits EPCs from a male. Our data on mate and site fidelity are incapable of revealing that type of influence of male traits.

At CNWR, the optimal strategy for a male appears to be to continue to display vigorously to attract additional females, to seek EPCs whenever possible, and to defend his nests, and the nests of other females with whom he has copulated, against predators. Male redwings do attempt to guard their mates, but their efforts appear to be relatively ineffectual because females regularly leave the nesting territories to gather food and nesting material, and several females are typically active on a male's territory at the same time. Also, preventing females from leaving would probably lower their nesting success by denying them access to valuable resources. Only when opportunities to attract new females have greatly declined and when renesting is nearly over does it pay to invest time in feeding offspring.

The nestlings of redwings, like those of most small songbirds, grow to nearly adult size within three to four weeks. During the latter parts of the nestling period, when nestlings eat more than their own weight in food each day, adults must capture and deliver each day several times the amount of food they would require for their own subsistence. If only one member of a pair feeds nestlings, the rate at which food can be delivered to the nest should be substantially less than if both members provisioned, even if the provisioning sex works so hard that its future survival is lowered. Therefore, if members of one sex do not feed nestlings, the benefits of alternative uses of time must exceed the benefits of the increased rate of food delivery to the nest. At CNWR, starvation is a minor cause of nestling mortality although fledging weights may be less than they would be if males also fed nestlings regularly. Nestlings hatched late in the breeding season may fledge at higher weights than individuals hatched earlier in the season, which may account for the higher rate of return of late-hatched males and females. Food shortages are most likely early in the season, when many new females are still arriving. Therefore, both the opportunity costs to males of feeding nestlings then and the value of doing so probably are relatively high. Our data suggest that high opportunity costs determine the decisions.

Males feed nestlings in all of the monogamous species of blackbird that have been studied, but males of many polygynous species feed neither nestlings nor fledglings. Patterns among the polygynous species in which males do feed nestlings tell us a great deal about the factors influencing male parental behavior. In eastern North America, where redwing harems are on average smaller and the nesting season is shorter and more synchronous than at CNWR, a much higher percentage of males feed nestlings, and the probability that a male does so increases with his age (Muldal et al. 1986; Patterson 1991; Yasukawa et al. 1993; Beletsky 1996). Under these conditions, opportunity costs of feeding nestlings decline rapidly while many nestlings are still present on territories.

Most male Yellow-headed Blackbirds feed nestlings, concentrating their efforts on the first nest to hatch on their territory, that is, at the nest whose contents have the highest reproductive value. Secondary and tertiary females are likely to receive help from the male only if the nests of higher-ranking females have failed. Male yellowheads also adjust their provisioning behavior in ways that increase the number of offspring they produce under current conditions. If a male continues to attract more females, he may not feed any of his nestlings (Gori 1984). All twelve yellowhead males shifted to feeding at their secondary nests when the number of eggs in their primary nests was reduced to two (Patterson et al. 1980).

THE CONTRASTS

For many years biologists have recognized that the fundamental distinction between males and females is the cause of many of the differences in the reproductive behavior of the sexes. Nonetheless, this book is, as far as we are aware, the first one in which decision-making during the breeding season has been analyzed by treating the sexes separately. The depth and breadth of the insights we have developed during our fieldwork and subsequent analyses have been increased by treating male and female redwings almost as if they were members of different species. The value of this separation is probably especially great in studies of polygynous species, but even investigations of monogamous species may benefit from separate consideration of the tactics of the sexes.

The causes of the profound sexual differences in breeding-season tactics of redwings have their roots in basic differences between males and females, combined with the environment in which redwings breed. Because sperm can be produced in large numbers, male redwings, as is typical of males of most species, can substantially increase their RS by mating with additional females, whether or not they invest in the offspring they have sired. In contrast, females can increase their RS by only a small amount by copulating with additional males. The potential benefits of EPCs include higher hatching success, genetic variability that may confer protection against pathogens, and additional parental investment by extrapair partners. Female redwings do realize at least some of these benefits, but their combined effects are much less than a male can achieve by mating with multiple females.

Because redwings breed in productive, low-stature marshes, males can readily defend territories that are large enough that males with high RHP can exclude other males from the breeding population. In so doing, they increase the probability that they can attract multiple females. The dramatic increase in fitness that is correlated with increasing harem sizes sets in motion a selective regime favoring large male size, and in which males devote their time to territory defense, mate attraction, and seeking EPCs rather than investing in already-sired offspring. The exception is nest defense, the benefits of which are shared by all nests on a male's territory. Also, because males cannot generally continue with other activities while predators are actively searching for nests or fledglings on their territories, the opportunity costs of predator mobbing are probably very low. Risks from mobbing are probably low as well because the major nest predators are not able to capture healthy adult redwings.

The redwing breeding system tends to favor site fidelity rather than mate fidelity on the part of both sexes, but for different reasons. Males are site-faithful because, provided their RHP remains relatively high, VA virtually guarantees their dominance over all challengers. Females are site-faithful because most of the information they can gather about other potential breeding locations has poor predictive power. There is, thus, an advantage to remaining in a known site, not only because, for males, knowledge may contribute to conferring dominance, but because familiarity improves ability to use an area.

INVARIANT BEHAVIORS

For several reasons we have concentrated our attention, both theoretically and empirically, on variable behavior, that is, behavior patterns whose expression depends on experience, physiological condition, and the environment. Variable behavior traits can be studied to determine the conditions that influence their expression and the consequences to their performers for having acted as they did. Observational and correlational analyses or experiments cannot be used to determine why some behaviors do not vary. Nonetheless, invariant behaviors are important components of the repertory of individuals, and they may strongly influence fitness. Determining why these behaviors do not vary requires analyses based on broad interspecific patterns of their expression rather than analysis of intraspecific patterns.

Redwings of both sexes have a number of invariant behavioral patterns. Males never build nests, incubate, courtship feed, or feed incubating females, and they do not defend more than one territory. Female redwings do not defend territories. Individuals of neither sex assist their parents or other adults with any reproductive activities.

Nest Building

In most orders and families of birds, nests are built by both sexes, but patterns among passerines are highly variable. Among icterines, females alone build the nest in most species, but male and female Melodious Blackbirds (*Dives dives*) share in building their nest (Orians 1983). The Yellow-hooded Blackbird (*Agelaius icterocephalus*) is the only icterine species in which the male is known to build the nest in its entirety (Wiley and Wiley 1980). In contrast, nests are built primarily or entirely by males in most species of weaverbirds (Ploceidae), a family whose social systems have many parallel features with those of blackbirds (Crook 1964; Collias and Collias 1984).

For males, the direct costs of building a nest include the time and energy expended to fly to and from appropriate places, gather materials, and incorporate them into the nest. Opportunity costs of nest building are potentially large because time devoted to building is not available for defense of territory, courting and copulating with additional females, caring for offspring already sired, and watching for predators. Potential benefits of building a nest include increased chance of attracting a female, allowing a present or future mate to devote more time to gathering energy for egg production, and shortening the interval between start of nest building and laying of the first egg. A female could be attracted to a male with a nest because she can save time and energy by using it. Furthermore, the presence of the nest may indicate that the male has a high enough RHP to be able to afford the opportunity costs associated with nest building.

The benefits to a male redwing of building a nest apparently are low. Females choose their breeding situations with little reference to the traits of the males holding the territories. Because they often wait for long periods after they settle before initiating nest building, the increase in seasonal RS from eliminating the nest-building phase would probably be very small. Male Crested Tits (*Parus cristatus*) most frequently help build late nests and second nests; only males in good condition help build late first nests (Lens et al. 1994). The benefit of male nest building is that pairs in which the male helped build the nest had shorter intervals between the start of nest construction and the onset of laying, the advantage of which may be greater later in the breeding season.

Male redwings do perform nest-site demonstration displays, but construction is not included as part of the inducement package. Females renesting after failure of their first nests do not lay fewer eggs or have lower RS than females initiating their first nests during the same time interval. Because the costs to females of building nests are not detectable in our demographic data, we doubt that by building nests a male would increase substantially the number of females he would attract or their RS.

In contrast, the opportunity costs of nest building for male redwings are probably high. Territorial boundary disputes with neighbors and intrusions by floaters are frequent, especially early in the breeding season. New females arrive for many weeks, fertile females are present on a male's territory much of the time, and opportunities for EPCs regularly exist. Because males never build nests, we cannot test our belief that opportunity costs exceed benefits, but our evidence is consistent with that view.

Similar arguments probably apply to other Temperate Zone marsh-nesting icterine males, none of which build nests. The value of a preconstructed nest to a female Yellow-hooded Blackbird may be relatively high because that species breeds in tropical marshes in regions with marked wet and dry seasons. Because water levels in these marshes fluctuate considerably depending on local rainfall patterns, rapid initiation of nesting may significantly increase the probability that a brood can be reared successfully before water levels either rise and flood the nest or drop, exposing the nest to terrestrial predators and lowering local food availability. Countering this argument is the fact that redwings also breed in tropical marshes having these characteristics, yet tropical male redwings do not build nests (Orians 1973). Data on little-known tropical species will be needed to evaluate these conjectures.

In tropical savannahs where most weaverbirds breed, food availability is lowest at the end of the dry season and the beginning of the rainy season. During the dry season, the seeds upon which the birds feed are gradually depleted and those that remain rapidly germinate and become unsuitable as food when the rains come. Colonies of weaverbirds are located in savannah trees, and males of most species defend only small portions of a tree branch that provide only nest sites. If females are under strong selective pressures to accumulate energy reserves in order to be able to breed quickly after the first rains fall, the value to them of a nest may be high.

Nuptial Feeding

Male redwings never feed females, either during courtship or after pair-bonding. Nuptial feeding is rare among icterines in general, having been reported only in the Melodious Blackbird (Skutch 1954). Nuptial feeding is widespread among birds, both among species that pair permanently and among those that pair seasonally. In passerines, nuptial feeding is common among antbirds, swallows, corvids, titmice, tree creepers, nuthatches, dippers, thrushes, Old World flycatchers, waxwings, shrikes, wood warblers, tanagers, and emberizids but is rare among furnariids, tyrant flycatchers, and wrens (Skutch 1976). Nuptial feeding during courtship may signal a male's foraging skills and his willingness to share food, both of which may improve a female's RS. Nuptial feeding may also enable the female to begin egg laying more quickly.

The lack of nuptial feeding by male redwings is not surprising given that a male's skill in foraging is not likely to influence a female's RS. Most females receive no help from a male in provisioning offspring, and the likelihood that he does so probably depends more on events that transpire after pair formation and are not predictable in advance, such as arrival patterns of other females and nest predation rates. As we just indicated, shortening the time between the arrival of a female and the initiation of her nest, a potential benefit of nuptial feeding, does not appear to be important among redwings, at least at CNWR. Why nuptial feeding is absent among monogamous icterines in which males do feed nestlings regularly, remains to be determined.

Incubation

In no population are male redwings known to incubate eggs. Incubation would have high opportunity costs for male redwings because territory defense and mate attraction are incompatible with incubation. Benefits from incubating would be very low because hatching success of eggs is high and we have no evidence to indicate that rates of nest predation would be lower if an adult were on the nest at all times during the incubation period. Nest predators are discovered quickly by the redwings in a marsh, and most of them are able to depredate a nest despite defensive actions of owners and neighbors.

Although lack of incubation by male redwings is not surprising, it is more difficult to explain the lack of incubation among icterines in general. In most orders and families of birds, incubation is shared by both sexes, and biparental incubation is the ancestral condition among birds (McKitrick 1992), but males are not known to incubate in any species of blackbird. Even if incubation by males is discovered in some of the little-known tropical species, incubation by males must be rare in the entire blackbird lineage (Orians 1985). Incubation by females only is the prevailing pattern among passerines and is the only known pattern among manakins, cotingas, tyrant flycatchers, wrens, wood warblers, honeycreepers, and tanagers (Skutch 1976). Whether the change to female-only incubation arose more than once in the passerine lineage cannot be determined from existing phylogenetic analyses (McKitrick 1992). The explanation probably lies in the basic reproductive biology of small songbirds whose nests can be concealed, where predation rates are reduced if traffic around the nest is minimized, and where hatching success is high under single-sex incubation.

Territorial Defense

Female redwings frequently engage in agonistic interactions, especially early in the breeding season, but extensive analyses and experiments have failed to uncover any evidence that they defend territories within the boundaries of the male territories on which they have settled (Searcy and Yasukawa 1995). Our data suggest that no advantage could accrue to females from defending a territory in the CNWR population because there is no correlation between rank in harem and annual RS, nor is there a negative correlation between total harem size and annual RS. Even if some advantage could be gained by preventing other females from settling, female redwings are constrained in their attempts to defend space by two factors. First, because males gain considerable advantage by increasing their harem sizes, they actively intervene to prevent already-settled females from attacking newly arriving females. Second, once a female is incubating, a persistent arriver can force her to chill her eggs, a price greatly in excess of any potential benefit of excluding her. Thus, there are ready explanations for an absence of territorial behavior among female redwings. Females of some monogamous species of tropical icterines do defend territories together with their mates. Settlement of a second female in a monogamous species poses a much more serious threat to a mated female than it does in a polygynous species.

Helpers

Recent intensive field studies of populations of individually color-marked birds have revealed that communal breeding and helpers at the nest are much more common among birds than previously supposed (Skutch 1987; Brown 1978, 1987; Stacey and Koenig 1990). Communal breeding systems are most common among birds living at low latitudes where they are permanent residents on their breeding grounds. Helpers at the nest are found among a number of species of South American icterines, including several in the southern part of the continent (Orians et al. 1977), but no North American species, even the most intensively studied ones, exhibit this form of social behavior. Although EPFs are common among redwings, and males and females may cooperate to defend their nests against predators, no observer has ever reported helpers at the nest in this species.

Any theory to explain helping must consider the risks and benefits to both partners in a helping situation. For helping to evolve, there must be individuals motivated to help and individuals willing to accept their help (Orians et al. 1977). The immediate benefits potentially accruing to individuals accepting help are improved care of offspring, increased future RS owing to reduced current investment in reproduction, enhanced detection of predators, and increased ability to drive away competitors and predators. A longer-term benefit may be the opportunity to hand down the territory to a close relative. Risks associated with accepting help include cuckoldry, attraction of predators because of higher densities of individuals and more activity at the nest, and greater local resource depression. Helpers should be permitted at nests only if the inclusive fitness of the breeders is increased. Benefits of accepting help are more likely to exceed costs if helpers are close relatives. Most birds may not allow extra individuals near their nests because the costs of accepting help exceed the benefits.

The lack of helpers at the nest in redwings cannot be due to a lack of individuals potentially available to help. There are few available non-breeding females, but many females whose nests have been destroyed could choose to help. During much of the breeding season, most females quickly renest after destruction of their own nests, but nestlings are still present in many nests when females no longer attempt to start new nests. Yet no female has been observed to feed nestlings at a nest other than her own. Redwings born at CNWR disperse far enough from their natal sites that nestlings available to be fed are unlikely to be closely related to potential helpers. Relatively low natal site fidelity also characterizes other redwing populations (Shutler and Weatherhead 1994). Therefore, inclusive fitness benefits are likely to be very small or nonexistent. Helping late in the breeding season is unlikely to improve a female's performance in subsequent years, and helping would delay initiation of molting, which may have negative consequences.

A substantial population of nonbreeding males exists in all populations of redwings that have been studied. Nonbreeding males may not help because inclusive fitness benefits are probably very small, survival is unlikely to be improved by helping, and territories cannot be inherited. In addition, however, those males may pose a substantial genetic threat to territorial males. Females arrive at and settle in territories over long time intervals, and because of high rates of nest depredation, most females are fertile more than once during a breeding season. Opportunities for cuckoldry are high under these circumstances. Even without the presence of helpers, males lose about one-third of their potential offspring to other males. One or more additional fertile males on a territory could well increase the proportion of EPFs considerably. Given that nestling loss due to starvation is low and that many individuals join to mob predators, potential benefits from allowing extra males on a territory are probably too low to compensate for the probable losses.

Although a number of South American icterines have helpers at the nest, two marsh-breeding species from temperate South America, the Scarlet-headed Blackbird (*Amblyramphus holosericeus*) and the Yellow-winged Blackbird (*Agelaius thilius*) do not (Orians 1980). Neither species is polygynous, so the arguments we have just advanced for redwings do not apply to them. Scarlet-headed Blackbirds are strongly territorial, and both males and females defend the territories. The Yellow-winged Blackbird is nonterritorial and several pairs may nest close together. Individuals regularly pass close to, and even may sit on the rim of, nests of other pairs, but helping has not evolved. Although no data are available, sex ratios may be close to unity and most individuals may be able to breed on their own, which generally has a better payoff than helping.

RESPONSES TO ENVIRONMENTAL INFORMATION

Many of our analyses have dealt with information that is potentially available to breeding redwings, the ease with which that information can be assessed, and the value of the information to individuals making breeding-season decisions. We do not know what information the birds actually possess, but we have assembled an array of evidence that allows us to say that the birds were acting "as if they possessed and used such information." We have also determined empirically, for the years in which we carried out field observations, the predictive value of different types of information. During the years of our field studies we assessed how well a particular type of information was correlated with future conditions that influenced redwing RS. This allowed us to distinguish between information that could benefit birds because it has good predictive power and information with low predictive power that is probably of little value to the birds (table 9.2).

Another key aspect of environmental information is the opportunity cost of acquiring it. The opportunity cost of acquiring information is the sum of fitness-enhancing activities that must be forfeited during the period an individual devotes to acquiring that information. Opportunity costs are influenced by both the time required to gain information and the extent to which gaining that information is an exclusive activity, that is, the degree to which it precludes doing or learning anything else. We cannot assess these costs quantitatively, but from our extensive field experience we have formed impressions about them that we use in evaluating the ways in which breeding redwings use information. Table 9.3 summarizes our evidence on how redwings use different types of environmental information during the breeding season.

INFORMATION ABOUT THE PHYSICAL ENVIRONMENT

The physical environment within and around breeding marshes offers information that could be used by blackbirds when making decisions. The opportunity costs of acquiring information about the weather are probably extremely low because no special behavior needs to be used to monitor the weather and because such monitoring is compatible with almost all other activities. However, because changes in the weather, on scales ranging from hours to months, are, for the most part, unpredictable, redwings on our study area apparently make little use of weather information in making strategic decisions. The tactical decisions of breeding redwings are also little influenced by weather patterns, but short-term behavior is highly weather-dependent.

TABLE 9.2. Value and use of information by breeding redwings

Type of information	Opportunity cost to assess	Predictive value	Decisions affected
Physical environment			
Weather	Zero	Short-term only	Short-term activity
Day length	Zero	Excellent	Initiation of reproductive behavior
Nonsocial biological environment			
Vegetation	Low	Seasonal	Habitat, territory, and nest-site selection
Food supplies	Low	Poor between seasons; moderate within seasons	Foraging location
Predators	Low	Poor	Short-term activity
Competitors (e.g., yellowheads)	Low	High	Territory location, aggression, nest sites
Cowbirds	Low to moderate	High	Defensive behavior
Intraspecific social environment			
Territorial males			
Identity	Low	Moderately high	Cooperation, female site-fidelity
Condition	High	High	Challenges to territory owners
Nonterritorial males	Moderate	High	Departures from territory; vigor of defense
Settled females			
Identity	Low	Low?	Interfemale aggression
Breeding stage	Low	High	Settling? Initiation of nesting
Prospecting females	Low	High	Male treatment of females
Information about self			
Age	Zero	High	Challenge vigor
Physiological condition	Low	High	Nest initiation, termination of breeding, when to challenge
Morphology	Moderate	High	Challenge vigor?

TABLE 9.3 Influence of environmental information on redwing breeding-season decisions

Information type	Male decisions influenced	Female decisions influenced
Physical environment		
Weather	Length of time on territory early in season	Nest initiation, length of bouts off eggs, brooding nestlings
Nonsocial biological information		
Vegetation structure	Habitat choice, territory choice?	Habitat choice, territory choice, nest-site choice
Food supplies	Foraging site choices, prey choices	Foraging sites, prey choices, load-size choices
Predators	Mobbing behavior, defensive behavior	Mobbing and other defensive behavior
Yellowheads	Territory choice, defensive behavior, territory shifts	Nest-site choice, renesting choices
Cowbirds	Nest defense	Nest defense
Intraspecific social environment		
Neighboring territorial males	Move options	Territory fidelity, Extrapair copulations
Floater males	Defensive behavior	—
Arriving females	Investment in advertising	Aggression to delay nest initiation?
Already-settled females	Courtship, guarding, seeking extrapair copulations	Territory choice, rank choice, nest-site choice, starting-time choice
Information about self		
Age	Vigor of effort to gain a territory	Degree of interfemale aggression
Physiological condition	Vigor of effort to gain a territory	When to start nesting, termination of reproductive effort, when to molt
Genotype	Habitat choice?	Habitat choice?

Males occupy their territories in eastern Washington during the early morning and evening hours beginning in late winter. This behavior is influenced by the weather because the males spend more time on their territories on days with fine weather than on days with stormy weather. They also spend less time displaying on exposed perches when winds are strong or it is raining.

During the years of our study, there was no empirical correlation between weather during February and March and weather one month later, when females have nestlings to feed. Not surprisingly, when females begin to build nests does not appear to be influenced by overall weather during those months. Nonetheless, females are influenced by current weather to the extent that they do not begin nest building on days of cold, stormy weather. Once a female is nesting, weather influences how tightly she incubates, the length of time she goes off to forage, and how much she broods nestlings, but these are all short-term decisions that depend only on current weather conditions.

During late winter and early spring, daylengths are increasing at a predictable rate. Redwings are probably typical of Temperate Zone passerines in coming into breeding readiness in response to increasing daylength although the actual initiation of breeding depends, for males, on getting a territory, and for females, on accumulating sufficient energy to begin nest construction and egg production.

INFORMATION ABOUT THE NONSOCIAL BIOLOGICAL ENVIRONMENT

The relevant nonsocial biological environment of breeding redwings is complex and varied. It includes vegetation structure, food supplies, predators, brood parasites, and competitors. This information is monitored by redwings and used to guide many breeding-season decisions.

Vegetation Structure

Vegetation structure is easy to assess when an individual settles. Vegetation structure changes during the breeding season as a result of growth of new vegetation, but these changes are relatively slow, are easily monitored, and are probably generally predictable from the state of overwintering vegetation.

In our study area, male redwings establish territories primarily in emergent aquatic vegetation or in riparian vegetation that may be dry underneath. Those few males that establish territories in other vegetation types do not attract females. Elsewhere in North America, upland agricultural fields are commonly used for breeding (Case and Hewitt

1963; Yasukawa and Searcy 1995; Beletsky 1996), but the dry uplands at CNWR are not suitable as redwing breeding areas (Orians 1980).

Within the array of suitable habitats, male redwings are quite insensitive to changes in the structure of vegetation on their territories. When we cut most vegetation on territories in late winter, before females arrived, we did not induce males to desert their territories (Beletsky 1992). Even after refuge personnel burned some of our peripheral study marshes in February for maintenance reasons, male redwings remained with their burned territories until the vegetation recovered in mid-spring, and they subsequently attracted mates. The reduction in number of territorial males on marshes undergoing deterioration in the quality and quantity of emergent vegetation was due primarily to the fact that not all territories vacated by former residents were occupied by new males rather than to a lower site fidelity of previously established males.

Females settle only on areas already defended by territorial males. Nonetheless, our data, as well as those of other observers, strongly suggest that the quality of the territory and its environs and not the identity of its defender is the major determinant of female settling decisions. Unfortunately, we have not been able to determine which clues are most important to females. Our experiments demonstrate that the presence, absence, and quality of old nests exert little influence on settling decisions of females (Erckmann et al. 1990). Return rates of females to Hampton Slough during the years when beavers were seriously damaging the emergent vegetation were similar to rates during years when the vegetation was in good condition, and new females continued to be attracted to the marsh when the vegetation was deteriorating. Not until the almost total destruction of emergent vegetation from 1990 to 1992 did females stop nesting on most parts of the marsh (chapter 4).

In the simple, relatively open marsh vegetation, most predators probably know approximately where nests are, and nest predation rates are high even in areas with tall, sturdy vegetation. Therefore, other factors influence settling decisions much more strongly than concealment provided by the vegetation itself, but we had limited success in determining the relative roles of other types of information.

Food Supplies

The rate at which food can be harvested and delivered to nestlings is a major determinant of redwing breeding success, but female redwings are able to fledge nestlings unassisted by their mates on all CNWR marshes. Starvation is an unimportant source of nestling mortality on our study area, although weight at fledging and, hence, survival to adulthood may be influenced by available food supplies. How much redwings can predict food abundance is uncertain because the food supply that will support breeding is not present when males establish territories or when females make their settling and nest-initiation decisions. A returning female could remember information about food supplies the previous year(s), but the amount of interannual variability in emergences of aquatic insects from our study lakes is so great that information gathered during one year is a poor predictor of emergence rates on the same marsh the next year (Orians and Wittenberger 1991).

Redwings may be able to gain some information about food supplies later in the breeding season by close inspection at the time they settle. When females first arrive at territories, they spend most of their time moving through the vegetation close to water level. They may be assessing both vegetation structure and food supplies in the water, but we have no direct evidence about the information they gather at that time or how they use it.

Although information about food supplies may not directly influence settling decisions, it does strongly influence where individuals forage, the kinds of prey they encounter, the prey choices they make, and the sizes of the loads they bring to their nests. At CNWR, where marshes are productive and uplands are dry and relatively unproductive, edges of marshes and emergent vegetation are the best foraging areas, especially during the morning hours, when large numbers of aquatic insects, the primary prey delivered to nestling redwings in the region, are emerging from the water (Orians 1980). The uplands receive their major input of aquatic insects during the afternoon. Redwings concentrate their foraging activities at the edges of marshes during mid- to late morning hours and shift to other locations at other times of day (Orians 1980).

Foraging occupies a large fraction of the day of females with nestlings, and because foraging is an exclusive activity, it has a high opportunity cost. Incubation of eggs and feeding of self and nestlings are very high priority activities of females that are interrupted only briefly when predators or competitors are present.

Predators

Predation is by far the most important source of mortality of redwing eggs and nestlings at CNWR and in most other areas (Beletsky 1996), but the probability that a nest will be lost to predators is unknowable at the time of settling and nest building. Once nesting is under way, monitoring the presence of predators and losses to them is easy. The presence of a predator co-opts the time of all individuals who either mob actively or observe the predator passively. Only a small amount of time needs to be devoted to assessing information about nest losses resulting from a predator's visit. Therefore, all individuals probably possess considerable information about predators and their local effects at all times during the breeding season.

Male redwings establish territories wherever there is a vacancy in suitable habitat; possible future nest predation rates apparently do not influence those decisions, nor do males abandon their territories when nest predation rates are high. However, males do monitor nesting success on neighboring territories and may move to one of those territories if success was better on it than on the males' own territories. Given that nest predation rates are a primary cause of differences in seasonal RS, predation does influence territorial shifts by males.

The arrival of a nest predator on a marsh exerts an immediate and powerful effect on male behavior. A predator in a marsh is mobbed by males, each male being most vigorous within the bounds of his own territory but continuing to mob the predator in neighboring territories. Males vary greatly in the vigor with which they mob predators. Some males attack and strike the predator (including a human "predator" near a nest), whereas others sit at a distance and simply utter alarm calls. The range of such behavior is puzzling, and existing data are equivocal about correlations between the vigor of mobbing and the probability of nest predation (Knight and Temple 1988; Weatherhead 1990).

Female redwings also mob predators but do so only in the immediate vicinity of their own nests. If a female loses her nest to a predator, she decides whether or not to renest and, if so, where. The distance females moved for their replacement nests was the same whether the nests were destroyed by mice or magpies (Beletsky and Orians 1991), predators with different searching strategies and probabilities of repeating the depredation at the same site.

Redwings are conspicuous in the low-stature marshes in which they breed. Territorial males typically perch high in the emergent vegetation, where they sing, call, and display at high rates. Female redwings also call frequently, and they typically vocalize when arriving at and leaving their nests. The lack of cryptic behavior around their nests indicates that nest predation rates are little influenced by conspicuous behavior, suggesting that the major diurnal predators know where the nests are and can find them easily. The lack of a need to behave cryptically around their nests influences a number of aspects of redwing breeding behavior. The length of incubation bouts and the number of trips to and from nests during incubation are free to evolve in response to factors other than predation. Rate of delivery of food to nestlings is potentially higher because adults with food do not need to approach and leave their nests slowly.

That male redwings never incubate and feed nestlings, or, if at all, at rates much lower than females do, cannot be explained by postulating an increased likelihood of nest predation if the conspicuously colored males were to attend them. Rather, the low investments by males in their nests and their contents must be the consequence of the high opportunity costs of doing so.

Yellow-headed Blackbirds

Yellow-headed Blackbird males defend their territories against both other yellowheads and redwings (Orians and Willson 1964). In eastern Washington, the migratory yellowheads arrive on the breeding grounds several weeks after all male redwings have established their territories and after many, but not all, female redwings have settled. When a male yellowhead evicts a male redwing from part or all of his territory, he also harasses already-nesting redwing females and may destroy nests with eggs or nestlings. Male redwings attempt to defend their territories and nests against invading yellowheads, but their efforts are nearly always unsuccessful. Therefore, avoidance of areas that will later be occupied by yellowheads would be adaptive if redwings could identify them.

Evidence that male redwings avoid areas traditionally occupied by yellowheads is provided by the failure of male redwings to establish territories on most of Morgan Lake. These areas are dominated by bulrushes, which are favored nesting substrates of yellowheads but are less preferred by redwings. Redwings did establish territories early in the season in other areas occupied by yellowheads, but the redwings were pushed back to the shoreward edge of the beds of emergent vegetation when the yellowheads arrived. Redwings achieved some success in these areas, and site fidelity was comparable to that in areas not invaded by yellowheads. This indicates that retaining even a reduced-size territory in a poor location was preferable to sustaining the costs of searching for new territories (chapter 8).

Brown-headed Cowbirds

Rates of nest parasitism by Brown-headed Cowbirds were high at CNWR, especially in nests started after the first of May (Røskaft et al. 1990). No sites were safe from cowbird parasitism, and parasitism appears not to influence settling behavior of redwings or locations of renesting attempts. Although female cowbirds are attacked by redwings if they are seen entering nests, cowbirds monitor the marshes from adjacent cliffs without being molested by redwings. Why redwings do not attempt more vigorously to prevent female cowbirds from parasitizing their nests is unclear because parasitized nests fledge, on average, one less redwing than unparasitized nests, primarily because a female cowbird usually removes one redwing egg when she lays her own (Røskaft et al. 1990). Male redwings may find it unprofitable to pursue cowbirds because nest parasitism occurs at times when the value of other uses of time is high.

Redwings accept cowbird eggs, make no attempt to eject them, and usually do not desert their nests when they are parasitized. The majority of acceptor species, including female redwings, are too small to eject a cowbird egg by grasping it. To eject a cowbird egg, therefore, a female redwing would have to puncture it, an act that risks damaging one or more of her own eggs. Because redwings do not attempt to puncture cowbird eggs, we have no estimate of the magnitude of that risk, but Bullock's and Baltimore (*Icterus galbula*) orioles, which are puncture-ejectors, damage between 0.24 and 0.38 oriole eggs per cowbird egg ejected (Rohwer and Spaw 1988; Sealy and Neudorf 1995). Our estimates of the reduction in RS a female redwing accepts when she incubates a cowbird egg and feeds the nestling, although imprecise, suggest that redwings would achieve no net benefit from attempting to eject cowbird eggs (Røskaft et al. 1990). The major loss—the eggs tossed out by the female cowbird—has already been incurred and cannot be recovered by ejection.

INFORMATION ABOUT THE INTRASPECIFIC SOCIAL ENVIRONMENT

Breeding redwings have conspecific neighbors of both sexes, some of which are settled and others of which are prospecting for places in which to settle. The presence and behavior of these individuals is important environmental information that influences the decisions made by individual redwings before, during, and after their settlement.

Territorial Males

The presence of a territorial male is necessary to induce a female redwing to settle, but our evidence strongly suggests that the quality of his territory and its environs rather than the traits of the male are the primary determinants of settling decisions of females. We did not measure directly the influence of male traits on mate choices of females, but other workers who have examined these traits have failed to find any correlations between the physical or behavioral attributes of males and the settling behavior of females (Searcy 1979a; Eckert and Weatherhead 1987a; Shutler and Weatherhead 1991a; Weatherhead et al. 1993). Our extensive data on site fidelity of females show that they are no more likely to nest on the same territory in a subsequent year if the former owner returns than if he does not. When males shift territories, even to ones nearby, their mates do not follow them. Females solicit from and copulate with neighboring territorial males, but males that participate in large numbers of EPCs in a given year are no more likely than other males to participate in large numbers in subsequent years (Gray 1996b). Thus, in contrast to the results of Weatherhead and Boag (1995), our evidence suggests that, at CNWR, particular males are not consistently especially attractive to female redwings.

The choice of a nesting territory does, however, constrain a female's copulatory opportunities. All CNWR females copulate with their mates, who, on average, sire about 66% of their offspring. EPCs in our population are almost exclusively with neighboring territorial males, and by copulating with them, females influence the parental behavior of those males. A male who has copulated with a female is more likely to permit her to forage on his territory and actively to defend her nest against predators than a male who has not copulated with her (Gray 1996c). These results may explain the surprising fact that, although females do not appear to select breeding territories on the basis of the traits of their owners, they are responsive to the number of familiar territorial neighbors. Reproductive success of females is higher if one or more neighboring territorial males were present the previous year than if all neighboring males are holding territories for the first time (Beletsky and Orians 1989b).

Male redwings also are influenced by the behavior of their territorial neighbors. Locations of boundaries are continually contested, and males have a communal system in which information on environmental events is communicated by changes in call notes, which are then copied by other males on the same marsh (Beletsky et al. 1986). However, we have no evidence that the identities of neighbors influence settling decisions by males. Our evidence suggests that males without territories usually take the first opening they find irrespective of who the neighbors are.

The behavior of territorial males is probably monitored by floater individuals to detect evidence of sickness or injury that would lower the RHP of territory owners. Limited evidence from territorial males carrying radio transmitters suggests that unusual behavior of a resident can trigger challenges from floaters. One territory owner who flew irregularly after we glued a transmitter to his back feathers was strongly challenged and ultimately evicted from his territory by a floater. Similarly, territorial males given antiandrogen implants were less vigorous in defense of their territories, with the result that they lost parts of their territories to challengers (Beletsky et al. 1990).

Floaters are probably alert for unstable boundaries, where an insertion attempt is more likely to be successful, than at a stable boundary (Beletsky 1992). As indicated by the rapid replacement of territory owners during most of our removal experiments, floaters also monitor marshes to detect vacancies resulting from the death or departure of territorial males.

Settled Females

The first female to arrive at a breeding marsh confronts only territorial males, but all subsequently arriving females find at least one female already established on the marsh, although none of them may yet have begun to nest. If the arriving female bred on that marsh the previous year, she may know some of those females, because between-year marsh fidelity is strong in our study area. Already-settled females constrain a female's options because they may act to discourage her from settling. Even if they do not, they determine the number of territories on which she could assume a particular rank in harem.

Our extensive data do not reveal any negative correlations between rank in harem and RS of females. In fact, on pocket marshes there is a positive correlation between harem size and average RS. The conspicuous aggression among females early in the breeding season may serve to delay the initiation of nesting by subsequent females, thereby reducing overlap in the time of heavy demand on the food supply, rather than to preserve rank per se or to prevent other females from settling.

Although we have evidence that where an experienced female settles is influenced by the presence of males who held territories on the marsh in previous years, we do not know whether females prefer to settle on territories with familiar females from previous years.

Prospecting Females

Prospecting females attract the attention of settled redwings of both sexes. Because a male's RS increases linearly with the number of females that nest on his territory, a prospecting female represents a potential increment to a male's fitness. Accordingly, a male invests considerable effort to induce a prospecting female to settle on his territory. Among his activities are song spreads, short territorial flight displays, chases, and nest-site demonstration displays (Orians and Christman 1968). The degree to which these displays influence female settling decisions is unknown, but the fact that males invest heavily in them suggests that they have some influence.

A prospecting female potentially increases the fitness of an already-settled female on a pocket marsh at CNWR. On other marshes she may not offer benefits, but she is not a threat either. Early in the season there is considerable aggression between already-settled and prospecting females, but as we have mentioned, the aggression evidently serves, at most, only to delay nest initiation by new females, not their ability to settle.

INFORMATION ABOUT SELF

Every redwing presumably possesses some information about its age, its physiological condition, and such genetically or developmentally controlled traits as its size, shape, color, and metabolic rate. This information influences such decisions as how and with what vigor a male attempts to gain a territory, when to start nesting, and when to terminate breeding.

Age

All physiologically mature females appear to breed every year. Yearling males, on the other hand, rarely hold territories even though they have functional testes and produce viable sperm. Males that acquired territories when they were one year old did not survive at higher rates, breed for more years, or fledge more offspring during their lifetimes than males that did not acquire territories until they were two years of age or older. Even when the population was declining and the number of replacement males was much less than the number we removed in our experiments, few yearling males established territories. Therefore, age strongly influences the vigor with which males compete for territories. Many yearling males apparently do not attempt to establish territories even if vacancies exist.

Physiological Condition

A bird's physiological condition changes as a function of the weather, food supplies, activity level, and stresses imposed by competitors and predators. Other than monitoring the general seasonal cycles of some plasma steroid hormones, we have not attempted to monitor physiological states of redwings. However, we know that territorial and floater males decline in body mass during the breeding season. Thus, breeding males invest so heavily in other activities that they do not spend enough time feeding to maintain their mass. Floaters also lose mass but at a slower rate than territorial males. Loss of mass might increase the probability that an owner loses his territory to a challenging floater, as suggested by our single-removal experiments (Beletsky and Orians 1987b). However, the results of our double-removal experiment in 1988 and our 1993–94 removal experiments suggest that loss of mass was not the cause of failure to regain territories by males held in captivity for periods of a week or more. Rather, the value of the territory to the replacement male, as influenced by the time he occupied it and, presumably, the assessment he made of it, exerted the strongest influence on whether or not the original male regained his territory.

Whether or not floaters can detect directly the amount of mass a bird has lost, the masses of territory owners do decline in a more or less regular way during the breeding season. Therefore, if loss of mass reduces the RHP of some territorial males to RHP levels of some floaters, increasing rates and vigor of challenges would be expected as the breeding season progresses. The reverse pattern appears to be the case, which suggests either that the reduction in RHP caused by normal mass losses of territorial males is too small to be of consequence or that acquiring a territory late in the breeding season has little value to challengers.

Genotypically and Developmentally Controlled Traits

Timing of breeding appears to be influenced by genotype, which thereby contributes to the great variability in starting dates of females in our study population, but we have no evidence that any of the decisions made by a female during the breeding season are directly influenced by her genotype.

Size and shape are determined by an interaction between an individual's genotype and the conditions under which it was raised. Thus, some aspects of an individual's RHP, its foraging ability, and its daily energy needs are determined prior to its reaching adulthood. The estimate a male has of his RHP probably influences the strategy he uses to attempt to gain a territory. Females may decide when to initiate and terminate nesting on the basis of an assessment of their status, but we cannot demonstrate that this is so.

Male and female redwings monitor and use strikingly different information when they make the sequential decisions that determine their behavior patterns during a breeding season. Males are overwhelmingly occupied with gaining and maintaining a territory. The information of greatest value to them is the location of vacant space, the RHP of owners relative to their own, and perhaps attributes of particular territories. To gather this information, floater males establish beats within which they observe territories from without and occasionally probe to determine whether a territory is really vacant or whether its owner is only temporarily absent. They may challenge an owner when they judge his RHP to be lower than their own, and they may attempt to insert themselves at unstable, contested boundaries, where owners have their attention diverted.

Once a male has gained a territory and females have settled, he leaves it only for brief periods to feed and to seek EPCs. Territorial males observe adjacent territories in order to monitor RS there. They may use that information to know when to seek EPCs and to decide whether or not to shift territories when a nearby vacancy arises. They actively court newly arriving females and apparently accept all settlers. Territorial males are alert for arriving predators and mob them at their own nests or at nests of females on adjacent territories with whom they have copulated. They watch for females from nearby territories that attempt to forage on their territories and evict those with whom they have not copulated.

Females explore a small but unknown number of territories before settling, but they do not establish beats because they do not need to search for vacancies. They do not evaluate male quality when settling. Despite many years of study, we still poorly understand the features of the territories and their environs that most strongly influence settling (Beletsky 1996). A female is more likely to return to the same territory on which she nested the previous year if at least one neighboring territorial male has returned, but she apparently does not care whether the former owner has returned. Once a female has settled she may wait for some time before initiating a nest, but we do not know the relative importance of environmental information and information about self in influencing the duration of delay.

Most females renest quickly if their nests fail, whatever the state of the local environment. They presumably monitor their own physiological condition, but we have no evidence to suggest that females decline in condition during the breeding season. At least they do not exert themselves to the point that future performances are affected.

BLACKBIRDS AND SEXUAL SELECTION

Although more than one hundred years have elapsed since Darwin (1859, 1871) proposed the concept of sexual selection, biologists have not yet agreed on a general version of the concept that is applicable to all living organisms (Arnold 1994). Darwin (1871, 256–8) attributed the elaboration of sexually dimorphic traits not involved with reproduction, primary sexual structures, structures used to feed and protect offspring, and male organs necessary for mating to natural selection rather than to sexual selection. The key concept in Darwin's view of sexual selection was the relative advantage some individuals have in mating success, which can accrue as a result of either male-male contests or female choice. A general definition of sexual selection, consistent with Darwin's view that fitness is the appropriate currency for measuring sexual selection, was proposed by Arnold (1994): "Sexual selection is selection that arises from differences in mating success (number of mates that bear or sire progeny over some standardized time interval)."

The relative variance in mating success, I_s, measured as the variance in success divided by the square of mean success, is called the "opportunity for sexual selection" (Wade 1987; Wade and Arnold 1980; Arnold and Wade 1984). The extent to which that opportunity is realized depends on the degree to which the variance in mating success is due to traits whose expression is thereby altered by selection. Here we use our data on age at first reproduction, LRS, and EPFs to consider which components of sexual size dimorphism and dichromatism in redwings can be attributed to sexual selection via intrasexual competition and via mate choice.

VARIATION IN REPRODUCTIVE SUCCESS

Although we cannot estimate it precisely, variance in RS is much higher among males than among females. Among individuals that bred, lifetime variance in RS was 195.65 for males versus 13.13 for females (Orians and Beletsky 1989). The true variance was certainly even more skewed because most males do not begin to breed until they are at least two years old, whereas females typically begin to breed when they are one year old. Therefore, a much higher proportion of males than females dies without reproducing. Once they begin to breed, males and females in our population breed, on average, for the same number of years, but because the breeding system is polygynous, males with large harems fledge many more offspring per year than males with small harems, resulting in an additional increase in variation in RS. In addition, individuals of both sexes engage in extensive EPCs, but only among males does this behavior have much potential for further increasing variance in reproductive success. Thus, the potential for sexual selection is much higher for males than for females, but is that potential realized?

SEXUAL SELECTION ON MALE REDWINGS

If the potential for sexual selection is to be realized, specific traits of males must contribute significantly to their probability of success, that is, size, mass, plumage, and behavior must contribute to success in male-male competition and to the ability of males to attract and copulate with females. A massive amount of evidence gathered by many students of redwings strongly suggests that sexual selection on males via female choice is very weak (Searcy and Yasukawa 1995). Females select their breeding situation on criteria other than the traits of the males holding the territories on which they settle. EPFs do not increase the variance in male RS in the CNWR population (Gray 1996b), but may do so elsewhere (Weatherhead and Boag 1995). On average, male redwings at CNWR gain about as much as they lose from EPFs, and there are no males that consistently gain substantially from EPFs.

Therefore, sexual selection on male redwings, to the extent that it occurs, must come via intermale competition. Competition for possession of a territory is intense, many males are unable to obtain territories, and males that fail to obtain a territory have no RS during that breeding season. If territory acquisition and maintenance were due entirely to a lottery mechanism, there would be no sexual selection on males. We have argued on theoretical grounds, however, that a lottery mechanism, although it may influence initial territory acquisition, cannot by itself explain maintenance of a territory. In addition, we have gathered observational and experimental evidence indicating that other factors, such as differences in RHP, contribute to the probability of gaining and maintaining a territory. The existence of substantial sexual dimorphism also suggests that the traits that are exaggerated in males influence the ability of males to obtain territories.

If sexual selection is responsible for the striking size dimorphism in redwings, size must confer an advantage in gaining and maintaining a territory. If so, territorial males should be, on average, larger than floaters, but this appears not to be the case (Eckert and Weatherhead 1987b,d; Shutler and Weatherhead 1991b). In laboratory experiments, however, larger males dominate smaller males in disputes over access to food (Searcy 1979c; Eckert and Weatherhead 1987c). Some of our removal experiments and our analysis of the tactics of floaters suggest that differences in RHP contribute importantly to the outcomes of contests for territories, but they do not enable us to determine which morphological traits strongly influence RHP. Traits other than the linear measurements usually used to estimate size may exert a stronger influence than size itself, masking weaker contributions of size to success in territorial contests.

Evidence that large size may be favored during adulthood was obtained by Weatherhead and Clark (1994), who found that survival rates of male redwings in Ontario were positively correlated with body size. If large size is even slightly advantageous to male redwings during adulthood, counterselection must be operating at some other stage during the life cycle. A likely candidate is the nestling stage, because sexual dimorphism is established early during nestling development, with the result that male redwings are more costly to rear than female redwings. This cost differential may account for the higher mortality rate of male nestlings (Weatherhead and Teather 1991). A logical corollary is that mortality rates of male nestlings should be positively correlated with size, but no data exist with which to test this prediction.

Also, if larger males fledge in generally poorer condition than smaller males, they may survive less well during the winter and enter the breeding season with lower RHP than smaller males. Males hatched early in the breeding season at CNWR are most likely to fledge at low weights because food supplies are poorer and bad weather is more frequent than later in spring. Such a relationship could explain the fact that males hatched early in the breeding season were less likely to become territory owners on the study area than males hatched later during the spring.

The high incidence of EPFs in redwings suggests a hypothesis to explain the striking sexual dichromatism of this species. Among birds, brightness of male plumage and extent of sexual dichromatism are positively associated with the degree of extrapair paternity (Møller and Birkhead 1994). The high incidence of extrapair paternity among redwings could favor brighter males even though extrapair paternity in CNWR redwings does not increase the variance in male RS. The necessary condition is that males with duller plumages are less successful in gaining EPCs than brighter males. We could not have detected such a relationship because we did not attempt to measure any small variations in brightness that may have existed among adult males.

An alternative hypothesis is that the striking sexual dichromatism in redwings is the result of strong selection for cryptic females rather than selection for conspicuous males (Irwin 1994). The basis for this view is that most tropical icterines, even polygynous species with considerable size dimorphism, are sexually monochromatic. Many of these tropical species are permanently resident on territories whose boundaries are defended by both males and females (Orians 1985). Among these species, widowed individuals of either sex sing to attract mates and defend their territories from intruders during the time they are unpaired.

The existence of a first-year male plumage similar to that of females may also be the result of selection for inconspicuousness. First-year males are able to intrude upon territories for longer time periods than adult males (Hansen and Rohwer 1986). They may learn things about the territory and its owner during that time, but very rarely are they able to copulate with females (Gray 1994).

SEXUAL SELECTION ON FEMALE REDWINGS

Although variance in reproductive success among females is relatively low, some opportunity exists for sexual selection. Mate choice by males does not appear to be a factor because males evidently accept all females that settle on their territories and they may intervene to prevent already-settled females from discouraging newly arriving females from settling. Males copulate with all their mates, and most clutches have offspring sired by the territory owner (Westneat 1993; Gray 1996a).

Does competition among females for breeding opportunities and status result in substantial sexual selection? As far as we have been able to determine, competition among females does not prevent females from settling wherever they choose or from breeding. At most, interfemale interactions may delay initiation of nesting by females of lower rank, but our extensive data reveal no consistent relationship between harem size, rank in harem, and date of initiation of breeding on seasonal RS. Therefore, even if some females delay initiation of their first nests of the season because of agonistic behavior of higher-ranked harem members, we cannot detect a significant potential for sexual selection on traits of females.

This conclusion leaves puzzling the fact that there are consistent age-related plumage changes among female redwings. First-year females lack red on their epaulets, are generally duller in plumage, and begin to nest later than older females. As a result, they are generally not present on territories when most of the agonistic interactions among females take place. This might suggest that the delay in acquiring the "adult" female plumage might be related to the value of the brighter colors in interfemale interactions, but we have failed to find evidence to support this view.

The "correlated response" hypothesis explains the presence of bright colors on females in the same locations in which males have conspicuous patches by postulating that selection on male coloration influences female coloration, resulting in brighter female colors than would otherwise be favored for females (Lande 1980; Muma and Weatherhead 1989). This hypothesis is supported by theoretical mathematical arguments that suggest that plumages of the sexes should be linked. In addition, if females have specific color patterns, they are usually paler versions of male coloration, even though females of many species do not use these colors in displays. Because females of many species engage in breeding activities very different from those of males, their color patches should often be located in places that differ from those of males if they were not influenced by selection on male coloration.

A problem with the "correlated response" hypothesis is that it results in female plumage patterns being maintained for long time periods in a suboptimal state. Under those circumstances, modifiers that break down the genetic correlation between the plumages of the sexes should be strongly favored (Scott and Clutton-Brock 1990). The spread of such modifiers would allow females to evolve a plumage adapted to their particular needs.

That female color patterns may be the result of selection acting directly on females is supported by the fact that females of many species lack any of the color patches found in males. Moreover, females of some species have plumage patterns dramatically different from those of males, including bright colors in places where they are lacking among males. And females of some species do use their color patches in displays.

If females are being dragged along by selection on males, then the temporal pattern of plumage changes should be the same in both sexes. Female redwings do, in general, become brighter with age and acquire reddish feathers on their epaulets. However, that they also acquire brighter colors on their throats, eye stripes, and backs—places where males are uniformly black—is difficult to explain by a "correlational" effect. Females that are brighter than average for their age and experience could have lower RS than females that are duller than average, whether the coloration has resulted from a "correlational" effect or direct selection on female plumage.

Female redwings display their epaulets during agonistic interactions with other females, and such displays are most common early in the season, when most breeders are adult females with reddish epaulets. Nonetheless, the RS of female redwings at CNWR improved very little with age and experience. Females with prior breeding experience fledged slightly more young than did inexperienced females in every year of our study, but this was due primarily to an average earlier start by older females. Mean annual fledging success was the same for yearling and adult females that began nesting during the same week. Whether older females are able to start earlier because they have brighter colors is uncertain. Therefore, why female redwings brighten with age and acquire reddish feathers on their epaulets is unresolved.

RED-WINGED BLACKBIRD INTELLIGENCE

Our long-term observational and experimental studies of breeding redwings were not designed to test redwing intelligence or to reveal the "cognitive maps" with which redwings may operate. Our data are also limited by the fact that, for the most part, we did not watch individual redwings acquire information and then use it to make their decisions. Our results are statistical: we know only the patterns of decision-making of many individuals whose particular experiences we know very incompletely. Nonetheless, our data do provide some insights into the abilities of redwings to assess and use environmental information, and they point to the existence of some aspects of cognition that might repay further investigation.

Animal intelligence consists of those processes by which animals obtain and retain information about their environments and use that information to make decisions (Kamil 1994). Our study has focused largely on these processes. In addition, we have attempted to determine the nature of information available in the environment of breeding redwings and have assessed the degree to which different components of that information reliably predict future conditions.

ASSOCIATIVE LEARNING IN REDWINGS

Much learning consists of forming associations between previously unassociated events (Dennett 1975; Abramson and Bitterman 1986). Most investigators study associative learning under circumstances where they expect to observe it, because positive results are generally regarded as more interesting than negative results. Nonetheless, some studies have shown that animals fail to develop associations between certain classes of stimuli. For example, animals readily associate intestinal illness with gustatory or olfactory stimuli but not with external stimuli (Garcia and Koelling 1966).

During our investigations we discovered that redwings fail to modify their behavior as a result of perceiving certain kinds of environmental information, that is, they appear not to engage in associative learning with respect to that information. For example, female redwings apparently do not adjust when they initiate breeding in response to early spring weather conditions. They do not use the presence of previous years' nests when making settling decisions. They are no more likely to return to the same territory on which they nested the previous year if the former owner is still present than if he is not. However, because they clearly remember the identities of neighboring males, they must know whether or not their former mate has returned.

Male redwings are very conservative in the face of variation in some kinds of environmental information but are very responsive to other information. They are highly site-faithful regardless of their RS in previous years, and they do not shift locations when vegetation on their territories has been seriously damaged. Site fidelity is, however, in large part the result of the formation of powerful associations between occupancy of a territory and willingness to escalate contests to defend it. They remember males that have held their territories briefly during a removal experiment and pursue them farther than they chase all other males. Males also remember which females they have copulated with and respond to them differently than they do to females with whom they have not copulated. Males associate success on a territory with its quality and preferentially move to territories on which breeding success was high and abandon territories on which breeding success was low.

REDWING COGNITIVE MAPS

Cognitive functions are typically partitioned into lower-level operations, such as simple learning, pattern recognition, memory, and spatial orientation, and higher-level cognitive operations, such as complex learning, problem solving, communication, and spatial representation (Real 1994). Redwings clearly learn, they remember past events, and they orient their behavior in space. In addition, they have complex communication systems, and they appear to have some mental representation of space. For the most part, our studies offer no insights into possible cognitive maps of redwings, but the results of our removal experiments point to something interesting.

A removal experiment creates an artificial situation in which two males have established behavioral dominance in a particular territory.

When we release the original owners, intense and sometimes prolonged contests over territory ownership typically ensue. Such intense contests are very rarely observed under natural conditions. In addition, defeated owners tend to remain in the vicinity of their former territories and are likely to reoccupy the same area in the future. These patterns suggest that a male redwing that owns a territory for even a short period develops a cognitive map that says, "I own this territory and it now has much higher value to me than any other piece of terrain." (But the "map" also retains sufficient flexibility that when territory owners switch marshes, their "allegiance" switches to the new sites.) By postulating the existence of such cognitive maps, we can account for the tenacity with which males fight for space they have occupied, a vigor that seems difficult to explain by assuming that they acquired enough knowledge of the space within a few days to raise the value of the territory so much that they risk serious injury to defend it and remain close to it even when defeated.

Development of such a cognitive map would be adaptive if it induced overt ownership behavior soon after an individual occupied a territory. The sooner a new occupant behaves as if he were a long-term resident, the lower the likelihood he will be challenged by floaters who would otherwise recognize that he is a new owner. Male redwings exhibit full ownership behavior within an hour of occupancy (Hansen and Rohwer 1986), long before they can have acquired enough information about the territory for its real value to them to have risen dramatically.

ARE REDWINGS INTELLIGENCE-LIMITED?

Redwings apparently do not use much of the information available in the environment when making their breeding-season decisions, and many decisions are made with incomplete information. These facts do not, however, necessarily imply that redwings could make better decisions if their abilities to acquire, store, process, and interpret information were better than they are. Or to put the problem differently, is natural selection currently favoring greater intelligence among redwings?

From a consideration of the results of our long-term study, we conclude that redwings are limited primarily by time to acquire information and by the poor predictive power of most environmental information, not by their mental capabilities. Male redwings appear to have excellent information about the success of nests on their own and neighboring territories, and they use that information in making territory-shift decisions, both within and between seasons. Thus, they clearly remember information from the previous breeding season, and doing so improves their RS. Male redwings remember with which females they have copulated and adjust their nest defense behavior and their responses to females from other territories that attempt to forage on their holdings. We doubt that male redwings could assess the RHPs of territory owners more rapidly or accurately if they were more intelligent. Similarly, female redwings appear to remember both neighboring territorial males from previous years and their own nesting success and adjust their settling decisions accordingly.

Although redwings remember many things about past events, they ignore much environmental information. Our results strongly suggest that they ignore much information not because they are incapable of processing and using it but because remembering that information would not improve their RS. Insect emergences on individual marshes vary tremendously among years, with the result that marshes with high emergences in one year may have relatively low emergences the next year. Nesting success also varies among and within marshes in a relatively unpredictable manner. Marsh vegetation that is physically damaged over the winter recovers to varying degrees during the next breeding season; thus, automatic abandoning of such areas will not necessarily lead to improved RS. The only significant exceptions we discovered are that (1) although nesting success was consistently better on pocket marshes than on strip marshes during our study, female redwings whose nests failed were not more likely to shift to pocket marshes; and (2) early-settling females should have avoided primary nesting status because, on average, primary females had lower seasonal RS than lower-ranked females. Whether these examples represent a limitation of cognitive abilities or a peculiarity of our study area for which no adaptive response has evolved we do not know.

FINAL REMARKS

In closing, we wish to place our long-term, single-species study into the broader context of investigations in animal behavior and ecology. What does our investigation tell us about the value of long-term field studies? What have we learned about hypothesis testing in behavioral ecology and about attention to appropriate scales of inquiry? What insights does our investigation offer for the integration of behavior and ecology and, eventually, for a better vertical integration of ecology?

INSIGHTS FROM OUR LONG-TERM STUDY

Long-term studies of marked individuals, which enable investigators to track the performance of particular individuals throughout their lives, are increasingly providing assessments of LRS. Interest in such studies is high because LRS is often a good approximation of fitness, a central evolutionary concept that is notoriously difficult to measure. Measures of LRS combine both survival and breeding success into a single measure of performance, they allow comparisons of individuals of the two sexes, and they enable investigators to determine the influences of life cycle, environment, genotype, and phenotype on variations in overall reproductive performance (Newton 1989).

Although long-term studies have clear scientific value, many important features of life-history tactics can be analyzed and interpreted adequately with studies of shorter duration. Because long-term studies are costly in terms of monetary and human resources, there is merit in assessing the results of long-term studies to determine which features of life-history tactics and LRS really require long-term studies and which do not. Here we present a retrospective analysis of our study that identifies which insights required our full data set and which did not.

Long-term studies are valuable for two rather different reasons. First, many years of data may be necessary to obtain sufficient sample sizes for statistical analyses of events that occur relatively infrequently. Analyses that require segregating individuals by age, location, timing of initiation and termination of breeding, individual reproductive effort, etc., also need sample sizes that are likely to be achieved only after many years of study. For some events, sufficiently large sample sizes can be obtained in a few years, but doing so may be prohibitively expensive or require a larger study area than is available to the investigator.

Second, long-term studies are essential for gaining an understanding of variability in reproductive performance and of how it responds to variations in environmental conditions. A short-term study may have been conducted during conditions that are not typical of the environment or the focal population in the long term. The value of a particular behavioral response may not be evident during a short-term study, and some behaviors may be missed entirely because the conditions that evoke them never arose.

Slowly Accumulating Sample Sizes

Although we monitored about eighty territories and several times that many females each year, we did not have sufficient sample sizes to analyze some important features of redwing reproductive biology even after ten years of fieldwork. For both sexes, because return rates of individuals banded as nestlings were so low, we needed our entire data set to determine the relationship between fledging date and probability of returning to become a breeder (for females, our sample was still small after sixteen years!). Because there was such high territory fidelity, we could not have provided valid estimates of the age at which males obtained territories, the time during the spring they did so, and the method of territory acquisition (replacement, insertion, etc.) without the data from our entire study. We also needed the entire data set to determine the size of floater beats and how far from their capture sites floaters obtained their territories.

For females, we needed the entire data set for some analyses in which we had to segregate individuals by age, size of harem in which they bred, their rank in harem, and when they started and terminated nesting. Included in this set are the effects of previous reproductive effort on RS in subsequent years, and mean annual fledgling production as a function of age, start time, rank in harem, and size of harem in which females bred. We also needed the entire data set to determine correlations between rank in harem and age.

Long-term Data and Environmental Variability

Marsh vegetation is dynamic, changing in response to water levels, intrinsic vegetation cycles, and disturbance by animals. Production of food that supports blackbird breeding is highly variable within and among marshes, within and between years. Without a long-term empirical record of such changes, we could not have estimated the predictive value of environmental information potentially available to redwings. Estimates of predictive value of information are the basis of our interpretations of why redwings appear to ignore some types of environmental information but respond to others.

Over the period of our study, the CNWR redwing population also changed. It remained fairly stable in size during the first decade of the study and then declined significantly. During that period the population of Yellow-headed Blackbirds breeding in the same marshes first increased and then also declined precipitously. We were able to estimate changes in the size of the redwing floater population during the population decline and the effect of temporarily high yellowhead breeding density on male redwing site fidelity. Our long-term data set also enabled us to observe variation in return rate as a function of natal year.

The removal experiments we conducted during the period of stable populations yielded results strikingly different from those of removal experiments we conducted when the population was declining and relatively few floater males were present on the study area. As a result, we altered our interpretations of causes of territorial dominance. Some animal behaviors are very sensitive to population density, being expressed or inhibited at particularly high or low densities. Thus, some potentially important behaviors may be amenable to detection and investigation only during a long study, which usually encompasses periods of varying population sizes. The influence of disease or extreme but infrequent weather conditions can be assessed only if those conditions appear during a study. In the middle of our investigations, ash from the eruption of Mount St Helens fell on our study area; from this event we were able to determine that the near absence of a year class had little influence on the number of breeding redwings the following year. In short, short-term studies risk missing important behavior, or missing the significance of seemingly minor or seldom-expressed behavior.

Where Short-Term Data Suffice

Although we required the full duration of our study to answer many important questions about decision-making among redwings and its consequences, answers to some of our questions did not requre the full data set. Our estimates of LRS using our sixteen-year data set do not differ from those we determined midway through the study (Orians and Beletsky 1989). At that point we had reliable estimates of site fidelity of territorial males, the success of males that made short-distance territory shifts, and the fates of males that lost their territories as a result of our removal experiments. Although we did not gather extensive data on floaters early during the study, we believe that our measures of floater site fidelity are representative of what a longer-term data set would show.

Because the number of females that bred each year on our study area was large, and because we could recognize yearling females by their plumage, we could determine, with a data set of less than ten years, the relationships between age and date of initiation of breeding and could establish that mean annual production of fledglings by females was independent of their age. Similarly, relationships between rank in harem and mate fidelity, the influence of reproductive effort on performance in subsequent years, and the influence of female interactions on temporal and spatial settling patterns were evident from a few years' data. We believe that experiments extending over two years were sufficient to determine that females ignored nests from previous years in making their settling decisions (Erckmann et al. 1990). Three years of data sufficed to reveal the extent of extrapair copulations and fertilizations and to show how females benefited from EPCs (Gray 1996a,b,c,d), but a longer-term data set might reveal as yet undetected interannual variation in the frequency with which females seek EPCs. The influence of familiar neighboring territorial males on settling decisions of females was evident from an analysis of only part of our data (Beletsky and Orians 1989b, 1991).

THE VALUE OF MULTIPLE TESTS OF HYPOTHESES

Many features of ecological systems are influenced by multiple processes whose influences are not mutually exclusive. Therefore it is unproductive to ask, say, whether the structure of ecological communities is determined by competition or predation. We need to determine the roles of competition and predation and to assess how their relative importance varies among species and environmental conditions. Similarly, it is unproductive to ask whether territorial dominance is caused by resource-holding potential (RHP) or value asymmetry (VA) because both processes may be influencing the outcome of interactions among territorial contestants.

The value of multiple tests to assess the relative roles of nonmutually exclusive processes influencing a particular outcome is illustrated by our analyses of territorial dominance. The results of our single-removal experiments were consistent with either a VA or RHP hypothesis of terrritorial dominance. The outcome of our double-removal experiment, on the other hand, was consistent with VA but not RHP. Lacking other evidence, we would have concluded that VA offered the best interpretation of why owners nearly always win territorial contests and, by implication, why they are able to acquire territories in the first place. However, our extensive evidence on floater behavior and our most recent removal experiments (1993–94) suggest important roles for RHP both in the regular dominance interactions between owners and floaters and in how floaters seek to acquire territories. We also monitored and manipulated hormone levels of territory owners and floaters to determine whether there was a correlation between RHP and plasma testosterone levels (Beletsky et al. 1990). Most floaters with experimentally elevated testosterone levels did not acquire territories, supporting the view that high testosterone levels are the result of, rather than a cause of, territory ownership. Finally, the behavior of males that lost their territories during removal experiments strongly points to the existence of cognitive processes that assign a high value to a territory that has been occupied.

Thus, our full data set suggests a complex interaction between VA and RHP that varies seasonally and with stage of occupancy, a pattern that we suspect may characterize many territorial species.

Similarly, although our data gathering and analyses of decision-making by female redwings were not designed to assess the relative importance of different hypotheses of female decision-making, our understanding of how and why females made the choices they did was greatly enhanced by analyzing our data from a number of different perspectives. Analyses of the dates on which females initiated nesting relative to other females provided some evidence consistent with an influence of genetics on timing of breeding. We also gathered extensive evidence that several factors influence a female's seasonal RS, but that rank in harem was not one of them. In combination, these data suggested plausible explanations of why females initiate nesting over such a long time period each spring and why they do not compete strongly for rank.

THE VALUE OF A DECISION-MAKING APPROACH

A comprehensive understanding of the evolution of behavior requires an integration of knowledge about its mechanistic foundations with measures of the consequences of performing the behavior in nature (Real 1994). Our study was designed to reveal how Red-winged Blackbirds make their major breeding-season decisions and to determine how and why those decisions influence survival and reproductive success. We examined a broad array of decisions, including intraspecific interactions (mate and site choice, competition for space), interspecific interactions (competition, brood parasitism, predation), and interactions with the physical environment. If students of breeding biology gather only population data that quantify average performances and statistical patterns, the underlying behavioral activities yielding those results remain obscure. Because most of the population phenomena studied by ecologists are the result of the decisions of large numbers of individuals, knowing how and why those decisions are made is a vital building block for understanding the life-history characteristics of species. Those traits are, in turn, the building blocks for analyses of population dynamics, interspecific interactions, community structure, and ecosystem dynamics.

Both the design of our field observations and experiments and the structure of our analyses were strongly guided by a game-theoretic approach to decision-making. We considered games against conspecifics, where the behavior of the interactants can be modified in response to

social cues, and games against the environment, whose behavior is uninfluenced by the actions of the birds. A game-theoretic approach especially influenced our investigations of the causes of territorial dominance. Our single-removal experiments were specifically designed to
distinguish between RHP and VA hypotheses. When we realized that
the results of those experiments were compatible with both theories,
we conceived of and designed a double-removal experiment whose result
clearly distinguished between the two hypotheses. The RHP and VA
models also led us to develop predictions about the behavior of floaters
and territorial owners expected in unmanipulated situations. Without
the theories, we might eventually have arrived at an equally insightful
explanation of why territory owners nearly always win challenges and
typically maintain their territories without being seriously challenged.
But we doubt it.

SCALES OF DECISION-MAKING

Decisions made by birds during the breeding season are based on information useful at variable temporal and spatial scales. The decisions also
affect and constrain other decisions at variable temporal and spatial
scales. Getting the scale right is a major problem in behavioral ecological
studies. If inappropriate scales of analysis are used, key factors influencing decisions and their consequences may not be detected and the role
of those factors that are recognized may be misinterpreted (Orians and
Wittenberger 1991).

Temporal Scales of Decision-Making

Choice of a location in which to establish a territory or build a nest
determines the array of environments that are available for exploitation
during the entire breeding cycle. Within-season territorial shifts do
happen, but they are sufficiently rare among redwings and most other
birds that occupancy of a territory can, to a useful approximation, be
viewed as a breeding-season-long decision. If considerable time is available during which to make that decision, if the costs of searching and
evaluating sites are low, and if high-quality sites do not become unavail-
able rapidly by being occupied by other individuals, then choice of a
territory should be made deliberately. For most small birds, however,
time has a high value. Delaying decisions reduces both options and
within-season RS. Nesting success of Pied Flycatchers, for instance,
declines so rapidly during the breeding season in northern Europe that
delays of even a few days reduce nesting success (von Haartman 1969;
Alatalo and Lundberg 1984; Harvey et al. 1985; Lundberg and Alatalo

1992) and reduce the number of unpaired individuals available for mating (Slagsvold et al. 1988).

Choice of a nest site constrains other decisions so long as the nest remains active. However, because nest destruction rates are high for most small birds, females often have additional opportunities to choose nest sites within a breeding season. Among monogamous species, replacement nest-sites are likely to be limited to those within the territory in which the first nest was built. In these species, therefore, choice of nest site typically constrains options for an entire breeding season just as territory choice does. Thus, female redwings have more within-season nest-site options than do females of most other small bird species.

Spatial Scales of Decision-Making

Breeding-season choices are usefully viewed as a nested hierarchy of decisions, each one of which constrains options at other levels. Choice of a general breeding situation determines which patches are available for use at varying distances from some central location. Choice of a patch, in turn, determines the types of objects that will be encountered within it. Some breeding-season activities, such as foraging, are extensive in nature, whereas others, such as selection of a nest site, are local but intensive in nature. The significance of location of resources depends on the mobility of the organism, the cost of moving a unit of distance, and the risks to which the organism exposes itself while moving. But there are inevitable costs of exploiting resources at a distance from a central location (Orians and Pearson 1979; Schoener 1979).

In general, the location of the resource with the most restricted distribution exerts the most powerful constraint on where individuals settle. In addition, if that resource is needed throughout the breeding season, it can influence the spatial distribution of use of the more extensively distributed resources. For redwings, as well as for yellowheads and many other species, the nest site, which is the local, intensively used resource, ultimately determines where males establish territories as well as where females settle. Food resources can be and are exploited at considerable distances from the nests. At CNWR, there are extensive undefended areas with abundant food supplies that are readily accessible to nesting birds within short and energetically affordable flying times. The small sizes of territories and the high densities of blackbird nests are the result of this spatial configuration of patches, combined with the high productivity of the CNWR lakes.

The situation is likely to be quite different if a species's breeding habitat is the dominant or exclusive habitat type over broad areas. In this situation, undefended foraging areas are scarce and the territory or home range must contain most, if not all, of the resources necessary to support successful breeding. The large territories and the restricted opportunities for nonbreeding individuals within the breeding habitat that prevail in these situations change many aspects of breeding-season decision-making. Floaters either may exist as furtive "underworld" individuals that persist by avoiding contact with territory owners (Song Sparrows [*Melospiza melodia*], Rufous-collared Sparrows [*Zonotrichia capensis*]—Smith 1978; Arcese 1987) or may live in spatially separate areas (Great Tits—Krebs 1971, 1982) from which they can make only occasional forays into breeding habitats to search for vacancies or evaluate the condition of territory holders. The slopes of the information-distance curves should also vary among habitat types. In the open environments in which redwings breed, locations of territories, their general features, and RHPs of owners are relatively easy to determine. Therefore, both territory owners and floaters probably possess fairly detailed information about conditions of many territories and their owners. In structurally complex vegetation where visibility is highly restricted, an individual's knowledge probably decreases rapidly with distance from its territory or home range.

Thus, we expect that the habitat a population occupies, the distribution of sites suitable for breeding within the habitat, and other natural-history features all strongly influence avian breeding-season decisions and behavior. Our findings on the relative roles of RHP, VA, and lottery hypotheses of territorial dominance may be specific to the natural-history features of redwings and the CNWR environment. The patchiness of breeding habitat, the presence of observation cliffs, and the low stature of vegetation allow floaters to monitor many territories from undefended vantage points. Floaters of species breeding in complex vegetation that is fully occupied by territories may have no options other than to wait as members of a furtive underworld or to help their parents raise subsequent broods. For species that are permanent residents on their territories, vacancies may result primarily from the deaths of individuals, which may happen at any time during the year, resulting in year-round monitoring by floaters. RHP and lottery may exert more influence on territory acquisition and maintenance among those species than among CNWR redwings.

The existence of a large number of floater males strongly influences the breeding tactics of redwings. Polyterritoriality is probably impossible under those conditions. If all males acquire territories, contests over space may be very brief, although variations in quality of available habitats may favor initial challenges for higher-quality sites. The length of the breeding season also influences temporal patterns of territorial contests and investments in mate attraction. Fortunately, a game-theoretic approach can be modified according to the features of the species and its breeding environments to yield situation-specific predictions. A rich array of such predictions and tests eventually will lead to a much deeper understanding of how and why factors that influence avian breeding-season decisions vary in space and time.

We do not claim to have demonstrated how linkages can be established between behavioral ecology and community structure, but we do hope to have provided some valuable insights into how and why individuals of one species use—or ignore—environmental information, and how their use of information influences a number of population processes. These insights constitute modest but useful building blocks for the eventual vertical integration of ecology. In addition, by focusing on decision-making we have derived some insights about redwing intelligence that may help guide studies of the internal mechanistic foundations of behavior. How useful these insights may eventually prove to be, only the future will tell.

REFERENCES

Abramson, C. I., and M. E. Bitterman. 1986. Latent inhibition in honey bees. *Anim. Learning Behav.* 14:184–9.

Alatalo, R. V., and A. Lundberg. 1984. Polyterritorial polygyny in the Pied Flycatcher *Ficedula hypoleuca*—evidence for the deception hypothesis. *Ann. Zool. Fenn.* 21:217–28.

Arcese, P. 1987. Age, intrusion pressure, and defense against floaters by territorial male Song Sparrows. *Anim. Behav.* 35:773–84.

Arnold, S. J. 1994. Constraints on phenotypic evolution. In *Behavioral mechanisms in evolutionary ecology*, ed. L. A. Real, 258–78. Chicago: University of Chicago Press.

Arnold, S. J., and M. J. Wade. 1984. On the measurement of natural and sexual selection: Theory. *Evolution* 38:709–19.

Aschoff, J., and H. Pohl. 1970. Der Ruheumsatz von Vögelen als Funktion der Tageszeit und der Körpergrösse. *J. Ornithol.* 111:38–47.

Beletsky, L. D. 1983. Aggressive and pair-bond maintenance songs of female Red-winged Blackbirds (*Agelaius phoeniceus*). *Z. Tierpsychol.* 62:47–54.

———. 1992. Social stability and territory acquisition in birds. *Behaviour* 123: 290–313.

———. 1996. *The Red-winged Blackbird*. London: Academic Press.

Beletsky, L. D., and G. H. Orians. 1985. Nest-associated vocalizations of female Red-winged Blackbirds. *Z. Tierpsychol.* 69:329–39.

———. 1987a. Territoriality among male Red-winged Blackbirds. I. Site fidelity and movement patterns. *Behav. Ecol. Sociobiol.* 20:21–34.

———. 1987b. Territoriality among male Red-winged Blackbirds. II. Site dominance and removal experiments. *Behav. Ecol. Sociobiol.* 20:339–49.

———. 1989a. Territoriality among male Red-winged Blackbirds. III. Testing hypotheses of territorial dominance. *Behav. Ecol. Sociobiol.* 24:333–9.

———. 1989b. Familiar neighbors enhance breeding success in birds. *Proc. Natl. Acad. Sci.* 86:7933–6.

———. 1989c. A male Red-winged Blackbird breeds for 11 years. *Northwestern Naturalist* 70:10–12.

———. 1990. Male parental care in a population of Red-winged Blackbirds, 1983–1988. *Can. J. Zool.* 68:606–9.

———. 1991. Effects of breeding experience and familiarity on site fidelity in female Red-winged Blackbirds. *Ecology* 72:787–96.

———. 1993. Factors affecting which male Red-winged Blackbirds acquire territories. *Condor* 95:782–91.

———. 1994. Site fidelity and territorial movements in a rapidly declining population of Yellow-headed Blackbirds. *Behav. Ecol. Sociobiol.* 34:257–66.

Beletsky, L. D., D. F. Gori, S. Freeman, and J. C. Wingfield. 1995. Testosterone and polygyny in birds. *Current Orn.* 12:1–41.

Beletsky, L. D., B. Higgins, and G. H. Orians. 1986. Communication by changing signals: Call-switching in Red-winged Blackbirds. *Behav. Ecol. Sociobiol.* 18:221–9.

Beletsky, L. D., G. H. Orians, and J. C. Wingfield. 1989. Relationships of steroid hormones and polygyny to territorial status, breeding experience, and reproductive success in male Red-winged Blackbirds. *Auk* 106:107–17.

———. 1990. Effects of exogenous androgen and antiandrogen on territorial and nonterritorial blackbirds. *Ethology* 85:58–72.

Birkhead, T. R., and A. P. Møller. 1992. *Sperm competition in birds: Evolutionary causes and consequences.* Orlando: Academic Press.

Bretz, J. H. 1959. Washington's channeled scablands. State of Washington, Division of Mines and Geology. *Bull.* 45:1–57.

Brown, J. L. 1964. The evolution of diversity in avian territorial systems. *Wilson Bull.* 76:160–9.

———. 1978. Avian communal breeding systems. *Ann. Rev. Ecol. Syst.* 9:123–55.

———. 1987. *Helping and communal breeding in birds: Ecology and evolution.* Princeton: Princeton University Press.

Bryant, D. M. 1979. Reproductive costs in the House Martin *Delichon urbica*. *J. Anim. Ecol.* 48:655–75.

Bryant, D. M., and P. Tatner. 1988. The costs of brood provisioning: Effects of brood size and food supply. *Proc. Intl. Ornithol. Congr.* 19:364–79.

Bryant, D. M., and K. R. Westerterp. 1983. Time and energy limits to brood size in House Martins. *J. Anim. Ecol.* 52:905–25.

Caccamise, D. F. 1976. Nesting mortality in the Red-winged Blackbird. *Auk* 93:517–34.

———. 1978. Seasonal patterns of nesting mortality in the Red-winged Blackbird. *Condor* 80:290–4.

Case, N. A., and O. H. Hewitt. 1963. Nesting and productivity of the Red-winged Blackbird in relation to habitat. *Living Bird* 2:7–20.

Charles, J. K. 1972. Territorial behaviour and the limitation of population size in Crows, *Corvus corone* and *C. cornix*. Ph.D. diss., University of Aberdeen, Scotland.

Charnov, E. L. 1973. Optimal foraging: Some theoretical explorations. Ph.D. diss., University of Washington, Seattle.

———. 1976a. Optimal foraging, the marginal value theorem. *Theoret. Pop. Biol.* 9:129–36.

———. 1976b. Optimal foraging: Attack strategy of a mantid. *Am. Nat.* 110:141–51.

Collias, N. E., and E. C. Collias. 1984. *Nest building and bird behavior.* Princeton: Princeton University Press.

Coombs-Hahn, T. P. 1993. Integration of environmental cues to time of repro-duction in an opportunistic breeder, the Red Crossbill (*Loxia curvirostra*). Ph.D. diss., University of Washington, Seattle.

Crawford, R. D. 1977. Breeding biology of year-old and older female Red-winged and Yellow-headed Blackbirds. *Wilson Bull.* 89:73–80.

Crook, J. H. 1964. The evolution of social organization and visual communica-tion in the weaver birds (Ploceinae). *Behav. Suppl.* 10:1–178.

Darwin, C. 1859. *On the origin of species by means of natural selection.* Lon-don: John Murray.

———. 1871. *The descent of man, and selection in relation to sex.* London: John Murray.

Davies, N. B. 1980. The economics of territorial behaviour in birds. *Ardea* 68: 63–74.

Davies, N. B., and A. I. Houston. 1981. Owners and satellites: The economics of territory defense in the Pied Wagtail, *Motacilla alba. J. Anim. Ecol.* 50: 157–80.

Dawkins, R. 1986. *The blind watchmaker.* New York: W. W. Norton.

Dennett, D. C. 1975. Why the law of effect will not go away. *J. Theor. Soc. Behav.* 5:169–87.

DeSteven, D. 1980. Clutch size, breeding success, and parental survival in the Tree Swallow (*Iridoprocne bicolor*). *Evolution* 34:278–91.

Dobson, S. F., and W. T. Jones. 1985. Multiple causes of dispersal. *Am. Nat.* 126:855–8.

Dolbeer, R. A. 1976. Reproductive rate and temporal spacing of nesting of Red-winged Blackbirds in upland habitat. *Auk* 93:343–55.

Drent, R. H., and S. Daan. 1980. The prudent parent: Energetic adjustments in avian breeding. *Ardea* 68:225–52.

Drilling, N. E., and C. F. Thompson. 1988. Natal and breeding dispersal in House Wrens (*Troglodytes aedon*). *Auk* 105:480–91.

Eason, P., and S. J. Hannon. 1994. New birds on the block: New neighbors increase defensive costs for territorial male Willow Ptarmigan. *Behav. Ecol. Sociobiol.* 34:419–26.

Eckert, C. G., and P. J. Weatherhead. 1987a. Male characteristics, parental quality and the study of mate choice in the Red-winged Blackbird (*Agelaius phoeniceus*). *Behav. Ecol. Sociobiol.* 20:35–42.

———. 1987b. Owners, floaters, and competitive asymmetries among territo-rial Red-winged Blackbirds. *Anim. Behav.* 35:1317–23.

———. 1987c. Ideal dominance distributions: A test using Red-winged Black-birds (*Agelaius phoeniceus*). *Behav. Ecol. Sociobiol.* 20:43–52.

———. 1987d. Competition for territories in Red-winged Blackbirds: Is re-source-holding potential realized? *Behav. Ecol. Sociobiol.* 20:369–75.

Ekman, J., and C. Askenmo. 1986. Reproductive cost, age-specific survival and a comparison of the reproductive strategy in two European tits (Genus *Parus*). *Evolution* 40:159–68.

Emlen, S. T. 1984. Cooperative breeding in birds and mammals. In *Behavioural ecology: An evolutionary approach,* 2d ed., ed. J. R. Krebs and N. B. Davies, 305–39. Oxford: Blackwell Scientific Publications.

Emlen, S. T., and L. W. Oring. 1977. Ecology, sexual selection, and the evolution of mating systems. *Science* 197:215–23.

Emlen, S. T., N. J. Demong, and D. J. Emlen. 1989. Experimental induction of infanticide in female Wattled Jacanas. *Auk* 106:1–7.

Erckmann, W. J., L. D. Beletsky, G. H. Orians, T. Johnsen, S. Sharbaugh, and C. D'Antonio. 1990. Old nests as cues for nest site selection: An experimental test with Red-winged Blackbirds. *Condor* 92:113–17.

Ewald, P. W., and S. Rohwer. 1982. Effects of supplemental feeding on timing of breeding, clutch-size and polygyny in Red-winged Blackbirds, *Agelaius phoeniceus. J. Anim. Ecol.* 51:429–50.

Falls, J. B. 1982. Individual recognition by sounds in birds. In *Acoustic communication in birds,* vol. 2, ed. D. Kroodsma and E. Miller, 237–78. New York: Academic Press.

Freeman, S. 1987. Male Red-winged Blackbirds (*Agelaius phoeniceus*) assess the RHP of neighbors by watching contests. *Behav. Ecol. Sociobiol.* 21: 307–11.

Fretwell, S. D., and H. L. Lucas. 1970. On territorial behavior and other factors influencing habitat distribution in birds. I. Theoretical development. *Acta Biotheoret.* 19:16–36.

Garcia, J., and R. A. Koelling. 1966. Relation of cue to consequences in avoidance learning. *Psychonomic Science* 4:123–4.

Garnett, M. C. 1981. Body size, its heritability and influence on juvenile survival among Great Tits, *Parus Major. Ibis* 123:31–41.

Garson, P. J., W. K. Pleszczynska, and C. H. Holm. 1981. The "polygyny threshold" model: A reassessment. *Can. J. Zool.* 59:902–10.

Gauthier, M., and D. W. Thomas. 1993. Nest site selection and cost of nest building by Cliff Swallows (*Hirundo pyrrhonota*). *Can. J. Zool.* 71:1120–3.

Getty, T. 1987. Dear enemies and the prisoner's dilemma: Why should territorial neighbours form defensive coalitions? *Am. Zool.* 27:327–36.

———. 1989. Are dear enemies in a war of attrition? *Anim. Behav.* 37:337–9.

Gibbs, H. L., P. J. Weatherhead, P. T. Boag, B. N. White, L. M. Tabak, and D. Hoysak. 1990. Realized reproductive success of polygynous Red-winged Blackbirds revealed by DNA markers. *Science* 250:1394–7.

Gill, F. B., and L. L. Wolf. 1975. Economics of feeding territoriality in the Golden-winged Sunbird. *Ecology* 56:333–45.

Gori, D. F. 1984. The evolution of paternal care patterns and coloniality in Yellow-headed Blackbirds (*Xanthocephalus xanthocephalus*). Ph.D. diss., University of Arizona, Tucson.

Gowaty, P. A., and S. J. Wagner. 1988. Breeding season aggression of female and male Eastern Bluebirds (*Sialia sialis*) to models of potential conspecific and interspecific egg dumpers. *Ethology* 78:238–50.

Grafen, A. 1984. Natural selection, kin selection and group selection. In *Behavioural ecology: An evolutionary approach,* 2d ed., ed. J. R. Krebs and N. B. Davies, 62–89. Sunderland, MA: Sinauer.

―――. 1987. The logic of divisively asymmetric contests: Respect for owner-ship and the desperado effect. *Anim. Behav.* 35:462–7.

Gray, E. M. 1994. The ecological and evolutionary significance of extra-pair copulations in the Red-winged Blackbird. Ph.D. diss., University of Wash-ington, Seattle.

―――. 1996a. Female control of offspring paternity in a western population of Red-winged Blackbirds (*Agelaius phoeniceus*). *Behav. Ecol. Sociobiol.*, 38: 267–78.

―――. 1996b. Extra-pair copulations in Red-winged Blackbirds: Behavior as an estimate of genetic paternity and the influence of extra-pair copulations on male reproductive success. *Behav. Ecol.*, in press.

―――. 1996c. Female Red-winged Blackbirds in a western population accrue ma-terial benefits from copulating with extra-pair males. *Anim. Behav.*, in press.

―――. 1996d. Extra-pair copulations as an important component of female Red-winged Blackbird reproductive success in western North America. *Anim. Behav.*, in press.

Greenwood, H. 1985. Sexual selection and delayed plumage maturation in the subadult male cohort of the Red-winged Blackbird (*Agelaius phoeniceus*). Ph.D. diss., McGill University, Montreal.

Greenwood, P. J., and P. H. Harvey. 1982. The natal and breeding dispersal of birds. *Ann. Rev. Ecol. Syst.* 13:1–21.

Gustafsson, L., and T. Pärt. 1990. Acceleration of senescence in the Collared Flycatcher *Ficedula albicollis* by reproductive costs. *Nature* 347:279–81.

Haartman, L. von. 1969. Nest-site and evolution of polygamy in European passerine birds. *Ornis Fenn.* 46:1–12.

Hamilton, W. D. 1964. The genetical evolution of social behavior. *J. Theoret. Biol.* 7:1–52.

Hammerstein, P. 1981. The role of asymmetries in animal contests. *Anim. Behav.* 29:193–205.

Hannon, S. J., R. L. Mumme, W. D. Koenig, and F. A. Pitelka. 1985. Replace-ment of breeders and within-group conflict in the cooperatively breeding Acorn Woodpecker. *Behav. Ecol. Sociobiol.* 17:303–12.

Hansen, A. J., and S. Rohwer. 1986. Coverable badges and resource defense in birds. *Anim. Behav.* 34:69–76.

Harms, K. E., L. D. Beletsky, and G. H. Orians. 1991. Conspecific nest parasit-ism in three species of New World Blackbirds. *Condor* 93:967–74.

Harris, M. P. 1970. Territory limiting the size of the breeding population of the Oystercatcher (*Haematopus ostralegus*)—a removal experiment. *J. Anim. Ecol.* 39:707–13.

Harris, M. P., D. J. Halley, and S. Wanless. 1992. The post-fledging survival of young Guillemots *Uria aalgae* in relation to hatching date and growth. *Ibis* 134:335–9.

Harvey, P. H., M. J. Stenning, and B. Campbell. 1985. Individual variation in seasonal breeding success of Pied Flycatchers. *J. Anim. Ecol.* 54:391–8.

Hausfater, G., and S. B. Hrdy. 1984. *Infanticide: Comparative and evolution-ary perspectives*. Chicago: Aldine Press.

Hinde, R. A. 1956. The biological significance of the territories of birds. *Ibis* 98:340–69.

Hochachka, W. M. 1990. Seasonal decline in reproductive performance of Song Sparrows. *Ecology* 71:1279–88.

Högstedt, G. 1981. Should there be a positive or negative correlation between survival of adults in a bird population and their clutch size? *Am. Nat.* 118: 568–71.

Holcomb, L. C. 1974. The question of possible surplus females in breeding Red-winged Blackbirds. *Wilson Bull.* 86:177–9.

Holm, C. H. 1973. Breeding sex ratios, territoriality, and reproductive success in the Red-winged Blackbird (*Agelaius phoeniceus*). *Ecology* 54:356–65.

Hrdy, S. B. 1977a. *The langurs of Abu.* Cambridge: Harvard University Press.

———. 1977b. Infanticide as a primate reproductive strategy. *Am. Sci.* 65: 40–9.

Hurly, T. A., and R. J. Robertson. 1984. Aggressive and territorial behaviour in female Red-winged Blackbirds. *Can. J. Zool.* 62:148–53.

———. 1985. Do female Red-winged Blackbirds limit harem size? I. A removal experiment. *Auk* 102:205–9.

Immelmann, K. 1973. Role of the environment in reproduction as a source of predictive information. In *Breeding biology of birds*, ed. D. S. Farner, 121–47. Washington, DC: National Academy of Sciences USA.

Irwin, R. E. 1994. The evolution of plumage dichromatism in the New World blackbirds: Social selection on female brightness? *Am. Nat.* 144: 890–907.

Kamil, A. C. 1994. A synthetic approach to the study of animal intelligence. In *Behavioral mechanisms in evolutionary ecology*, ed. L. A. Real, 11–45. Chicago: University of Chicago Press.

Kermott, L. H., L. S. Johnson, and M. S. Merkle. 1991. Experimental evidence for the function of mate replacement and infanticide in a north-temperate population of House Wrens. *Condor* 93:630–6.

King, J. R., and D. S. Farner. 1961. Energy metabolism, thermoregulation, and body temperature. In *Biology and comparative physiology of birds*, vol. 2, ed. A. J. Marshall, 215–88. New York: Academic Press.

Knapton, R. R., and J. R. Krebs. 1974. Settlement patterns, territory size, and breeding density in the Song Sparrow (*Melospiza melodia*). *Can. J. Zool.* 52:1413–19.

Knight, R. L., and S. A. Temple. 1988. Nest-defense behavior in the Red-winged Blackbird. *Condor* 90:193–200.

Krebs, J. R. 1971. Territory and breeding density in the Great Tit, *Parus major*. *Ecology* 52:2–22.

———. 1977. The significance of song repertoires: The Beau Geste hypothesis. *Anim. Behav.* 25:475–8.

———. 1982. Territorial defense in the Great Tit (*Parus major*): Do residents always win? *Behav. Ecol. Sociobiol.* 11:185–94.

Labov, J. B., V. W. Huck, R. W. Elwood, and R. J. Brooks. 1985. Current problems in the study of infanticidal behavior of rodents. *Quart. Rev. Biol.* 60:1–20.

REFERENCES 277

Lack, D. 1954. *The natural regulation of animal numbers.* Oxford: Clarendon Press.

————. 1966. *Population studies of birds.* Oxford: Clarendon Press.

————. 1968. *Ecological adaptations to breeding in birds.* London: Methuen.

Lande, R. 1980. Sexual dimorphism, sexual selection, and adaptation in polygenic characters. *Evolution* 34:292–305.

Langston, N. E., S. Freeman, S. Rohwer, and D. Gori. 1990. The evolution of female body size in Red-winged Blackbirds: The effects of timing of breeding, social competition, and reproductive energetics. *Evolution* 44:1764–79.

Laux, L. J. 1970. Nonbreeding surplus and population structure of the Red-winged Blackbird (*Agelaius phoeniceus*). Ph.D. diss., University of Michigan, Ann Arbor.

Lenington, S. 1980. Female choice and polygyny in Red-winged Blackbirds. *Anim. Behav.* 28:347–61.

Lens, L., L. A. Wauters, and A. A. Dhondt. 1994. Nest-building by Crested Tit *Parus cristatus* males: An analysis of costs and benefits. *Behav. Ecol. Sociobiol.* 35:431–6.

Lessells, C. M. 1991. The evolution of life histories. In *Behavioural ecology: An evolutionary approach,* 3d ed., ed. J. R. Krebs and N. B. Davies, 32–68. Oxford: Blackwell Scientific Publications.

Lewontin, R. C. 1970. The units of selection. *Ann. Rev. Ecol. Syst.* 1:1–18.

Lorenz, K. 1966. *On Aggression.* New York: Harcourt Brace Jovanovich.

Lundberg, A., and R. V. Alatalo. 1992. *The Pied Flycatcher.* London: T. and A. D. Poyser.

Marshall, A. J. 1970. Environmental factors other than light involved in the control of sexual cycles in birds and mammals. In *La Photorégulation de la Reproduction Chez les Oiseaux et les Mammifères,* ed. J. Benoit and I. Assenmacher, 53–64. Paris: Cent. Natl. Rech. Sci.

Masman, D., S. Daan, S. and H. J. A. Beldhuis. 1988. Ecological energetics of the kestrel: Daily energy expenditure throughout the year based on time-energy budget, food intake and doubly labeled water methods. *Ardea* 76:64–81.

Maynard Smith, J. 1974. *Models in ecology.* Cambridge: Cambrige University Press.

————. 1978. Optimization theory in evolution. *Ann. Rev. Ecol. Syst.* 9:31–56.

Maynard Smith, J., and G. A. Parker. 1976. The logic of asymmetric contests. *Anim. Behav.* 24:159–75.

Maynard Smith, J., and G. R. Price. 1973. The logic of animal conflict. *Nature* 246:15–18.

McKitrick, M. C. 1992. Phylogenetic analysis of avian parental care. *Auk* 109:828–46.

Miskimen, M. 1980. Red-winged blackbirds: I. Age-related epaulet color changes in captive females. *Ohio J. Sci.* 80:232–5.

Mock, P. J. 1991. Daily allocation of time and energy of Western Bluebirds feeding nestlings. *Condor* 93:598–611.

Møller, A. P., and T. R. Birkhead. 1994. The evolution of plumage brightness in birds is related to extrapair paternity. *Evolution* 48:1089–1100.

Moreno, J. 1989. Variation in daily energy expenditure in nestling Northern Wheatears (*Oenanthe oenanthe*). *Auk* 106:18–25.

Moreno, J., and J. J. Sanz. 1994. The relationship between the energy expenditure during incubation and clutch size in the Pied Flycatcher *Ficedula hypoleuca*. *J. Avian Biol.* 25:125–30.

Morton, M. L., M. W. Wakakamatsu, M. E. Pereyra, and G. A. Morton. 1991. Postfledging dispersal, habitat imprinting, and philopatry in a montane migratory sparrow. *Ornis. Scand.* 22:98–106.

Muldal, A. M., J. D. Moffatt, and R. J. Robertson. 1986. Parental care of nestlings by male Red-winged Blackbirds. *Behav. Ecol. Sociobiol.* 19:105–14.

Muma, K. E., and P. J. Weatherhead. 1989. Male traits expressed in females: Direct or indirect sexual selection? *Behav. Ecol. Sociobiol.* 25:23–31.

———. 1991. Plumage variation and dominance in captive female Red-winged Blackbirds. *Can. J. Zool.* 69:49–54.

Murphy, M. T. 1986. Temporal components of reproductive variability in Eastern Kingbirds (*Tyrannus tyrannus*). *Ecology* 67:1483–92.

Nero, R. W. 1954. Plumage aberrations in the Redwing (*Agelaius phoeniceus*). *Auk* 71:137–55.

———. 1956a. A behavior study of the Red-winged Blackbird. I. Mating and nesting activities. *Wilson Bull.* 68:5–37.

———. 1956b. A behavior study of the Red-winged Blackbird. II. Territoriality. *Wilson Bull.* 68:129–50.

Newton, I. 1973. *Finches.* New York: Taplinger.

———. 1989. Synthesis. In *Lifetime reproduction in birds,* ed. I. Newton, 441–69. New York: Academic Press.

Nolan, V. 1978. The ecology and behavior of the Prairie Warbler, *Dendroica discolor*. *Ornithol. Monogr.* 26:1–595.

Nolan, V., and C. F. Thompson. 1975. The occurrence and significance of anomalous reproductive activities in two North American nonparasitic cuckoos *Coccyzus* sp. *Ibis* 117:496–503.

Nur, N. 1984. The consequences of brood size for breeding Blue Tits. I. Adult survival, weight change and the cost of reproduction. *J. Anim. Ecol.* 53: 479–96.

———. 1988a. The consequences of brood size for breeding Blue Tits. III. Measuring the cost of reproduction: survival, future fecundity, and differential dispersal. *Evolution* 42:351–62.

———. 1988b. The cost of reproduction in birds: An examination of the evidence. *Ardea* 76:155–68.

O'Connor, E. 1976. Response of female Red-winged and Brewer's Blackbirds to the presence of intruding female conspecifics near their nests. Master's thesis, University of Washington, Seattle.

Orians, G. H. 1961. The ecology of blackbird (*Agelaius*) social systems. *Ecol. Monogr.* 31:285–312.

———. 1969. On the evolution of mating systems in birds and mammals. *Am. Nat.* 103:589–603.

———. 1972. The adaptive significance of mating systems in the Icteridae. *Proc. XV Int. Orn. Conv:* 389–98.

———. 1973. The Red-winged Blackbird in tropical marshes. *Condor* 75:28–42.

———. 1980. *Some adaptations of marsh-nesting blackbirds.* Princeton: Princeton University Press.

———. 1983. Notes on the behavior of the Melodious Blackbird (*Dives dives*). *Condor* 85:453–60.

———. 1985. *Blackbirds of the Americas.* Seattle: University of Washington Press.

Orians, G. H., and Beletsky, L. D. 1989. Red-winged Blackbird. In *Lifetime reproduction in birds*, ed. I. Newton, 183–97. New York: Academic Press.

Orians, G. H., and G. M. Christman. 1968. A comparative study of the behavior of Red-winged, Tricolored, and Yellow-headed Blackbirds. *Univ. Calif. Publ. Zool.* 84:1–81.

Orians, G. H., and N. E. Pearson. 1979. On the theory of central place foraging. In *Analysis of ecological systems*, ed. D. J. Horn, R. D. Mitchell, and G. R. Stairs, 155–77. Columbus: Ohio State University Press.

Orians, G. H., and Willson, M. F. 1964. Interspecific territories of birds. *Ecology* 45:736–43.

Orians, G. H., and Wittenberger, J. F. 1991. Spatial and temporal scales in habitat selection. *Am. Nat.* 137:S29–S49.

Orians, G. H., C. E. Orians, and K. J. Orians. 1977. Helpers at the nest in some Argentine blackbirds. In *Evolutionary Ecology*, ed. B. Stonehouse and C. Perrins, 137–51. New York: Macmillan.

Orians, G. H., E. Røskaft, and L. D. Beletsky. 1989. Do Brown-headed Cowbirds distribute their eggs at random in the nests of potential hosts? *Wilson Bull.* 101:599–605.

Parker, G. A. 1974. Assessment strategy and the evolution of fighting behaviour. *J. Theor. Biol.* 47:223–43.

Parker, G. A., and D. I. Rubinstein. 1981. Role assessment, reserve strategy and acquisition of information in asymmetric animal conflicts. *Anim. Behav.* 29:221–40.

Patterson, C. B. 1991. Relative parental investment in the Red-winged Blackbird. *J. Field Orn.* 62:1–18.

Patterson, C. B., W. J. Erckmann, and G. H. Orians. 1980. An experimental study of parental investment and polygyny in male blackbirds. *Am. Nat.* 116:757–69.

Payne, R. B. 1965. The breeding seasons and reproductive physiology of Tricolored Blackbirds and Red-winged Blackbirds. Ph.D. diss., University of California, Berkeley.

———. 1969. Breeding seasons and reproductive physiology of Tricolored Blackbirds and Red-winged Blackbirds. *Univ. Calif. Publ. Zool.* 90:1–137.

Payne, R. B., and L. L. Payne. 1993. Breeding dispersal in Indigo Buntings: Circumstances and consequences for breeding success and population structure. *Condor* 95:1–24.

Peek, F. W. 1971. Seasonal change in the breeding behavior of the male Red-winged Blackbird. *Wilson Bull.* 83:383–95.

Perrins, C. M. 1970. The timing of birds' breeding seasons. *Ibis* 112:242–55.

———. 1979. *British Tits.* London: Collins.

Perrins, C. M., and R. H. McCleery. 1989. Laying dates and clutch size in the Great Tit. *Wilson Bull.* 101:236–53.

Petrie, M., and Møller, A. P. 1991. Laying eggs in other's nest: Intraspecific brood parasitism in birds. *Trends Ecol. Ev.* 6:315–20.

Pianka, E. R. 1976. Natural selection of optimal reproductive tactics. *Amer. Zool.* 16:775–84.

Picman, J. 1980. Impact of marsh wrens on reproductive strategy of Red-winged Blackbirds. *Can. J. Zool.* 58:337–50.

———. 1981. The adaptive value of polygyny in marsh-nesting Red-winged Blackbirds; renesting, territory tenacity, and mate fidelity of females. *Can. J. Zool.* 59:2284–96.

———. 1987. Territory establishment, size, and tenacity by male Red-winged Blackbirds. *Auk* 104:405–12.

Picman, J., M. Leonard, and A. Horn. 1988. Antipredation role of clumped nesting by marsh-nesting Red-winged Blackbirds. *Behav. Ecol. Sociobiol.* 22:9–15.

Pitelka, F. A. 1958. Timing of molt in Steller Jays of the Queen Charlotte Islands, British Columbia. *Condor* 60:38–49.

Pyke, G. H. 1979. The economics of territory size and time budget in the Golden-winged Sunbird. *Am. Nat.* 114: 131–45.

Real, L. A. 1994. Information processing and the evolutionary ecology of cognitive architecture. In *Behavioral mechanisms in evolutionary ecology,* ed. L. A. Real, 99–132. Chicago: University of Chicago Press.

Ricklefs, R. E. 1966. The temporal component of diversity among species of birds. *Evolution* 20:235–42.

———. 1983. Comparative avian demography. *Current Orn.* 1:1–32.

Ricklefs, R. E., and J. B. Williams. 1984. Daily energy expenditure and water-turnover rate of adult European Starlings (*Sturnus vulgaris*) during the nesting cycle. *Auk* 101:707–16.

Robinson, S. K. 1986. Three-speed foraging during the breeding cycle of Yellow-rumped Caciques (Icterniae: *Cacicus cela*). *Ecology* 67:394–405.

Rohwer, S. 1982. The evolution of reliable and unreliable badges of fighting ability. *Amer. Zool.* 22:531–46.

———. 1985. Replacement male Red-winged Blackbirds fail to kill unrelated offspring. *Murrelet* 67:37–43.

———. 1986. Selection for adoption versus infanticide by replacement "mates" in birds. *Current Orn.* 3:353–95.

Rohwer, S., and G. S. Butcher. 1988. Winter versus summer explanations of delayed plumage maturation in temperate passerine birds. *Am. Nat.* 131: 556–72.

Rohwer, S., and C. D. Spaw. 1988. Evolutionary lag versus bill-size constraints: A comparative study of the acceptance of cowbird eggs by old hosts. *Evol. Ecol.* 2:27–36.

Rohwer, S., S. D. Fretwell, and D. M. Niles. 1980. Delayed maturation in passerine plumages and the deceptive acquisition of resources. *Am. Nat.* 115: 400–37.

Røskaft, E. 1985. The effect of enlarged brood size on the future reproductive potential of the Rook. *J. Anim. Ecol.* 54:255–60.

Røskaft, E., and S. Rohwer. 1987. An experimental study of the function of the red epaulettes and the black body colour of male Red-winged Blackbirds. *Anim. Behav.* 35:1070–7.

Røskaft, E., G. H. Orians, and L. D. Beletsky. 1990. Why do Red-winged Blackbirds accept eggs of Brown-headed Cowbirds? *Evol. Ecol.* 4:35–42.

Schartz, R. L., and J. L. Zimmerman. 1971. The time and energy budget of the male Dickcissel (*Spiza americana*). *Condor* 73:65–76.

Schoener, T. W. 1979. Generality of the size-distance relation in models of optimal feeding. *Am. Nat.* 114:902–14.

Scott, D. K., and T. H. Clutton-Brock. 1990. Mating systems, parasites, and plumage dimorphism in waterfowl. *Behav. Ecol. Sociobiol.* 26:261–73.

Sealy, S. G., and D. L. Neudorf. 1995. Male Northern Orioles eject cowbird eggs: Implications for the evolution of rejection behavior. *Condor* 97: 369–75.

Searcy, W. A. 1979a. Female choice of mates: A general model for birds and its application to Red-winged Blackbirds. *Am. Nat.* 114:77–100.

———. 1979b. Sexual selection and body size in male Red-winged Blackbirds. *Evolution* 33:649–61.

———. 1979c. Morphological correlates of dominance in captive Red-winged Blackbirds. *Condor* 81:417–20.

———. 1986. Are female Red-winged Blackbirds territorial? *Anim. Behav.* 34: 1381–91.

———. 1988. Do female Red-winged Blackbirds limit their own breeding densities? *Ecology* 69:85–95.

Searcy, W. A., and K. Yasukawa. 1983. Sexual selection and Red-winged Blackbirds. *Am. Sci.* 71:166–74.

———. 1995. *Polygyny and sexual selection in Red-winged Blackbirds.* Princeton: Princeton University Press.

Shields, W. M. 1982. *Philopatry, inbreeding, and the evolution of sex.* Albany: State University of New York Press.

Shutler, D., and P. J. Weatherhead. 1991a. Basal song rate variation in male Red-winged Blackbirds: Sound and fury signifying nothing? *Behav. Ecol.* 2: 123–32.

———. 1991b. Owner and floater Red-winged Blackbirds: Determinants of status. *Behav. Ecol. Sociobiol.* 28:235–41.

———. 1992. Surplus territory contenders in male Red-winged Blackbirds: Where are the desperados? *Behav. Ecol. Sociobiol.* 31:97–106.

———. 1994. Movement patterns and territory acquisition by male Red-winged Blackbirds. *Auk* 104:405–12.

Skutch, A. F. 1954. Life histories of Central American birds. *Pacific Coast Avifauna* 31.

———. 1976. *Parent birds and their young.* Austin: University of Texas Press.

———. 1987. *Helpers at birds' nests: A worldwide survey of cooperative breeding and related behavior.* Ames: University of Iowa Press.

Slagsvold, T. 1984. Clutch size variation of birds in relation to predation; on the cost of reproduction. *J. Anim. Ecol.* 53:945–53.

Slagsvold, T., J. T. Lifjeld, G. Stenmark, and T. Breiehagen. 1988. On the cost of searching for a mate in female Pied Flycatchers *Ficedula hypoleuca*. *Anim. Behav.* 36:433–42.

Smith, D. G. 1972. The role of the epaulets in the Red-winged Blackbird social system (*Agelaius phoeniceus*). *Behaviour* 41:251–68.

———. 1976. An experimental analysis of the function of Red-winged Blackbirds song. *Behaviour* 56:136–56.

Smith, J. N. M. 1981. Does high fecundity reduce survival in Song Sparrows? *Evolution* 35:1142–8.

Smith, J. N. M., R. D. Montgomerie, M. J. Taitt, and Y. Yom-Tov. 1980. A winter feeding experimentation on an island Song Sparrow population. *Oecologia* 47:164–70.

Smith, S. M. 1978. The "underworld" in a territorial sparrow: Adaptive strategy for floaters. *Am. Nat.* 112:571–82.

———. 1987. Responses of floaters to removal experiments on wintering chickadees. *Behav. Ecol. Sociobiol.* 20:363–7.

Stacey, P. B., and W. D. Koenig. 1990. *Cooperative breeding in birds: Long-term studies of ecology and behavior.* Cambridge: Cambridge University Press.

Stamps, J. A. 1990. The effect of contender pressure on territory size and overlap in seasonally territorial species. *Am. Nat.* 135:614–32.

Stearns, S. C. 1976. Life history tactics: A review of the ideas. *Quart. Rev. Biol.* 51:3–47.

———. 1992. *The evolution of life histories.* New York: Oxford University Press.

Strehl, C. E., and J. White. 1986. Effects of superabundant food on breeding success and behavior of the Red-winged Blackbird. *Oecologia* 70:178–86.

Stutchbury, B. J., and R. J. Robertson. 1988. Within-season and age-related patterns of reproductive performance in female Tree Swallows (*Tachycineta bicolor*). *Can. J. Zool.* 66:827–34.

Teather, K. L., K. E. Muma, and P. J. Weatherhead. 1988. Estimating female settlement from nesting data. *Auk* 105:196–200.

Temeles, E. J. 1994. The role of neighbors in territorial systems: When are they "dear enemies"? *Anim. Behav.* 47:339–50.

Trivers, R. 1972. Parental investment and sexual selection. In *Sexual selection and the descent of man,* ed. B. Campbell, 136–79. Chicago: Aldine Press.

Van Balen, J. H. 1979. Observations on the post-fledging dispersal of the Pied Flycatcher, *Ficedula hypoleuca. Ardea* 67: 134–7.

Veiga, J. P. 1990. Infanticide by male and female House Sparrows. *Anim. Behav.* 39:496–502.

Verner, J., and M. F. Willson 1966. The influence of habitats on mating systems of North American passerine birds. *Ecology* 47:143–7.

Wade, M. J. 1987. Measuring sexual selection. In *Sexual selection: Testing the alternatives,* ed. J. W. Bradbury and M. B. Andersson, 197–207. Berlin: John Wiley & Sons.

Wade, M. J., and S. J. Arnold. 1980. The intensity of sexual selection in relation to male behaviour, female choice, and sperm precedence. *Anim. Behav.* 28: 446–61.

Wahba, G. 1990. *Spline models for observational data.* Philadelphia: Society for Industrial and Applied Mathematics.

Walsberg, G. E. 1983. Avian ecological energetics. In *Avian Biology,* vol. 7, ed. D. S. Farmer and J. R. King, 161–220. New York: Academic Press.

Watson, A. 1967. Population control by territorial behaviour in Red Grouse. *Nature* 215:1274–5.

Weatherhead, P. J. 1990. Nest defense as shareable paternal care in Red-winged Blackbirds. *Anim. Behav.* 39:1173–8.

Weatherhead, P. J., and P. T. Boag. 1995. Pair and extra-pair mating success relative to male quality in Red-winged Blackbirds. *Behav. Ecol. Sociobiol.* 37:81–91.

Weatherhead, P. J., and R. G. Clark. 1994. Natural selection and sexual size dimorphism in Red-winged Blackbirds. *Evolution* 48:1071–9.

Weatherhead, P. J., and R. J. Robertson. 1977. Harem size, territory quality, and reproductive success in the Red-winged Blackbird (*Agelaius phoeniceus*). *Can. J. Zool.* 55:1261–7.

———. 1981. In defense of the sexy son hypothesis. *Am. Nat.* 117:349–56.

Weatherhead, P. J., and K. L. Teather. 1991. Are skewed fledgling sex ratios in sexually dimorphic birds adaptive? *Am. Nat.* 138:1159–72.

Weatherhead, P. J., K. J. Metz, G. F. Bennett, and R. E. Irwin. 1993. Parasite faunas, testosterone, and secondary sexual traits in male Red-winged Blackbirds. *Behav. Ecol. Sociobiol.* 33:13–23.

Weathers, W. W., and K. A. Sullivan. 1989. Juvenile foraging proficiency, parental effort, and avian reproductive success. *Ecol. Monogr.* 59:223–46.

Webster, M. D., and W. W. Weathers. 1990. Heat produced as a by-product of foraging activity contributes to avian thermoregulation. *Physiol. Zool.* 63:777–94.

Westneat, D. F. 1992a. Do female Red-winged Blackbirds engage in a mixed mating strategy? *Ethology* 92:7–28.

———. 1992b. Nesting synchrony by female Red-winged Blackbirds: Effects on predation and breeding success. *Ecology* 73:2284–94.

———. 1993. Polygyny and extra-pair fertilizations in eastern Red-winged Blackbirds (*Agelaius phoeniceus*). *Behav. Ecol.* 4:49–60.

———. 1994. To guard mates or go forage: Conflicting demands affect the paternity of male Red-winged Blackbirds. *Am. Nat.* 144:343–54.

Whittingham, L. A. 1989. An experimental study of paternal behavior in Red-winged Blackbirds. *Behav. Ecol. Sociobiol.* 25:73–80.

Wiley, R. H., and S. A. Hartnett. 1976. Effects of interactions with older males on behavior and reproductive development in first-year male Red-winged Blackbirds *Agelaius phoeniceus. J. Exp. Zool.* 196:231–42.

Wiley, R. H., and M. S. Wiley. 1980. Spacing and timing in the nesting ecology of a tropical blackbird: Comparison of populations in different environments. *Ecol. Monogr.* 50:153–78.

Williams, G. C. 1966. *Adaptation and natural selection.* Princeton: Princeton University Press.

Williams, J. B. 1987. Field metabolism and food consumption of Savannah Sparrows during the breeding season. *Auk* 104:277–89.

Williams, J. B., and B. Dwinnel. 1990. Field metabolism of free-living female Savannah Sparrows during incubation: A study using doubly labeled water. *Physiol. Zool.* 63:353–72.

Willson, M. F. 1966. Breeding ecology of the Yellow-headed Blackbird. *Ecol. Monogr.* 36:51–77.

Wimberger, P. H. 1988. Food supplement effects on breeding time and harem size in the Red-winged Blackbird (*Agelaius phoeniceus*). *Auk* 105:799–802.

Wingfield, J. C., T. P. Hahn, R. Levin, and P. Honey. 1992. Predictability and control of gonadal cycles in birds. *J. Exp. Zool.* 261:214–31.

Wingfield, J. C., R. E. Hegner, A. M. Dufty, and G. F. Ball. 1990. The "Challenge Hypothesis": Theoretical implications for patterns of testosterone secretion, mating systems and breeding strategies. *Am. Nat.* 136:829–46.

Wittenberger, J. F. 1976. The ecological factors selecting for polygyny in altricial birds. *Am. Nat.* 110:779–99.

Wynne-Edwards, V. C. 1962. *Animal dispersion in relation to social behaviour.* Edinburgh: Oliver and Boyd.

Yasukawa, K. 1979. Territory establishment in Red-winged Blackbirds: Importance of aggressive behavior and experience. *Condor* 81:258–64.

———. 1981. Male quality and female choice of mate in the Red-winged Blackbird (*Agelaius phoeniceus*). *Ecology* 62:922–9.

———. 1989. The costs and benefits of a vocal signal: The nest-associated "chit" of the female Red-winged Blackbird, *Agelaius phoeniceus. Anim. Behav.* 38:866–74.

Yasukawa, K., and W. A. Searcy. 1981. Nesting synchrony and dispersion in Red-winged Blackbirds: Is the harem competitive or cooperative? *Auk* 98:659–68.

———. 1982. Aggression in female Red-winged Blackbirds: A strategy to ensure male parental investment. *Behav. Ecol. Sociobiol.* 11:13–17.

———. 1986. Simulation models of female choice in Red-winged Blackbirds. *Am. Nat.* 128:307–8.

———. 1995. Red-winged Blackbird (*Agelaius phoeniceus*). In *The birds of North America,* no. 184, ed. A. Poole and F. Gill. Philadelphia and Washington, DC: The Academy of Natural Sciences and the American Ornithologists' Union.

Yasukawa, K., F. Leanza, and C. D. King. 1993. An observational and brood-exchange study of paternal provisioning in the Red-winged Blackbird, *Agelaius phoeniceus. Behav. Ecol.* 4:78–82.

Yasukawa, K., L. K. Whittenberger, and T. A. Nielsen. 1992. Anti-predator vigilance in the Red-winged Blackbird (*Agelaius phoeniceus*): Do males act as sentinels? *Anim. Behav.* 43:961–9.

Ydenberg, R. -C. 1989. Growth-mortality trade-off, and the evolution of juvenile life histories in the Alcidae. *Ecology* 70:1494–1506.

Ydenberg, R. -C., L. A. Giraldeau, and J. B. Falls. 1988. Neighbors, strangers, and the asymmetric war of attrition. *Anim. Behav.* 36:343–7.

Yom-Tov, Y. 1974. The effect of food and predation on breeding density and success, clutch size and laying date of the Crow (*Corvus corone* L.). *J. Anim. Ecol.* 43:479–98.

Young, H. 1963. Age-specific mortality in the eggs and nestlings of blackbirds. *Auk* 80:145–55.

Zack, S., and B. J. Stutchbury. 1992. Delayed breeding in avian social systems: The role of territory quality and "floater" tactics. *Behaviour* 123:194–219.

INDEX

movements
  between marshes, 17, 76–7, 204–6,
    214, 223
  between nests, 6, 11, 35
  between territories, 7–8, 10, 135–6,
    188–9, 191–3, 202–8, 213–5, 266
  breeding season, 5, 10
  of floaters, 131, 135, 163, 165–6,
    168–75
  and geography, 17
  hypotheses to explain, 189
  and nest failure, 6
Muskrat (*Ondatra zibethica*), 20

natural selection, xvii, 124, 220
nest initiation patterns
  and female age, 61
  and female genetics, 63–4
  and female reproductive effort, 61–3
  and female reproductive success,
    49–50
  and food supply, 56–8, 66–7
  influences on, 47–8, 53–69, 101
  and nest success, 49–50
  starts by week, 48
  variation in, 48–51, 66–9
nesting
  decisions, 5, 47–103, 114–20, 224–5,
  delays, 51–2, 60, 66
  effort, 43, 104–14
  initiation, xix, 5, 43, 47–69
  intervals, 91–5
  substrate, 7
nesting termination, 43, 114–20
  influence of breeding exhaustion,
    117–9
  influence of food supply, 115
  influence of molt, 118–20
  influence of offspring quality, 117
  influence of predation rates, 115–7, 119
nests
  building of, 5, 61, 224, 232–4
  causes of termination of, 27
  number built per year, 22, 24, 105
  old, 13, 75–6, 223, 242
  site of, xix, 3, 5, 8, 15, 43, 70, 224
  spacing of, 6
  success of, 28, 49–50
  synchronization of, 44, 60–1, 101, 104
  termination of, 27, 114–20
New Jersey, 86

New York, 86, 123, 224
nonbreeders. *See* floaters
North Juvenile, 24
nuptial feeding, 234

Ontario, 84, 89, 123, 153, 187, 198–9,
  224
opportunity cost, 238–9

pair bond 5
Para Lake, 22
parental care, 104, 133, 221
parental investment, 104
paternity, 8, 28
phenotypic gambit, 219
physical environment, 3, 7, 68, 220,
  238–41
physiology, 129–30, 155, 200–1, 220, 249
Pied Flycatcher (*Ficedula hypoleuca*), 47,
  82, 187, 266
plumage
  female, 106, 254–7
  male, 144, 254
polygyny, 5–6, 226
polyterritoriality, 268
predation
  and marsh shape, 35
  and nesting termination, 115–7
  on nests, 6, 115
  patterns, 13, 37–9
  rates, 37–9
predators, 3, 37, 223
  information about, 134, 243–5
  mobbing of, 9, 35, 231, 236, 244
  swamping of, 81
predator dilution, 60
prospecting
  female, 6, 43–5, 70–3, 103
  male, 131, 137, 139–40, 153, 164–86,
    175–6, 183–6, 227

Raccoon (*Procyon lotor*), 37, 39
radio telemetry, 143, 173–5, 248
removal experiment, 13, 95, 138–9, 143,
  176–81, 188–90, 194–9, 201–4,
  210–3, 250, 262
renesting, 9, 64–6, 102, 105, 251
reproduction, cost of, 61, 104–14
reproductive effort, 9, 61, 104–14
reproductive energy investment score
  (RE), 105–12